Endorsements

Inspiring… intriguing… thought provoking… Nineteen interactional roles are introduced in creative and provocative ways that will challenge how you respond to others in highly charged emotional situations. Through true-to-life case scenarios, reflection, and guided practice, you will learn how to risk and flexibly adopt new international roles to help you feel less obstructed with a general feeling of happiness and well-being. The true essence of how to positively change your self is captured within these pages… Read now!

Jeanne E. Jenkins, Ph.D., Associate Professor, John Carroll University. Cleveland, Ohio.

Refreshing…..magical…..provocative. Lars Brok and Audrey Ellenwood have done it again in their new book. They have taken the sting out of change and explained the mystery of how to transform oneself when in difficult relationships. They have introduced a cast of nineteen magical characters that can be used in the drama that can occur between key relations when differences arise. In reading this book, I often heard their voices prompting me to risk assuming a different character, a more effective character when in the face of conflict. As a result, I appreciate more than ever the richness of interactions that occur in and between people.

Marc B. Dielman, Ph.D., Psychologist, Center for Solutions in Brief Therapy, Inc., Sylvania, Ohio.

This book presents the reader with an excellent tool for developing self-awareness, changing unuseful behaviors, and, through adopting new behaviors, creating more constructive relationships. The authors, both experienced therapists, lead the reader on this journey in a detailed, step-by-step manner. However this is not a one-size-fits-all recipe. The book presents a range of choices for making changes, with a guide that allows the reader to make individualized choices based on the reader's own preferences and personal style. It helps the reader to recognize, in the heat of the moment, that there are a variety of possibilities for handling the situation instead of being caught in a habitual response. Among the important underlying themes are the ways in which our development within our families forms our habits of interacting with others, that these habits can lead us into rigid and unsuccessful reactions to others in adulthood, that any habit learned can be unlearned and replaced with more successful behavior, and that changing ourselves can often change the relationships we have with others, even if the other person does not set out to change.

Phoebe Prosky, MSW, Director Center for the Awareness of Pattern
Freeport, Maine

This book in your hands is very special. The authors of the most inspiring "Shake-Up" have now written a book about different interactional roles. Writing about how to change oneself is more than a difficult task. In this book the authors Drs. A. Ellenwood and L. Brok have really succeeded in this task – they write about ways in which to make your life more effective in a very practical, interesting, and sensitive way. A lot of our interactional roles and styles are learned in childhood. Even though they would be unconscious to us, they can greatly impact present life situations. They can even block us. That is why it is so important to try to be aware of them. This book has a great amount of wisdom within its pages. Wisdom about life, how to analyze it, and if need be, how to change your interactional roles in various situations that you may encounter to be more effective.

The book is open-minded - without prejudices. One of the main messages is that to become happier you need to take an intensive look at yourself. You must look at how you have responded to others throughout your life, the past and the present, especially when in highly charged emotional situations. The book is handy for people in different kinds of life and occupational situations. Also, it is a good resource for therapists to use with their clients to promote change.

Ellenwood and Brok invite you into a journey of your our own life experiences, especially those in which you interact with one another. By learning about your own interactional styles or roles or how you behave in different living situations. You can try to make an effort to go beyond yourself in the future – to learn more effective ways of relating especially in very intense and uncomfortable situations with other people. With the help of this book you can learn new kinds of interactional roles and have a richer interactional future leading to being happier and more content from within.

Sari Sundvall-Piha, Familypsychotherapist, Reverend, Master of Theology, Director at the Family Counseling Centre, Turku and Kaarina Parish Union, Finland

EXPAND

A Self-HelpWorkbook for Changing Your Role in Relationships

Audrey E. Ellenwood, Ph.D.
Lars Brok, M.D.

Jan van Gastel, Illustrator

Glenn —
Believe in
yourself that you
do not need to
"run" and that
"life is "safe"

Audrey Ellenwood

EXPAND

A Self-HelpWorkbook for Changing Your Role in Relationships

Title: EXPAND: A Self-Help Book For Changing Your Role in Relationships

Printed in the United States of America

ISBN Number-13: 9780990814108

Library of Congress Control Number: 2013920778

Writing, Publishing and Distribution of the book made possible by:
ISSOOH, Institute for System Approach; Training and Research
Institute Learning Around the World, Institute for Enhancing International Education for Children

Publisher Information
C & E Ltd
6400 Monroe Street, St. E
Sylvania, Ohio 43560
USA Phone: 419 885-4121
Fax Number: 419 885-6121
Europe Phone: +32 497189219

Cover Design and Illustrations: Jan van Gastel
E-Mail: elbrok@shake-UP.us
Webpage: www.shake-up.us

$1.00 from each book sold will be donated to www.platw.org, 501 3c charity, which provides funding to build playgrounds and provide educational materials for children in developing world countries

Dedication

To those within our living culture, especially John and Marijke, our spouses, children, friends, extended family, and co-workers, who have taught us about the releasing of our own personal power through the interactional roles that we activate with them each day.

To Stacey Lynn Osborn, our editor, you are special beyond belief and many of your ideas and creativity hold steadfast in our book. We wish you well.

Acknowledgements

We would like to thank the following people for their support, encouragement, and guidance throughout the completion of this book:

Marc Dielman, Sylvania, Ohio
Sandra Emerson, Washougal, Washington
Jeanne Jenkins, Ritchfield, Ohio
Russell and Karen Haber, South Carolina
Phoebe Prosky, Freeport, Maine
Rick Snyders, South Africa
Frances Sternberg and Rick Whiteside, New Zealand
Sari Sundvall-Piha, Finland

A special thank-you is extended to those whose creativity helped to bring our ideas alive:

Marilynne Greenberg, *Proof Reader*
Jan Van Gastel, *Illustrator*
Susan Panning, *Graphic Designer*

Special acknowledgement is extended to:

Janet Amid who encouraged writing from the heart in order to help and guide others to understand highly complex emotional situations.

Attya Rahimtoola and her family for teaching us about taking different interactional roles with people from different cultures.

Babs and Kees van Hussen who provided training on how to reconsider interactional roles in one's own family.

Special salutations are extended to **Dawn Freeman and Doug Shelton** of Toledo, Ohio and **Frank Tol, The Netherlands,** for their hours of work helping to bring this book to a published format.

And, most of all,

To *our clients*, who provided examples for this book, taught us the real meaning of life, and reaffirmed for us that one can **EXPAND** themselves, creating change and happiness from within.

How to USE THIS BOOK

We have written this book as a self-help tool to assist you in learning a number of various interactional roles in order to become more comfortable when in a stressful relational situation. As it is a self-help book, you do not need to read this book from cover to cover. Rather, the book should be read in sections overtime and studied as new interactional roles are desired in your personal or professional relationships.

It is recommended that you begin by reading Part One Chapters1 through 4. Then read Part Two Chapter 5 which serves as an overview of all the roles within each of the four quadrants. The quadrants are divided according to a particular interactional style which describes how you respond to and manage information from others. After taking the short quiz presented in chapter 3 we suggest you read the chapters related to the interactional roles located in the quadrant(s) that you seem to endorse the most from the quiz. From the quadrant you select, you will learn new interactional roles which may assist you in times of highly charged emotions which are within other quadrants. You are encouraged to then read the chapters associated with the new interactional roles of which you are curious about and would like to learn.

After reading about a new interactional role located in Chapters 6 through 24, we would like to direct you to Part Three Chapter 25 which is a teaching chapter. This chapter will guide you on how to practice the new interactional role. Here we describe the actions you will need to take to practice this new interactional role and teach you about the benefits of the interactional role. Also you can read a short scenario of the interactional role in action.

The above process should be repeated each time you want to expand your repertoire and acquire a new interactional role with others. Self-help reflection questions have been interspersed among the chapters to help you reflect on the acquisition of preferred interactional roles, learning of new interactional roles, and if you are happy in life.

Part Four, Chapter 26, deals with how to change your role when involved in highly complex relationships with others when various types of mental or physical health concerns are present. This chapter present various stories of how people in difficult emotional situations EXPANDED their interactional roles and moved from a point of stuckness in their relationships to feeling freer and more in control when in highly complex emotionally draining situations with little to no hope of change.

Finally, you should conclude by reading Part Five, Chapter 27 as this chapter addresses how you learned an interactional role, and tells you something about your "living and presenting culture". We explain what happens in emotional differences and when dealing with abusive situations. We end with a special note from the authors.

Table of Contents

Table For Figures

Table For Tables

Making of YOU

Part of life is hardship; it's a journey through a maze
You will not make it out alive, but will learn from every day.
Your family truly impacts the roles you choose in life
These connections may bring joy, happiness, and even cause some strife
You may try to forget where you came from and who you are within
But the past will always follow; your history is your kin.
The people you relate with may have their ups and downs,
They may fight, argue and bicker, or even have emotional breakdowns
But the most important aspect these encounters hold
Is that they set up who you are
and shape your particular interactional role(s).

So, from life's experiences and connections
Your interactional role(s) were fostered
Which are often used in highly charged situations
Sometimes engulfed with anxiety, sadness, grief, and/or depression
You seek answers and reasons for your distress that results in regression
Changing of your interactional role(s) with others
Holds the secret from within
That you alone have the answers to heal
And positive resolutions will be revealed.

Kara McCourt, 2013

Introduction

Imagine you are in the presence of two people, could be family members, spouse, friends, co-workers, acquaintances, and they begin to disagree. At first they are relatively cordial toward each other, but as the discussion pursues they become angry, upset, and strong emotions lead to a very intense situation, you begin to feel despair and are very uncomfortable. Suddenly, they turn to you....what do you do? How do you respond? Do you watch and do nothing? Do you try to lecture? Do you step in and try to "save" them? Do you try to make everyone happy? Do you try to make peace, or do you panic and leave the situation without saying anything? Whatever choice you make, will determine the emotional impact that the situation has on you. Most of the time you can handle situations well, but there are times when in the presence of highly charged emotions you may experience shame, sadness, anxiety, guilt, helplessness fear, stress, panic, depression, and hopelessness. IT is during these moments that you are prone to becoming rigid and inflexible and display behaviors or responses that tend to unbalance you.

As a child, you learned early in life how to respond in highly charged emotional situations from Key-Relations (family members) who were influential to you. Overtime their messages became engrained within and without knowing you developed a particular response style, or what we call your interactional role, when in the presence of highly stressful situations. You eventually conformed to what you believed your interactional response should be in the public persona and engaged in behaviors that were approved of and considered acceptable responses by others. As a result, you habitually began to display a similar behavior pattern (interactional style or role) towards friends, in various school situations, in the society at large, and eventually into your work setting when you felt under duress. During these moments you feel out-of control and powerless. It is not uncommon that emotionally charged situations often result in people freezing and not knowing how to respond.

This book presents to you the distinctive recognition that you hold within yourself the *power to change*. The book encourages you to think about your preferred interactional style (role) with others when under emotional duress and how your preferred interactional role(s) has become cyclic in nature. Within these pages, we present to you 19 interactional roles that can help you to EXPAND your response behavior when under duress in more practical and effective ways. We will guide you through small manageable steps how to respond to various people, when in various situations.

You may be thinking to yourself, it is hard to change old or habitual behavior. Stop and think; be courageous and ask yourself, "Am I happy"? If not, then you need to learn how to become more flexible, to think logically, and respond from a position of strength when in highly charged situations. Through the reading of this book, you will adapt and form new behavior, which will help you to change. When you broaden your repertoire of interactional response styles and roles, as well as become aware through personal guided reflection, the impact that your developmental years had on your response style toward others, you will think differently. You will also begin to perceive chaotic situations differently and interject hope, which will allow you to *EXPAND* and change in a more effective ways your interactional role(s) in your personal and professional relationships.

PART ONE

Getting to Where You are Today

Chapter 1

Help! How Did I Get Into This Position With Others?

"Here we go again," Melanie thought at the dinner table. Her mother brought up the subject of going on a summer trip and of course, her parents were unable to come to any agreement as to where they wanted to go. "I think the Smokey Mountains have a lot to offer; and we could walk, explore, and see waterfalls. They also have Elk also live in the mountains," her mother stated. Melanie's father sat quietly, tapping his fingers on the table and then began to state in a raised voice, "I told you that our next vacation would be to Nashville to the Grand Ole Opry."

"But I am not fond of country music," said her mother, and, "I am not fond of hikes," her father declared in a raised and irritated voice. Angry, Melanie's father arose from the table, shoving his chair back until it fell over, "You are so damn self-centered". Melanie's mother began to cry softly.

Melanie excused herself from the table. While doing the dishes, her mother approached her, and brought up the subject of the Smokey Mountains. "Listen Mom, I have been thinking, why could we not do both? How about if we go to the Smokey Mountains for three days, and then drive to Nashville for a long weekend? I think Dad would go along with that idea." Her mother thought for a minute and then suggested that Melanie go and speak to her father, as he would, "Listen to her." As usual, Melanie attempted to relieve the tensions between her mother and father.

In the above scenario as the tension built between her parents Melanie tried to negotiate a common agreement where both parents would feel satisfied in the final decision. It is not unusual when tensions and disagreements arise, especially between parents, that a third person (child) will step into the conflict by negotiating an agreed upon the decision for the two parents. This interactional stance (intervening on other's behalf) can be helpful in many situations. However when this becomes a habitual response between the parents with the child intervening, the parents in disagreement may never learn how to negotiate a common ground and therefore their true conflict remains buried below the surface. In addition, the child learns early in life that in order to stop tension in the family he/she needs to step in and make the decision for the parents.

In the above case, the interactional role of The *Mediator* was unconsciously enacted by Melanie as she used the skills associated with this role; (1) She listened to her parents present their wishes; (2) She observed their reactions to each other; (3) She inhaled the tension; (4) She removed herself from the discomfort; (5) She then thought about how to make both parents happy; and, (6) she then discussed her thoughts with her parents. Melanie came to the aid of both parents saving them from further disagreement. In the interactional role of the Mediator, Melanie appeased them both. The primary unconscious belief of Melanie in this situation was, "I cannot let my parents be unhappy." As The Mediator, she did a very good job as she found a way to resolve her parents' issues so they would not fight. Of course, Melanie was unaware of how her interactional role and actions "saved" the parents and lessened the tensions within the family atmosphere. Melanie was also unaware of how her behavior and interactional role resulted in blocking her parents' ability to learn negotiation skills themselves.

Growing up in your family, there may have been situations where you tried to relieve, protect, and/or even save others from pain, hurt, sickness, or sadness. Interactional roles played out within families are not mindfully acquired behaviors and/or actions that are used when tensions arise, and family members become stuck in certain response behaviors towards each other. The effect is to step in to alter, change or "save" the family's relations in some way which can result in blocking communication between others in the family thus relieving the tension and returning the family back to a level where the atmosphere is more comfortable (homeostatic level).

Children, in particular, are quite aware of parent's verbal interactions and behaviors (nonverbal behaviors) and know when parents are upset, angry, hurt, or annoyed. This awareness can create fear, anger, anxiety, concern, or even excessive worry within a child. To compensate for these negative feelings, the child responds with certain interactional roles in order to alleviate these internal fears and worries.

Now let us be honest, of course there are times when as a child it was important to intervene in some way in other family members' disagreement often with a successful outcome. The issue arises when you adhere to a particular interactional role which may become habitual overtime. Because of this, you may unconsciously start or continue to play this interactional role ascribed by your family members in other settings and with other people. Then, without realizing it, you begin to play out this habitual interactional role of responding whenever tensions arise across many social settings in your life such as with peers, in school social situations, in various social organizations. You will begin to transfer these interactional roles into your employment setting as well as your immediate family as an adult. Even though you may have left your childhood family, you find that you still continue to play out certain preferred, or assigned, interactional roles with your extended family members in person, over the phone, or through social media.

These habitual interactional roles can result in your becoming "extremely rigid" and possibly experiencing feelings of being helpless, stuck, anxious, uncomfortable, overwhelmed, unhappy, and/or even depressed.

In healthy families, where parents model various ways to resolve conflict, children will automatically move into effective interactional roles, which allow them to experience a number of effective ways to resolve tensions between family members. However, there are times when family members seduce a child into rigidly adhering to a particular interactional role. This results in a lack of growth and the child becomes stymied into a particular behavioral response. This eventually plays out across all social situations throughout their life when tensions arise and the individual becomes uncomfortable.

To break these unconscious interactional roles within you the task is to:

(a) See how your preferred interactional role has protected you and others when tensions or strong emotions arise,

(b) Learn about the strengths and positive effects of your preferred interactional role,

(c) Learn how this interactional role can also be detrimental to you and your relations in life when this role becomes too rigid,

(d) Learn about how the various interactional roles described in this book can help you acquire more personal power when in a face-to-face, emotionally charged situation, and how these interactional roles help free you from feeling "stuck", helpless or overwhelmed by others,

(e) Become aware of the risks you need to take when you leave your preferred interactional role in order to adopt other interactional roles prescribed in this book, and,

(f) Practice new interactional roles in various situations in order to learn new ways of coping when emotional situations are encountered. This means that you will need to learn the necessary skills for these roles.

By assuming one or more of the interactional roles described in this book, you will become free to EXPAND and change in a more effective ways your interactional role(s) in your personal and professional relationships. You will learn more effective ways of handling tension between yourself and others which will result in you becoming freer, much happier, and having less anxiety. In the end, you will be able to develop more effective relationships in both your personal and professional relationships.

A healthy dose of curiosity is needed to jump-start or "EXPAND" new ways of responding to others when tensions and differences occur. Through the process of becoming aware of the nineteen interactional roles introduced in this book you will begin moving yourself to a higher level of functioning that will assist you in being more effective and responsive in all relationships.

This book was written from the view point of a psychiatrist and psychologist trained in family therapy approaches. With over 60 years of combined experience in the field of psychotherapy, we partnered to introduce you to a process of acquiring internal power and growth that is clear and distinctive. We will guide you into new interactional roles that are interesting for you. Each interactional role introduced in this book can be visualized and adapted for use by most individuals.

We present the interactional roles in a practical way rather than through an analytical approach. The stagnant interactional role patterns within an individual is addressed and identified. When you habitually implement the same interactional role under duress, the ineffective interactional role can be identified, visualized, and you will know when you need to shift to a more effective interactional role.

This book presents to you the distinctive recognition that you hold within yourself the power to *change* in more effective ways your interactional role(s) in your personal and professional relationships.

The book encourages you to think about your preferred interactional style (role) with others when under emotional duress. Our guidance will help you to move out of your preferred interactional role(s) that have become cyclic in nature through learning:

(a) How a preferred interactional role is developed,

(b) How this preferred interactional role is sustained,

(c) What does the preferred interactional role looks like to others?

(d) Under what circumstances can this preferred interactional role be beneficial for you?

(e) How a particular interactional role plays out when tensions develop with and between others through the use of case examples.

(f) How to shift into other more effective interactional roles using presented cases.

(g) What other interactional roles can you initiate when tensions arise to become more powerful and effective in creating change.

(h) What risks you will need to take to change your preferred
     interactional role, and,

(i) What skills you need for to practice a new interactional role.

(j) How to reframe your thinking in highly emotional complex situations.

By altering your preferred interactional role, you make a change in the behaviors and responses of the other members in your social system. This change will help you become less anxious, tense, and happier with your interactions with others. This book presents to you a contemporary way of understanding and explaining human behavior when tensions arise in various social situations.

When you can easily shift from one interactional role to another an alternative space develops in which new conversations are created. These new conversations assist you and others to produce healthier exchanges. You will have the ability to overcome various situations, which appear in-tenable. When you change your interactional role with others, you EXPAND options and your response style towards others will become more flexible and enriched.

The content within the book is provocative. It will encourage you to reflect on your personal growth and development as you re-think your positions within all social situations. The reflection section of each chapter was designed to help you challenge your current preferred interactional role(s), and thereby promote long-term personal development.

The book is an easy read and can serve as a life-long guide. The content will help you analyze your preferred interactional roles within your own family of origin and various social circles. You will learn how to visualize, easily, when you are employing a particular interactional role, when engaged in tense, uncomfortable situations. As you examine your own patterns of behavior and the needs of those you come into contact with, you will notice how you quickly assume a prescribed interactional role with others. This knowledge helps you to move freely between the various interactional roles as necessary to meet the concerns of others as well as protect yourself. Further, the text includes descriptions of how particular interactional roles can specifically lead to unhealthy emotional responses within you. The interactional roles are created from recognizable visual images that you can easily imprint and transfer into real life scenarios. The case studies and applications are realistic and sometimes humorous, making the text readable and compelling.

The nineteen interactional roles described in this book are the:

The Angel, The Bird Watcher, The Clown, The Construction Worker, The Detective, The Doctor, The Firefighter, The Journalist, The Judge, The Mediator, Potato Hot-Head, The Peacemaker, The Preacher, The Referee, The Recorder, The Runaway, The Savior, The Superman, and The Teacher.

Of course, there are many other interactional roles that can be assumed, but the interactional roles described in this book are those most often employed by a large number of people. We encourage you to add your own chapter and interactional role to the back as you proceed through this book. The interactional roles identified above can have a dramatic impact on the way in which you interact with, gather information from, and intervene on behalf of others in your immediate, extended, and general social circles.

In each chapter, we guide you into a higher level of understanding of your own interactional development, preferred interactional roles. New interactional roles to shift into when tensions arise in others will be taught. Of special note, throughout the book we use the terminology *he* or *his* to refer to both genders. We also refer to family members, spouse, significant others, friends, co-workers and acquaintances as *Key-Relations*.

All together, the purposes of this book are to:

(a) Help you identify through personal reflection and self-awareness, the type of interactional role(s) you have assumed from a developmental stand.

(b) Provide a discussion of a number of personal interactional roles you can assume when faced with highly charged emotional situations.

(c) Describe the social interactions which tend to encourage you to use a particular interactional role within various social settings.

(d) Discuss what happens within you when tensions arise between you and others;

(e) Identify the risks you will need to take to get out of a preferred interactional role.

(f) Identify alternative interactional roles which may be more effective in various highly emotionally charged social situations.

(g) Introduce the skills needed to learn new interactional roles.

(h) Help you reframe your interactional role(s) in highly intense emotionally charged situations.

Part Three or chapter twenty-five is a teaching chapter for each interactional role. Within this chapter you will discover a list of questions that will allow you to (a) reflect on how an interactional role may have developed throughout your personal and professional growth and (b) your overall response to the adoption of new interactional roles. Part Four will discuss how to change your interactional role(s) when faced with highly complex emotional situations in your personal and professional life that seem hopeless. Part Five or chapter twenty-seven will address how your interactional role was developed.

Chapter 2

How Will I Know Which Interactional Role is Best to Use in Stressful Situations?

Previously, it was noted, most of you have adopted through life a preferred interactional role with others when tensions arise. There is a unique group of personal characteristics, attributes, behaviors or style in each interactional role. Tensions emerge and you display a <u>level of control</u> in regards to the type and amount of information shared. Further you engage in a <u>level of personal involvement</u> with other people. Figure One, *Level of Personal Involvement with Others*, depicts how each interactional role falls upon a continuum related to level of involvement with others from being overly involved to extremely disengaged. Figure Two, *Level of Control Towards Others*, illustrates how each interactional role falls upon a continuum related to level of control with others from being particularly authoritarian to quite passive.

Figure One
Level of Personal Involvement With Others

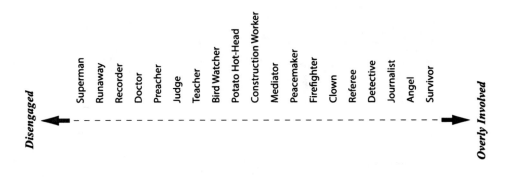

Level of Control Towards Others

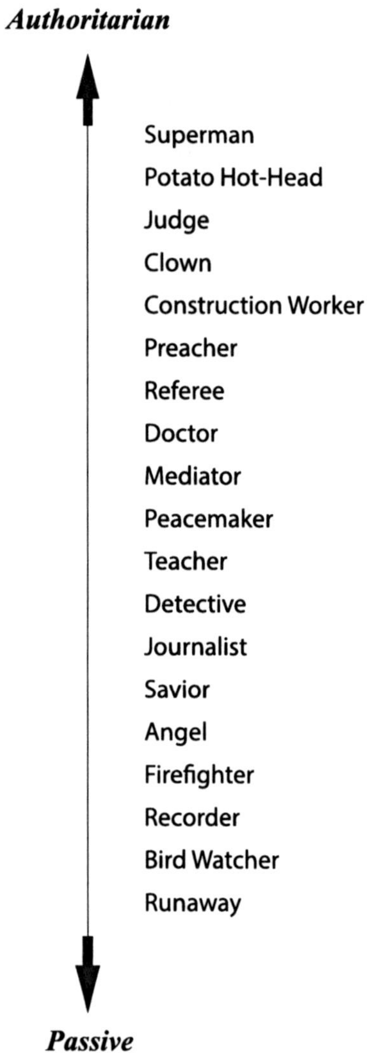

Authoritarian

Superman

Potato Hot-Head

Judge

Clown

Construction Worker

Preacher

Referee

Doctor

Mediator

Peacemaker

Teacher

Detective

Journalist

Savior

Angel

Firefighter

Recorder

Bird Watcher

Runaway

Passive

Each interactional role was placed on a continuum, or a cross map (Figure Three, Cross Mapping of Interactional Roles and Interactional Styles), to provide an index of your level of control toward others (e.g., authoritarianism) and level of involvement (e.g., overly involved) with others. The following cross map demonstrates the plotting of each interactional role in relation to the degree of authority displayed and level of personal involvement with others.

Figure Three

Cross Mapping of Interactional Roles

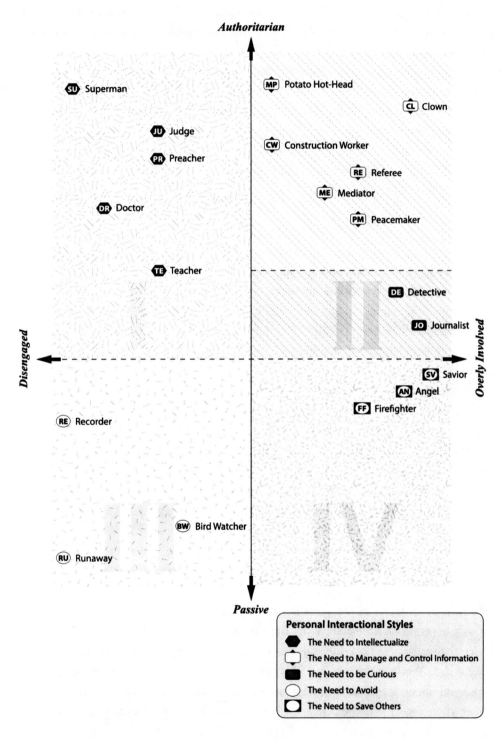

In figure three, the dotted line (--) indicates a continuum of interactional roles ranging from over-involvement to disengagement with others. The heavy line (-) represents the level of control towards others associated with each interactional role and which ranges from a very authoritarian approach to an extremely passive approach. We also depict each role in relation to the five key interactional styles (Quadrants: I Need to Intellectualize; Quadrant II Need to Manage and Control Information or Need to Be Curious; Quadrant III Need to Avoid; and Quadrant IV Need to Save Others) which are portrayed to others, especially when tensions arise. This cross map can be used to help you determine your personal dynamics related to these variables. You can also discover alternative interactional roles or styles that may be more productive when you believe you are out-of-control in a situation.

For example, let's imagine you are using the interactional role of The Bird Watcher (Quadrant III; Need to Avoid) with a friend. Your friend shares a deeply emotional situation, you are quiet and rarely say a word. It is apparent to you that your friend is becoming very annoyed and upset with your lack of perceived involvement, which is being interpreted as lack of caring. In order to connect with your friend on a different level, you will need to rethink your interactional role. As The Bird Watcher, you distance your friend and you risk losing the friendship if he believes he cannot count on you for help or guidance in time of stress. When you view the cross map, you become aware that The Bird Watcher is a very passive, somewhat uninvolved interactional role, and you do not take responsibility to help develop ideas or solutions for your friend's situation. The cross map helps you to examine alternative interactional roles within the same quadrant or other quadrants, offering opportunities for responding in ways that are more consistent with the needs of your friend. The cross map can be used to select a new interactional role which will assist you in becoming more involved at a personal level by displaying more control and by becoming more assertive in the situation. In addition, the cross map helps you to think about what interactional roles would be too risky for you to try and might even further alienate your friend from you.

After you review the cross map, you decide you should be more involved and more assertive in this particular situation. A decision is made to leave the interactional role of The Bird Watcher (which is in the third quadrant; Interactional Style: Need to Avoid) and adopt the role of The Teacher which is in quadrant I; Need to Intellectualize. The interactional role of The Teacher, (which will not be too risky) allows you to give advice to your friend, which demonstrates more concern and involvement with your friend's situation. You could also shift to the role of The Angel (Quadrant IV; Interactional style Need to Save Others). This shift allows you to become more connected with your friend while not becoming too authoritarian. You could also switch into the interactional role of The Detective in Quadrant II; Need to be curious. This interactional role allows you to become more curious about the situation via asking questions. By asking questions, your friend will experience you as more involved. The Detective would help you to become more active and assertive in helping your friend find solutions to his problem. The cross map also demonstrates shifting to the interactional role of The Judge (Quadrant I; Need to Intellectualize) places you in a higher controlling situation but would further disengage you from your friend who already feels alienated by your perceived lack of involvement. This interactional role would not be helpful in this particular situation.

You can use the cross map as a reference guide for analyzing each interactional role: its level of personal involvement with others, its level of control in relation to how much information is imparted and the interactional style connected to each role. The cross map serves as a quick reminder of various options available to you when face-to-face tense situations with others. This helps you to EXPAND and will guide you on how to change your interactional role(s) in your personal and professional relationships in order to be more effective.

Chapter 3

So, How Can I Determine What Is My Preferred Interactional Style With Others?

According to Koenig (2001) an interactional style is, "As unique as someone's fingerprint and as distinctive as a voice or a gait". Over time, each of you has developed a personal interactional style (role) of relating to others. Your personal interactional style forms a backdrop which reveals your life's historical information. Your interactional style is derived from your experience, heredity, and unique individual characteristics such as talents, aesthetic taste, physical strengths, weaknesses, appearance, education, intelligence, disposition, and sense of humor. Taken together, these dynamics help to define your personal persona and interactional role (level of involvement and control) with others.

Although your interactional style is instinctive, it plays a crucial part in establishing rapport and obtaining positive relations with others. When you are willing to explore your interactional style you can effectively learn to connect, empathize, and respond in a more positive effective way to others in your surroundings at several levels (e.g., acquaintance to more intimate engagements); especially when tensions and disagreements arise. If you do not take this step you may underestimate *the power which is within you* and will have no idea about the impact that your interactional style can have on effectively altering your own level of anxiety, tension, worry, fear, or anger that can develop with others in stressful situations.

The following scenarios will help you to identify your personal interactional style. Read each of the situations below and select the letter that *most likely* represents how you think you might respond. If you are not 100% sure of how you might respond or if you are having difficulty selecting one of the responses, select the option that feels *most* comfortable for you:

Situation I

Why don't you hear me?

Linda has just learned that she has fibroids in her uterus and the doctor is suggesting that she needs a partial hysterectomy. She is fearful the operation may cause her to lose her womanhood and; that she may never have a satisfying sexual encounter. She believes, based on her limited knowledge, that she will grow old quickly and become unattractive. She responds with tears and anger to the news. She immediately phones you and is near hysteria.

How you might respond?

A. You try to calm Linda by sharing that she will be fine. This is an operation that is done every day, and she will feel so much better after the operation.

B. You do not respond to her fears, but start asking curious questions about the details of the operation. When it will occur, exactly what was the diagnosis, what the recovery time will be, if her employer will pay her for sick time, etc.

C. You interrupt her and tell her that being emotional is not helpful, and she needs to think about her situation before speaking again. You remain silent and have no idea what to tell her.

D. You share with Linda that she needs to be stronger and stop being so emotional every time she goes to the doctor.

E. You look at her and in a firm voice share that many people have this operation and they are perfectly content. Maybe she needs to accept she is aging.

Situation II

Why Does My Sister Not Listen?

Susan entered the house terribly upset about her recent visit at her sister's home. Susan's sister Anne is five years younger. When together, they have a tendency to resort to sibling competitiveness arguing over what others may consider to be trivial situations. They bicker constantly to the point where there is no resolution and usually one or the other leaves upset. Susan drove to her sister's house unexpectedly, and they began to argue about the differences concerning the care of their mother, who has recently become ill with cancer. Anne wants her mother to go to assisted living and Susan does not agree. She thinks her mother should stay at home. Susan looks to you for answers.

How you might respond?

A. You try to calm Susan by saying how wonderful it is that she and her sister care so much about her mother's well-being.

B. You begin to inquire, through questions. Have they looked at various assisted living places? When might their mother move? Have they spoken to their mother? In what part of the city do they want to locate their mother?

C. You share that the sisters need to meet face-to face-with you. You will help them discuss their concerns so they do not interrupt each other.

D. You walk away without responding and leave the room upset that she came over without calling first.

E. You begin to share that placing one's parent's into assisted living is beneficial and that over 65% of people who go into assisted living live 6-12 months longer.

Situation III

Tell me what I can do for you?

Carol had the desire and dream to go to college and be a teacher. You know from your experiences with Carol that she loved small children and would often volunteer at day schools. As an adolescent, she worked as an aide in a convalescent home as she wanted to bring "sunshine" to others. You remember that her friends always called upon her to borrow money, clothes, or take her places in her car, but they never offered to pay for the gas. At times, Carol would become angry at her friends as her parents did not have much money and she complained that they were "using" her but she could never say, "No" to them. Carol had now gone to college, and she was really happy, probably for the first time in her life. But, Carol has just received a phone call that her mother is depressed and she needs to leave college and come home to take care of her mother. Carol does not know what to do and calls you for advice.

How you might respond:

A. You share that she must immediately leave college and go home to take care of her mother.

B. Share your mother's story with me. When did she become depressed? Has she always been depressed? Is this new behavior? Is she seeing a doctor?

C. In order to make sure that her mother and father are doing well she needs to go home and organize their life for them.

D. You do not say much, but you begin to write down about Carol's situation so you can think about it and tell her you will call her back.

E. You tell her that her mother has severe depression, and may even be suicidal and it is best she go home immediately.

Situation IV

I am a what?

Susan was upset with Harry as he did not confront their daughter, Kathy, about staying out after her curfew and not calling. Susan sat up worried most of the night. When Kathy arrived home, Susan began to yell at her for being so inconsiderate which woke-up Harry. Harry without getting the details of Susan's anger came out of the room and told Susan to, "Shut-up". When Susan tried to explain her anger and how worried she was about Kathy as she had not called and came in late, Harry called her a, "Bitch" and told her she was, "Acting like her mother". Susan phoned you to say that they had a huge fight, and she had been throwing up all night.

How you might respond?

A. You share that she might have the flu, and you will come to make her some tea and soup.

B. You begin to ask several questions; has Harry always been like this? How have you handled his behavior in the past? When did he start calling her names? Did he not like her mother? How soon after the fight did she start throwing up.

C. You can see why both she and Harry are upset and you begin to explain each other's perspectives.

D. You do not reply; you just listen.

E. After listening to Susan you tell her that Harry had every right to be upset that she woke him up, he needed to go to work and he has a stressful job

Situation V

The Runaway

Emily had arrived home from school in a very good mood and was singing when she entered the door. Her eyes widen with disbelief. The living room was in chaos; there was broken glass, lamps smashed, and furniture turned over. She knew instantly that her parents had another fight, and she became overwhelmed with fear and worry. Where was her mother? Where was her father? She ran to the bedroom and saw her father leaning up against the closet and was breathing heavily. She knew he had smashed the furniture and lamps. When she asked where her mother was; "She left", her father replied. Emily filled with fear, ran out of the room, out of the house and she just kept running. She had no idea of where to go, or whom to go to, but she knew she had to get away. You learn of what happened and you decide to take action.

How you might respond:

A. You immediately try to find Emily; and when you do you bring her home and tell her that she can live with you full time.

B. You begin to investigate the story by asking a number of questions; what happened? Why she ran away? Has this happened before? Was she scared?

C. You start yelling at her and tell her what a stupid thing she did and you plan to call the police to punish her.

D. You listen to her story and only respond with, "hmm" and later journal about your thoughts.

E. Do not question me. I am telling you what you do. You need to go home. Do not say a word and clean up the house. After all, I study psychology, and I know what is best for you to do.

Now analyze your responses and see which letter(s) has the most frequent endorsement. Match your most frequent circled letter(s) to the descriptions below, there can be more than one set of letters endorsed. If this is the case, read both sections.

Interactional Style: Need to Intellectualize (Quadrant I)

If you primarily circled the **E** responses your interactional style may be to remain aloof from others. You have a tendency to 'escape into reason' by focusing on facts and logic. If you find yourself frequently in this position when tensions arise you may benefit by beginning to read part II chapter five (overview of all interactional roles and styles), and then Quadrant I chapters six, seven, eight, nine and ten; the interactional roles of *The Doctor, The Judge, The Preacher, The Teacher,* and *The Superman.*

Interactional Style: Need to Control and Manage Information (Quadrant II)

If you primarily circled the **C** responses, your interactional style may be to control who speaks to whom and then make decisions as to how others should behave or what actions they must take in order to solve a particular situation. If you find yourself frequently in this position when tensions arise you may benefit by reading chapter five (overview of all interactional roles and styles), and then read Quadrant II of part II chapters eleven, twelve, thirteen, fourteen, fifteen and sixteen; the interactional roles of *The Construction Worker, The Clown, The Mediator, The Peacemaker, Potato Hot-head,* and *The Referee.*

Interactional Style: Need to be Curious (Quadrant II)

If you primarily circled the **B** responses, your interactional style may be one of believing that the most important aspects of your interactions with others has been to help them understand the underlying dynamics of their presenting problems by asking questions. If you find yourself frequently in this position when tensions arise you may benefit by beginning to read chapter five (overview of all interactional roles and styles), and then read Quadrant II of part II chapters seventeen and eighteen; the interactional roles of *The Detective and The Journalist.*

Interactional Style: Need to Avoid (Quadrant III)

If you primarily circled the **D** responses, your interactional style may indicate that you have trouble controlling information and knowing how to get control, especially when there is a lot of tension in others and too much information is communicated in a short period of time. If you find yourself frequently in this position when tensions arise you may benefit by beginning to read chapter five (overview of all interactional roles and styles), and then read Quadrant III of part II chapters nineteen, twenty, and twenty-one; *The Birdwatcher, The Recorder,* or *The Runaway.*

Interactional Style: Need to Save Others (Quadrant IV)

If you primarily circled the A responses, your interactional style may be to guide, strengthen, assist, and encourage others. If you find yourself frequently in this position when tensions arise you may benefit by beginning to read chapter five (overview of all interactional roles and styles), and then Quadrant IV of part II chapters twenty-two, twenty-three, and twenty-four; the interactional roles of; *The Angel, The Firefighter,* and *The Savior.*

By examining adherence to the above interactional styles, you will gain insights as to how to improve your relations with others especially in tense situations. You will be able to know when you are engaging in a particular interactional style and how to select other more effective interactional roles or styles if conflict should develop. By becoming familiar with the nineteen interactional roles presented in this book and knowing your preferred interactional style, you will have very important information. You will learn to (a) assess if an interactional style or role is being effective with others (b) make the decision of when you are overly-relying on a particular interactional style or role and (c) know when you need to tailor, adjust, or select an alternative interactional style or role with others in order to be more effective.

Begin now to read about your interactional roles and styles

Table 1. Interactional Role Response Matched to Quadrant

Situation 1	Interactional Role Response	Quadrant
	Savior	IV
	Detective	II
	Construction Worker	II
	Bird Watcher	III
	Preacher	I
Situation 2	**Interactional Role Response**	**Quadrant**
	Angel	IV
	Detective	II
	Referee	II
	Run Away	III
	Teacher	I
Situation 3	**Interactional Role Response**	**Quadrant**
	Firefighter	IV
	Journalist	II
	Peace Maker	II
	Recorder	III
	Doctor	I
Situation 4	**Interactional Role Response**	**Quadrant**
	Savior	IV
	Detective	II
	Mediator	II
	Bird Watcher	III
	Judge	I
Situation 5	**Interactional Role Response**	**Quadrant**
	Savior	IV
	Journalist	II
	Potato Hot-Head	II
	Recorder	III
	Super Man	I

Chapter 4

How is this Book Organized So I Can Learn About the Interactional Roles?

In Part 2 of this book we present nineteen classical interactional roles. In chapter 5, we provide an overview of each quadrant and the interactional roles. Chapters 6 through 24 are divided into four parts, representing the quadrants which are associated with the cross map introduced in chapter 2. We begin each part by providing a general overview of the interactional roles described within the quadrant section. Each interactional role is then specifically described. We have structured each chapter in the following format:

a. Each chapter begins with an overview of the specific characteristics of a particular interactional role.

b. **How Did I Learn This Role?** Provides information about how you learned to use a particular interactional role when tensions arose with others.

c. **Is this Interactional Role Ever Good For Me to Use?** Shares how useful an interactional role can be as your preferred interactional role.

d. **Help I am Stuck:** Provides you with an overview how an interactional role can create a feeling of helplessness with others.

e. **What Happens Within You:** This section discusses feelings that you experience when face-to-face in a tense or emotional situation.

f. **The Case Scenario:** Presents composites of situations presented by actual clients from our extensive clinical experiences and portrays how a particular interactional role described in a session led to anxiety, worry, fear, or depression within the clients.

g. **Changing of the Interactional Role:** Here we discuss the presented case scenario and how other interactional roles within the cross mapping quadrants could actually be used to diffuse or "EXPAND" the situation into a positive stance.

h. **What Interactional Roles Can I Try to Give Me Personal Power?** We identify interactional roles within the cross mapping of interactional roles and styles that could be implemented to help release the *power from within you* when face-to-face in a tense situation with others. We also share the interactional roles that we believe may be too risky for you to try initially.

i. **The Risk:** We delineate the specific risks you will need to take to breakout of a particular interactional role.

j. **The Reflection:** Encourages you to develop self-awareness by examining your interactional roles and styles in light of guided exercises and questions.

We now encourage you to select and read the interactional roles you believe you display (from chapter 3). The interactional roles described in Part II will guide you into reading other interactional roles which can help release your inner power. Lastly, read those interactional roles you believe are most risky for you, and think about how to engage these roles positively into your daily repertoire of behaviors with others, when tensions arise. In so doing, you will be able to respond to tensions, anxiety, and difficult situations with more freedom and ease. Part Three, chapter 25, is a teaching chapter and will guide you step-by-step on how to acquire and practice a new interactional role. Part Four, chapter 26, will share stories of highly complex rigid relationships and how you can change very rigid interactional role(s) to create hope in what seems like hopeless personal and professional situations. The book concludes with Part Five, chapter 27, which overviews how you developed your preferred interactional role and if you are unhappy how to change your interactional role(s) in your personal and professional relationships in order to be more effective.

PART TWO

Enhancing Effectiveness

Chapter 5

How Can The Interactional Roles Help Me Be More Effective?

There are a number of interactional roles you can utilize to become less reactive when you find yourself in a highly charged emotional situation with family members, spouse, significant other, friends, co-workers or acquaintances. If you look at the cross map on page 13 you will notice that there are four quadrants; each pertaining a particular interactional style (e.g., Need to Intellectualize, Need to Control and Manage Information, Need to be Curious, Need to Avoid, Need to Save Others) and each containing various interactional roles. The interactional roles listed will help you determine how engaged you need to be with others, as well as the degree of passivity or level of authority you may need to display in times of stress or highly charged emotional situations. This will help you and others work through the presenting situations or differences. Each interactional role is unique and will be defined in subsequent chapters classified according to their interactional style. The following charts overview each of the interactional roles according to their quadrants.

As you grew in life and were exposed to different interactional experiences, you developed a preference for a particular style as described above and you may quickly change from one interactional role to another within your preferred style. This is very healthy, and a good approach to take when under duress. The problem arises when you engage solely on a particular interactional role and do not alter or change that role. It is during these moments that you feel stuck and need to be able to *EXPAND* your power by moving to alternative interactional roles either within the same quadrant or another quadrant.

The following charts overview each of the interactional roles according to their quadrants. The charts provide a description of the uniqueness of each interactional role, how it provides personal power to you, and the danger associated with each role is highlighted. Through the skillful adoption of these alternative interactional roles, you will learn to become more effective through being able to EXPAND and change your interactional role(s) in your personal and professional relationships which will instill hope into situations which are characterized by chaos, sadness, anger, and hopelessness. These interactional roles could help you to be more effective and improve your communication skills with Key-Relations during highly emotionally charged situations.

Quadrant I: Need to Intellectualize

These interactional roles allow you to impart your knowledge or provide the necessary resources (e.g., books, online sites, magazines etc.) to promote awareness. You believe that education and knowledge are paramount for everyone. You rely on your readings or acquired knowledge to identify what is good for others. You may tend to impart your universal principles, beliefs, and morals with others who are under duress. Operating in these interactional roles will help you to take charge when emotional situations or differences appear to be out-of-control and others may not know how to respond. These interactional roles would help you portray to others in duress a sense of calmness, control, and trustworthiness that you can react to emotional duress and take responsibility while remaining aloof and calm.

Table 2 – Quadrant I Roles

Interactional Role	Description	Uniqueness	Effectiveness	Danger Associated With This Role
The Doctor	You remain disengaged but reactive to the concerns of others. You present an all knowing medical stance with others	You assume responsibility for solving the intense emotional situation around somatic concerns	You demonstrate to others that you care and can take responsibility for direction in times when they feel helpless	You may want to label others with a somatic concern and if not supported by the mental health or medical fields you will lose face with others
The Judge	You hear all sides of a situation before rendering an opinion or judgment to others	You listen to and clarify ambiguous information surrounding situations	You take the emotion out of the situation as each person is able to speak in turn. You then impart what you believe in your judgment the best course of action for everyone	Your judgment may not be agreed upon by all and some may distance from you or get angry
The Preacher	You remain disengaged by lecturing others based on your beliefs, morals, and value system	You determine how others *should* behave based on your morals	You provide a level of stability for those who tend to use poor judgment or lack internal controls	You may come across as too authoritarian and others' beliefs, morals, and values are discounted which can lead to passive aggressiveness or oppositional behavior in others

Table 2 – Quadrant I Roles Continued

Interactional Role	Description	Uniqueness	Effectiveness	Danger Associated With This Role
The Superman	You assume an all knowing stance with others	You assume full responsibility for solving the intense emotional situation around highly charged emotional situations	You demonstrate to others that you can take responsibility and they can count on you in times where they feel helpless	You may be too overpowering which would alienate or make others very dependent on you
The Teacher	You provide understanding by teaching others how to organize themselves around a highly charged emotional situation	You help to educate those around you about the development, maintenance, and general understanding of their differences	You offer advice to (or teach) others as how to behave or respond differently in a situation and help to diffuse tension by taking the emotion out of the situation through introducing logic	You may come across as too logical and aloof which will keep others from growing close to you

Quadrant II: The Need to Manage and Control Information

When you use the interactional roles described below, you are able to alter the flow of the conversation between others, so less emotion is displayed during highly charged situations. Operating in these interactional roles lends a sense of sincerity and caring to others as you respond by monitoring the flow, control, and level of information. By interjecting humor or deciding who speaks and when you (a) lighten the atmosphere and (b) allow others to speak without interruptions which can help calm the atmosphere when intense anger is present. In these interactional roles, you would be perceived as authoritarian and actively involved with others. Through these interactional roles, you show respect for others feelings and reactions during highly charged emotional situations.

Table 3 – Quadrant II Roles (Need to Manage)

Interactional Role	Description	Uniqueness	Effectiveness	Danger Associated With This Role
The Clown	You interject humor into tense and painful situations	You alleviate tensions typically present in intense situations and helps others view their concerns from a different perspective	Your humor helps others be less reactive as the atmosphere is lightened which will allow others to be less serious	Your comments may be perceived as snide, rude, or hurtful

Table 3 – Quadrant II Roles (Need to Manage) Continued

Interactional Role	Description	Uniqueness	Effectiveness	Danger Associated With This Role
The Construction Worker	You abruptly halt conversations or interruptions being displayed between others who are in highly reactive or emotional situations	You alleviate tensions or anger by encouraging others to first listen to each before responding	You block erroneous information that is igniting and kindling emotion and bring a sense of calmness and respect to the presented situations or differences	You may cut off conversation too soon resulting in additional anger being directed at you
The Mediator	You assist others in coming up with comprises and ways to be more effectively handle their emotional differences	You lower people's emotions so that they can openly discuss their differences	You model for others how to communicate clearly and assertively thereby creating a safer atmosphere	You may be too quick to want to mediate a compromise; the true differences between others may not be understood
The Peacemaker	You listen to others, express their thoughts, ideas, and reactions to the situation while maintaining an atmosphere of mutual respect and calmness between them	You allow for the concerns of other's to be acknowledged and create peace in situations	You present to others as calm, helpful and caring during times of intense emotional situations	You may be so concerned about creating a peaceful atmosphere that you do not allow others to openly express their concerns or differences so issues become buried and surface again in other ways

Table 3 – Quadrant II Roles (Need to Manage) Continued

Interactional Role	Description	Uniqueness	Effectiveness	Danger Associated With This Role
The Referee	You determine who speaks and when during times of highly charged emotions	You decide how others will discuss differences through giving space for everyone to speak; You decide the rules as to how information will be imparted and discussed	Your rules will assist in maintaining a calmer atmosphere. You create trust by others toward you	You must be careful that your rules do not hinder the process
Potato Hot-Head	You use anger or a controlled intense voice to obtain other's attention during a highly charged situation	You stop the flow of conversation that could be hurtful to others and gain immediate attention in highly charged situations	When you gain people's attention, you show that you are serious about their emotional concerns and halt the disruptive blame game that goes on between people	Your use of anger is always a risk as others may distance or cut themselves off from you if you are overly intimidating

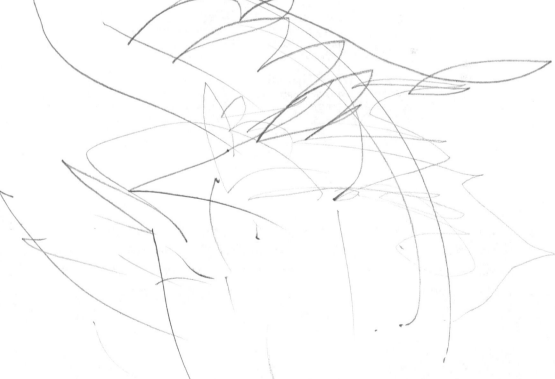

Quadrant II: The Need to Be Curious

These interactional roles described below would require you to demonstrate curiosity and would be quite useful for you to employ with others who are under duress. When you use these interactional roles, you give a sense of sincerity and caring to others, as you respond by asking questions. By allowing others to speak, you would be perceived as being actively involved with others. These interactional roles would demonstrate respect, interest, and warmth to others.

Table 4 – Quadrant II Roles (Curious)

Interactional Role	Description	Uniqueness	Effectiveness	Danger Associated With This Role
The Detective	You ask pertinent questions about the presenting concerns	You uncover hidden agendas that fuel the behavior of those present. The clues may help to explain the true issues between people and therefore suggestions made by you might encourage others to think about themselves and result in lasting change	You display concern, caring, interest, and warmth to others. Others feel important around you	When you ask too many questions may irritate and distance others from you
The Journalist	You gather, without interruption, people's stories regarding their differences	You objectively gather sufficient information regarding differences between others so the root of the problem can be uncovered	You display interest, genuine concern, and curiosity towards others giving a sense of importance to others	You may get lost in stories which can overwhelm the situation if clarity is not offered

When you work in an integrated role of The Detective and The Journalist you provide a balance of asking probing questions coupled with storytelling. These interactional roles would create opportunities for others to tell their stories so they can express, without interruption, their worries and concerns underlying problematic behaviors.

Quadrant III: Need to Avoid

The interactional roles described below allow you to remove yourself from situations that are out-of-control or are filled with highly charged with emotion. In these interactional roles you have time to reflect and analyze how you might want to respond to others. These interactional roles would help you remain calm, keep your cool, and remain aloof during very complex highly charged situations.

Table 5 Quadrant III Roles

Interactional Role	Description	Uniqueness	Effectiveness	Danger Associated With This Role
The Birdwatcher	You observe, watch, and analyze the behaviors of others while remaining somewhat passive in highly emotional charged situations	You have time to think and gain a solid perspective on others differences or concerns before acting	You present to others as calm, helpful and nonreactive during times of intense emotional situations	Others may perceive you as aloof, uncaring and unhelpful during highly charged emotional situations
The Recorder	You analyze, watch, and observe the behavior of others and then records what is observed through a diary or journal	You remain calm and somewhat aloof during situations with intense emotion	The process of journaling will assist you in uncovering the root of differences and you will become aware of your own reactions and emotions during highly charged emotional situations	If you use this role as an escape; you never learn a safe way to openly express your feelings so your emotions become buried and can lead to depression
The Runaway	You physically remove self from a highly charged situation	You remove yourself from the situation temporarily so that you can gain composure and allow others to calm down so that they can more easily speak about differences	During the temporary removal of yourself, your are able to calm down, reason through a situation and decide a course of action or response to others	When you use this role as an escape; problems or differences with others will never be resolved. Your emotions become buried and can lead to depression

Quadrant IV: Need to Save Others

The interactional roles described below help you to guide, strengthen, assist, and encourage others during desperate or intense emotional situations. In these interactional roles you are highly involved in the lives when you try to make them happy or comfortable. Operating in these interactional roles lends a strong sense of caring to others.

Table 6 – Quadrant IV Roles

Interactional Role	Description	Uniqueness	Effectiveness	Danger Associated With This Role
The Angel	You interject hope into highly charged emotional situations	You help others to view their situation more optimistically. You calm highly charged emotional situations or differences	You present to others as calm, helpful, caring and optimistic during times of intense emotional situations	You may be so concerned about creating hope in others that you may overlook the seriousness of concerns or situations
The Firefighter	You take charge of a highly emotional situations (e.g, death) in crisis situations	You provide purpose and direction to people who are fraught with emotion	Others know they can count on you in times of emotional duress or crisis	In your haste to take quick action you may become perceived by others as heeding the process rather than helping
The Savior	You have strong tendency to seek out people who desperately need help and will assist or protect them at all cost	You are highly involved with others, work very hard, and take full responsibility for making everyone happy and safe.	You create a highly supportive, caring environment. Others perceive you as soft, sensitive and very much involved in their well-being	You often sacrifice your own personal needs for those of others

Reflection Effectiveness Exercise:

At this point list the interactional roles suggested above that you are most willing to try out when in a highly charged emotional situation: _____

_____

Now list the interactional roles suggested above that you believe are somewhat risky but open to try when in highly charged emotional situations: _____

_____

_____

_____

Now list the interactional roles suggested above that you believe are very risky and you are uncertain how to use these interactional roles when in a highly charged emotional situation: _____

_____

_____

_____

Now proceed to reading about the nineteen interactional roles described in chapters 6-24

Quadrant I

The Need to Intellectualize

When you reflect about your interactional roles and style you become aware that you believe that the most important aspect of your interactions has been to lecture or provide educational experiences for other people. In this style, you work hard to create an environment in which others learn about their relationships how to resolve their problems. If Key-Relations appear to lack knowledge or understanding of an issue, you are quick to impart your knowledge or provide the necessary resources (e.g., books, online sites, doctor suggestions etc.) to promote awareness.

You believe that education and knowledge is paramount for everyone. You rely on your readings or acquired knowledge to identify what is good for others. You may tend to impart your universal principles, beliefs, and morals unto others and expect others to follow your beliefs without questioning. In general you do not like to be challenged and as a result you may have a tendency to fight back by using verbal derogatory comments or resort to other forms of defense if questioned. You may also have a tendency to talk down to others and assume that you are always right. In these interactional roles you tend to respond to stress or highly charged situations in a more disengaged and authoritarian way. If your interactional style involves the need to educate or rely upon your knowledge with others consider reading Part 2, Quadrant I chapters six, seven, eight, nine and ten: *The Doctor, The Judge, The Preacher, The Teacher, or The Superman.*

Quadrant I - The Need to Intellectualize

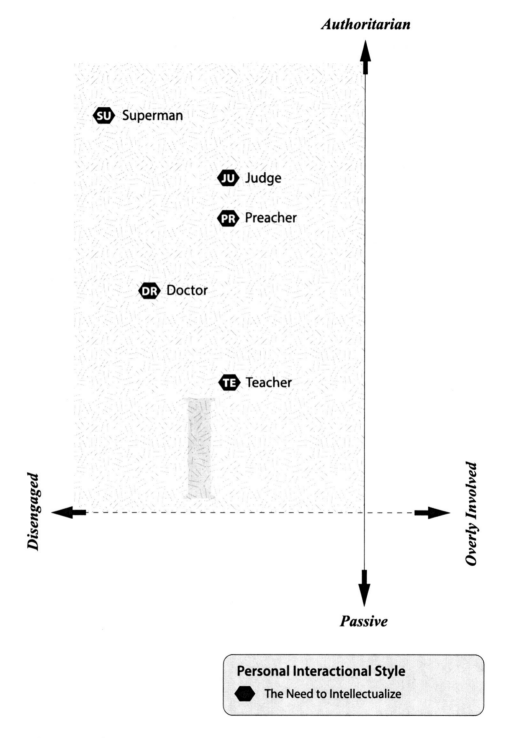

Chapter 6

The Doctor

"I think she is depressed and needs medication if you ask me." This interactional role derives its power from the use of medical terminology when differences appear between Key-Relations over the care of another or self. As the "The Doctor" you frequently use medical or psychological terminology to describe those that seem to have emotional, behavioral, or social concerns. You view one person as sick or mentally ill while the other family members or those in social circles are healthy. You believe that others must be helped to cope and understand the psychological or medical illness associated with the behavior of themselves or others.

You often define the patient's illness for the family or themselves while remaining emotionally detached from the situation. Frequently, you will give advice about diet, exercise, and sleep to others or simply labels someone as "crazy".

How Did I Learn This Role?

As a child, you may have been curious about and wanted to help those who were sick or more helpless than you. As a result, you began to educate yourself about various somatic or psychological concerns and overtime, offering advice to parents or family members about how to become less helpless in various situations. When friends began to discuss issues around feelings of helplessness or as having despair you would research and then offer suggestions how to make them stronger. You soon realized that people respected you for your knowledge, and through the process you noticed that others began to listen to you. As an adult, you are engaging yourself into action with others when they present with either somatic or psychological complaints or who clearly present behaviors in others that are confusing to them. In order to bring meaning to observed behaviors, you try to label the behavior or symptoms based on your (limited) expertise. In your own mind, your diagnosis is paramount, and others may not question your diagnosis.

Is this Interactional Role Ever Good For Me to Use?

Quite often this interactional role can be very beneficial for you to use as your preferred way of responding in various highly charged emotional situations. In this interactional role, you can introduce flexibility and hope through new ways of looking at medically or psychologically based concerns with knowledge. This interactional role can be extremely powerful as it provides direction for those facing the challenges of medical or psychological concerns and guides them into action. However, you become stuck when you habitually use this interactional role very rigidly as it can result in medical or psychological blaming. At this point, your Key-Relations may become angry, and relationships with those around you begin to suffer.

EXPAND:

In the next part of this chapter, we reveal to you what happens when this interactional role becomes rigid. We will guide you to other more useful interactional roles.

Help I am Stuck:

In an attempt to shield your Key-Relations from emotional duress, you label and educate others about someone's condition and the impact of the "illness" or behavior on others. Confident in your interpretation of the concerns, you frequently make a diagnosis and suggest various pharmacological interventions or recommendations for treatment to alleviate their presenting concerns. However, you must be careful, as you lack adequate training and your diagnoses could actually lead to more harm than help. Problems arise with others when you offer medical or mental health diagnoses that misrepresent the presenting issues. Sometimes, in order to stop strong emotion or anger you inadvertently may throw out a diagnosis which belittle others and/or cuts off all discussion. Sometimes your diagnosis can escalate a discussion to the point of no resolve (e.g., if you declare, "You are bi-polar, and you are crazy"). When you begin to talk down to others, communication breaks down quickly. As a result, you become stuck as hopes for coming to any form of resolution are sabotaged, and the root of the problem is never investigated; or people may stop listening to you and walk away.

Even though your wish is to make others stronger by offering understanding, your information may actually result in others believing that their situation is more hopeless than they thought. Especially, when they feel powerless over the problem or its solution. When those around you fail to experience change, feel belittled, or invalidated by you, they may end the relationship with you.

What Happens Within You:

When tensions or differences arise you may begin to feel very uncomfortable, anxious, and have a strong sense of being out-of-control. At times, you may even have trouble arguing with another in a logical fashion. If challenged too much, you may resort to using an emotional derogatory medical terminology to describe the other (e.g., "You are a Borderline"). This tends to turn a heated discussion into an argument. When this happens, you must stop and remember that when you use a label – it more accurately describes how you feel about the other person than what you actually think about the other person, and this can escalate the differences between you. In general, you are insecure in your ability to relate to others with empathy, genuineness, and positive regard. You lack confidence in your ability to respond effectively to others' presenting concerns or differences. Your efforts are shadowed when you impart knowledge to cover your insecurities. You offer advice to "protect" yourself from other's discussing serious concerns or expressing strong emotions around you.

The Case Scenario:

Rick and Kerry had a heated discussion over Rick's lack of help around the house. Kerry was in a cleaning mood and asked Rick to please take out the garbage. Rick ignored her request and continued to read the newspaper. After five minutes, Kerry asked him again to please help. At this point, Rick began to say she was a, "nag", and he would do it on his time. Kerry pointed out that the sanitation crew would be soon here, and it may be too late. At this point, Rick began to yell that she was obsessive compulsive and demanding. Kerry tried to explain that she was not obsessive compulsive but wanted to get the house clean for her family's' arrival in three days, which she was quite excited about. At this point, Rick said she was "crazy like her mother" and needed "medication" to help her with her "out-of-control" anxiety. He continued saying that her issues were not his concern nor would he make her wishes top priority. She could go pout like a baby or get pissed off; he really was tired of her immature, childish behavior. At this point, Kerry became quite furious and shared that her mother was a good person; she did not need medication nor was she immature.

Changing of the Interactional Role:

Based on information provided in the case scenario above, Rick did not like being told what to do. As a result, he was very instrumental in deflecting his lack of engagement to Kerry's request by making snide comments and remarks about both herself and her mother. When he labeled her "obsessive compulsive", he was referring to a mental health condition located within the DSM-IV-TR. By adding the word, "crazy" he was being hurtful and insensitive to Kerry's wishes and request for assistance. By bringing her mother into the conversation, he deflected the communication further and placed

Kerry in a position of having to protect and be loyal to her mother, as well as defend her own state of mind. Furthermore, as her family was arriving in three days, this comment would also put Kerry in an uneasy position about what might be said in front of her family about her mother, creating worry and tension within her. In this case, the interactional role of The Doctor was not beneficial and resulted in a breakdown of communication along with hurt feelings. In order to release his inner power, Rick would have been more effective had he shifted into the interactional role of The Mediator in order to negotiate a time and place to take out the garbage that coincided and was conducive with his "relaxation" time.

What Interactional Roles Will Give Me Personal Power?

There are a number of interactional roles you can utilize to replace the interactional role of the "The Doctor" in order to become less reactive when tensions arise. In The Doctor role, you tend to react to any and all emotional situations with some aloofness and interject medical terminology or diagnoses in order to save yourself and others from emotional pain or duress. As The Doctor, you may also make snide medical or mental comments towards another when the emotion becomes too intense. You need to practice interactional roles where you can learn to listen, observe, support, remain present, and be less verbally reactive and intellectual toward others. Through the skillful adoption of the alternative interactional roles described below, you will instill hope into situations which are characterized by chaos, sadness, anger, and hopelessness. The following chart suggests the best interactional roles for you to select from each quadrant:

Table 7 – Alternate Interactional Roles for The Doctor

Quadrant	Roles to Best Try	Roles to Initially Shy Away From
Quadrant I; Need to Intellectualize	The Judge The Teacher	The Preacher The Superman
Quadrant II: Need to Control and Manage Information	The Clown The Construction Worker The Mediator The Peacemaker The Referee	Potato Hot Head

Table 7 – Alternate Interactional Roles for The Doctor Continued

Quadrant	Roles to Best Try	Roles to Initially Shy Away From
Quadrant II: Need to Be Curious	The Detective The Journalist	
Quadrant III: Need to Avoid	The Bird Watcher The Recorder	The Runaway
Quadrant IV: Need to Save	The Angel The Firefighter The Savior	

*Please see Chapter 5 for a quick overview of the interactional roles or read Part III, How Do I learn a New Interactional Role? Part III will introduce and teach the skills of the new interactional role(s) that you selected from the above chart when you are stuck in the interactional role of The Doctor.

The Risk:

When you want to move out of the interactional role of The Doctor, you must become more self-aware of the hubris that too often maintains this role, and is often connected to a more egocentric way of looking at relations. You have to learn to demonstrate empathy by interacting in more caring ways with others. You need to work diligently to understand the concerns of others from holistic viewpoints (e.g. taking into consideration all elements around a situation or a request). You must practice asking questions that will lead to a clearer understanding of others' interactions with those around them who may be maintaining or exacerbating somatic concerns. You must also learn to be more tolerant of others rather than labeling someone when in a heated argument, listening and understating of their viewpoint. Such changes are extremely risky because in the interactional role of The Doctor you are quite comfortable presenting to others as knowing all the answers. Admitting that you do not have all the answers can feel quite threatening.

The Reflection:

In order to determine if The Doctor is your preferred interactional role in tense situations with others, it would be helpful to ask yourself the following questions:

Family: Was I the person in the family who read books to learn if my family members were sick or had a mental illness?

Social Circles: When friends acted strange, was I the person trying to figure them out by diagnosing them? Was I often thinking that my friends were sick or had a mental illness? If I were actively engaged in social clubs, was I the person trying to allay others' fears by educating them about phobias or unusual behaviors?

School Experience: As a student, was I the one who took interest in reading about medical or psychological problems and reporting back to classmates? Co-Workers: Do I have a tendency to classify or diagnosis others or situations with labels, when co-workers speak of their concerns about the workplace environment or issue with management?

Co-workers: Do I have a tendency to classify or diagnose others, or situations with labels, when co-workers speak of their concerns about the workplace environment or issue with management?

Spouse or Significant Other: Do I quickly want to help my spouse or significant others understand the reactions of others by using labels or classifications for them? Do I often "label" my spouse or significant other with a medical or psychological diagnosis especially during a heated exchange?

In General: Do I rely on labels to diagnose others? Do I regularly suggest that others need to see a specialist for additional medical or pharmacological assessment and treatment? Do I often find myself saying, "They need medication" when tensions arise rather than allowing the conflict and tension to direct me?

Chapter 7

The Judge

"Watch out!" Here comes the gavel and a decision is imparted to Key-Relations, "You are right; you are wrong!" One person is angry and in tears, while the other smiles, knowing that s/he has joined in a coalition with the Judge. The interactional role of The Judge is often activated when others present opposing positions in an emotional conflict. As the "The Judge", you have a tendency to make decisions and place a value on others' behaviors (e.g. good, bad, right wrong). You typically display effective listening, communication, analytical, and problem-solving skills. You present as a highly ethical, trustworthy, patient, hardworking, and detail-oriented person. You demand respect from those around you, and they demonstrate such respect by not questioning your decisions. In the interactional role of The Judge you tend to listen impulsively to opposing sides presented by others, render a verdict as to who is right or wrong in the situation, and make a determination how each person "should" or "should not" act. You only ask questions of others so that fair and sound judgments can be made.

How Did I Learn This Role?

As a child, you may have become quite anxious when parents or family members argued and in order to reduce the tension in the home you may have offered a "judgment" and demanded that others behave or respond in accordance with your judgment. With friends, you began to organize them in terms of right and wrong behavior. You noticed that they listened to your "judgment" and would do what you said which put you in a position of power. As an adult, you have a tendency to engage in the interactional role of The Judge when three situations happen around you; (1) People close to you quarrel frequently and present their opposing opinions to their differences to you, (2) Your children run to you to tattle each time they fight and argue, or (3) Friends in the process of separation or divorce tend to come to you and want you to be an ally in supporting their viewpoints. In all cases, people are saying to you *"Help me by supporting me!"* Through the process, your Key-Relations may subtly or actively work to entice you to their way of looking at an issue.

Typically, those around you often demand for you to provide a ruling for their issues. Often you do not use negotiation or mediation techniques with those who present with distress. Rather, you listen to presenting arguments (while often disregarding words or behaviors of those involved in the situation), offer value-laden feedback (e.g., "You are right; you are wrong"), and tell people what they must do to resolve their differences. For example in the above situations, with a spouse or significant other you tend to judge their action or opinion with some explanation but you tend not to let others question your decisions. You are eager to stop the fighting and to resolve the problems, and you investigate on your own terms the presenting issues in detail. In the end, it is you who makes a decision as to how define a problem and resolve it. This can result in those around you becoming, angry, annoyed, and resistant toward your suggestions and they may back away from you.

Is this Interactional Role Ever Good For Me to Use?

Quite often this interactional role can be very beneficial for you to use as your preferred way of responding in various highly charged emotional situations. In this interactional role, you sort out the differences of others through detailed questioning, the questions are based on your value system and rules. You then present a judgment and people, without questioning, must accept your ruling. This interactional role is very powerful as those around you see you as very, logical, wise, and fair. However, you become stuck when you habitually use this interactional role rigidly as others may not listen to your advice or be willing to obey your rules. At this point, your relations with those around you begin to suffer, as you get angry with those who appear to be disrespecting of your decisions.

EXPAND:

In the next part of this chapter, we reveal to you what happens when this interactional role becomes rigid and guide you to other more useful interactional roles.

Help I am Stuck:

As The Judge you may notice that you rarely encourage communication or negotiation among those who quarrel around you. Instead, you encourage your Key-Relations to direct their differences to you directly in an attempt to gather facts quickly for later use in rendering a decision. If in the process, you collect very basic information, lacking sufficient breadth about the development of the problem you can get stuck. When you feel you have heard enough from each opposing side, you render an opinion, with the goal of putting a halt to the incessant, annoying quarreling or complaining. Through the process, your Key-Relations can feel slighted and perceive that a union between you and the one you agree with was created. By failing to encourage communication and negotiation skills among those in differences, you become stuck as your Key-Relations become angry, may shy away from you or even cut-off from you. When you collect basic information the differences between others are not truly understood, and as a rendered decision is not questioned, the concerns become buried only to resurface at a later time.

What Happens Within You:

When your Key-Relations disagree or argue you may have a tendency to become annoyed, uneasy, uncomfortable, and/or experience anxiety. As people come to you, especially children, looking to help them with their differences you tend to feel responsible to handle the decision. In order to try to retain peace, fulfill the expectation that you will handle the differences, and reassure people that you are right. Through rendering a decision, the response is not questioned, and people return to a level where disagreements are no longer on the surface, helping to reduce your annoyance and anxieties.

Case Scenario:

Bobbie, age 14, has begun to walk to his home every day with three of his friends and two of their older siblings. When they arrive at Bobbie's house they often will sit in the TV room where they joke, laugh, and have something to drink. They wait an hour at Bobbie's house to be picked up by their parents after work. Their parents are co-workers and friends of Bobbie's mother. This has become a routine and the adolescents enjoy the time after school together. Typically Bobbie's mother is at home when they arrive, but there are times when she arrives home from work approximately 15 minutes after the adolescents arrive from school. Bobbie's younger sister, Linda, age 8, tries to "hang out" with the older children who are annoyed by her, but they let her stay with them. This has become an issue for the family as Linda has started to go to her father and share that one of the older boys may have sworn in front of her, told dirty jokes, and that they drank some pop which the father has said they can no longer have as it is too costly for the family. At times, Linda is not always truthful and embellishes situations to her father. After the father hears Linda's side of the story, he calls Bobbie into the room to question him. When Bobbie tries to explain what happened, the father focuses on the fact that Bobbie broke his previous rule sand forbid his friends to come again to his house. When Bobbie is found guilty by his father, Linda smiles and will go play in her room. Bobbie has begun to yell at Linda when the father is not around and refuses to do anything with her. Bobbie is beginning to spend more time in his room, away from the family, especially when the father is home. When Bobbie's mother tries to "save" him, as she is aware of Linda's behaviors and embellished stories, the mother and father tend to get into serious arguments. The father tends to stick to his judgment that he sees as fair and holds to his decision that adolescents are no longer welcomed in "his" home. The mother tries to explain she is committed to their parents that the adolescents could come to their home until they finished work. His decision places her in an awkward position, therefore she will not agree with his decision. This makes the father angry toward her and their relations suffer (e.g., mother refuses his advances for sex during this intense time).

Changing of the Interactional Role:

In the above case scenario, the father was clearly acting like a Judge towards his children and wife. This created a rift between the children as one child (the daughter) was elevated to a position where her word was golden and the son was found guilty, breaking the rules of the arents. The father inadvertently was reinforcing the daughter's "tattling" behavior as he was not aware that her "stories" were not always true. The son believed he was unfairly judged and grew to be resentful towards the younger sister. He viewed his father as favoring his sister. The wife was living as if she were on egg shells trying to make everyone happy. She felt the need to protect her son, was beginning to hide things from her husband, and as a result, the husband and wife had begun to argue putting discord and distance in their marriage. When the father told his wife his decision that the adolescents were not welcomed in "his" home, the wife was placed in a difficult situation with her friends and began to feel like a punished "child". In order to become more effective in this situation, it would be helpful for the father to use the interactional roles of The Detective, The Journalist and The Mediator with his children. This would allow him to hear both sides of the story presented and to refrain from making a judgment. Instead, he could teach and model for the children how to work out their differences and help them negotiate how to handle the friends coming over after school in a more positive way. By shifting into the interactional role of The Angel with his wife, he would display empathy toward her situation and promises to her co-workers, while being able to negotiate new terms and rules when the adolescents' visit. Through this process the parents would not fight; the mother would not need to protect the children and agreements could be negotiated, and the wife would feel on equal terms in her marriage with her husband, replacing discord with harmony.

What Interactional Roles Will Give Me Personal Power?

There are a number of interactional roles that you can utilize to replace "The Judge" and become less responsible when differences among others are presented to you. As The Judge, you tend to react to any and all differences with aloofness and authoritative, decision-making behavior in order to save others from emotional pain, conflict, or duress. You take complete control of emotional situations by telling others how to behave or not behave. Therefore, you need to practice interactional roles where you can learn to listen, observe, support, remain present, be curious about situations, and become less judgmental toward others. Through the skillful adoption of these alternative interactional roles, you may instill hope into situations which are characterized by chaos, sadness, anger, and hopeless. The following chart suggests the best interactional roles for you to select from each quadrant:

Table 8 – Alternative Interactional Roles for The Judge

Quadrant	Roles to Best Try	Roles to Initially Shy Away From
Quadrant I; Need to Intellectualize	The Teacher	The Doctor The Preacher The Superman
Quadrant II: Need to Control and Manage Information	The Clown The Construction Worker The Mediator The Peacemaker The Referee	Potato Hot-Head
Quadrant II: Need to Be Curious	The Detective The Journalist	
Quadrant III: Need to Avoid	The Bird Watcher The Recorder	The Runaway
Quadrant IV: Need to Save	The Angel The Savior	The Firefighter

*Please see Chapter 5 for a quick overview of the interactional roles or read Part III, *How Do I learn a New Interactional Role?* Part III will introduce and teach the skills of the new interactional role(s) that you selected from the above chart to use when you are stuck in the interactional role of The Judge.

The Risk:

Perhaps the greatest risk for you to get out of the interactional role of The Judge is to "become more human", more of a mediator, and allow others to interact with each other. You choose the interactional role of The Judge, because you are so stressed when people are fighting and disagree. You need to put away your gavel and be willing to explore presenting problems, differences of others, and be open to listening to all viewpoints while not judging. This means that you will need to engage with others by learning to ask questions. You have to find out what happened prior to the behaviors being reported, what the behavior specifically looked like, and what those reporting to you did in the situation. How did they contribute to the situation and what happened? Questioning will help to reveal hidden agendas that maintain the differences of those around you. You will also appear more "human" as all people will feel as if they could share with you their perspectives on the situation. Of course, you must be courageous and allow yourself to cope with strong emotions of fear because you have to leave the solution of the problems to them.

The Reflection:

In order to determine if The Judge is your preferred interactional role in tense situations with others it would be helpful to ask the following questions:

> **Family:** Did I often listen to family members and then present a judgment or decision regarding how each member should act in a certain situation?

> **Social Circles:** When with friends, did I tell them who was right or wrong when a disagreement emerged? When actively engaged in social clubs, was I the person listening to all options and then rendering a judgment as to the proper course of action?

> **School Experience:** On group assignments, did I assume responsibility for making decisions regarding how assigned projects or tasks would be completed, especially if classmates had different ideas?

> **Co-Workers:** Do I have a tendency, when co-workers are dismayed, to make decisions for them as to how they should respond or whom they should contact to resolve their concerns?

Spouse or Significant Other: Do I often tell my spouse or significant what they should or should not do in a particular situation? Do I become annoyed or angry if I am questioned or my judgment and decisions are not implemented?

In General: Do I find myself listening to opposing sides and then directing others how they should respond in various situations? Do I often find myself saying, "After carefully considering both sides and only one side of the issue, I believe that you should …."

Chapter Eight

The Preacher

"Home schooling? I believe that is a very irresponsible choice of you to home school Alfredo. If you truly care about your child, you will send him to school. Children need socialization, to play with others and, by the way, do you possess the education credentials required to home school your children?" The interactional role of The Preacher stems from a belief that those around you need to receive direction in life based on established moral or ethical principles. Consequently, as "The Preacher" you may have a tendency to "preach" to your Key-Relations about what you perceive to be right. You demonstrate strong communication and organizational skills, which you use to motivate others to change their behaviors by following your guidance. You present to others as very dependable, yet passionate about projecting strong religious, ethical, and moral beliefs onto those around you for their own good. You typically advise people in emotional conflict or differences to respond to their problems or dilemmas in a dichotomous, either-or manner. Advice is solely based on your belief system. When values are contrary to your belief system, the values of others are often marginalized or discounted. Throughout the exchange with others, you remain blissfully unaware of your overbearing attitude. You typically collect only limited information from others about their conflicts. You are more interested in those present listening to you, and as a result, conversation is directed towards you.

How Did I Learn This Role?

As a child, you may have been around those who had very strong convictions. Whenever you misbehaved you were lectured to and reminded of how you *should* behave. You may even have been a strong follower of the church and believe in the preaching of the church. As you grew older you adopted the values of those around you, especially a parent. As an adult, you are often engaged into action by others who lack strong ethical beliefs and value systems. Your social contacts and friends may be limited to only those who have the same beliefs and values compatible to your own. When you encounter others who oppose your prevailing family, political or religious value system, you may tend to spend a lot of time trying to "convince" them to adopt your values and beliefs. In this process, you may inadvertently interrupt, cut-off, or minimize others' ideas. You may tend to gather only minimal information before launching into a "sermon" designed to help those around you understand the best way to resolve their problems. By preaching answers and solutions for disagreements between (you and) your Key-Relations, differences are held in check but rarely resolved.

Is this Interactional Role Ever Good For Me to Use?

Quite often this interactional role is useful for you to use as your preferred role in various highly emotional situations. In this interactional role, you can provide moral guidance to others. Also, you are a beacon of light for those who feel insecure. In this role you feel strong and important as you rely on the moral values and principles that you see as universal. However, you become stuck when you habitually use this interactional role very rigidly. This is especially true when you use this interactional role with other people who do not share your morals or belief system. At this point, your relations with those around you begin to suffer as you become upset and angry with those who do not listen to you.

EXPAND:

In the next part of this chapter, we reveal to you what happens when this interactional role becomes rigid. We will guide you to other more useful interactional roles.

Help I am Stuck:

As you have a tendency to instill your values unto others and gather only limited information about the differences or emotional concerns of others, you rarely take time to understand the family, political, or religious values of others. When this happens you may find yourself caught in a double bind, as others may want to find resolution for their differences. However, you insist the resolutions match your value and belief system. Faced with an untenable situation of trying to convince others to your way of thinking, you may become aloof or demonstrate disinterest in others. As a consequence, solutions are rarely developed. This results in a disconnection between you and others which is exacerbated if they reject your values; others may become verbally angry or act out even more aggressively against you or the "system." At this point, you become stuck as those around you may distance from you, ignore you, or if they agree with you, personal growth may become stilted as there are only limited, if any, new ideas or suggestions.

What Happens Within You:

When strong values and beliefs are at the core of your thinking, you have a tendency to present a rigid thought style characterized by a need to order the world in a manner consistent with your own personal beliefs and values. When opposing views are presented you may become anxious, feel threatened, and somewhat powerless. During periods of intense stress, you may become overly rigid and want to take immediate control by insisting others follow your advice. As you tend not to consider the viewpoints of others, you may become angry, annoyed, and irritated. You may respond by degrading others who have contrary points of view.

The Case Scenario:

Marion is the 18-year-old daughter of a foreign diplomat. Demonstrations of gracious attitudes and proper behaviors are very important to her parents. Both parents, but especially her father, have declared that Marion only engage in behavior conducive to their family's "social status" when in the presence of others. Weary of what she refers to as her parents' "hypocrisy," Marion begins to act out. She is rude to her parents, and their houseguests, has several parts of her body pierced and wears gaudy eyebrow rings and navel studs. She purchases a facial tattoo and refuses to attend social gatherings in her parents' home. Marion's anger intensifies when her grandfather tries to speak to her and further reinforces her parent's value system.

Her grandfather speaks of how they have a predominant role in the political events of their country, and she must comply at all times to her parent's requests. She must wear the dress of her country; her shoulders can never be revealed and the wearing or display of jewelry is not allowed. Marion must remember to stand quietly next to her mother in social gatherings and politely smile to all guests when she is greeted. She is not to shake hands with another or speak until she is granted permission to do so by her mother. She must remove all body piercings and rings immediately. Her grandfather has made arrangements for the facial tattoo to be removed. He goes on to tell Marion that she is acting like an immature "brat" and has been overly spoiled by her parents. Marion responds to her grandfather's "lecture" by crossing her arms and staring at the floor. She refuses to make eye contact or respond to any of his questions. When her grandfather finishes speaking to her, she simply gets up from her chair, turns on her Pandora radio, and goes to her room. When she comes out of her room she is wearing very large pierced earrings, a short mini-skirt, and a top that displays her shoulders.

Changing of the Interactional Role:

After observing Marion's behavior, the grandfather realized he was not effective in helping Marion change her behavior. Rather, he alienated her further. At first he was angry towards her for not listening to him, but he then began to reflect; he was acting like her parents, and he needed to shift his approach to the situation. He felt disparate, as his son had confided in him that if Marion, his oldest granddaughter, did not change her behaviors; they would send her to a boarding school. The grandfather decided he would try a different approach with Marion, instead he asked for her permission to speak to her. Reluctantly she shut off her radio and turned to him. The grandfather, in the interactional roles of The Journalist and The Detective, began to explore Marion's behaviors with the goal of understanding her perspective. He asked Marion why she had refused to attend the last dinner party given by her parents. Marion reported that she was not permitted to speak at these parties and that her parents had demanded her to stay at the table until all guests had finished eating (sometimes as long as 3 hours). She said that she did not mind helping her parents with their diplomatic duties, but that her mother had become so engrossed in supporting her father's career that she no longer had time for her only daughter. Marion cried as she discussed earlier times when she and her mother would shop and have lunch together. She said that she was afraid that her mother no longer loved her and that she had behaved badly in recent months in order to "hurt" her mother. The grandfather began to understand that Marion was afraid that she was losing her mother. As she spoke more, he understood it was not about the family values; in fact she respected the family's traditions and beliefs. She even wanted to support her father, but she also wanted her mother to spend time with her. With this new understanding, the grandfather knew that his job was to reunite mother and daughter in a healthy way so that Marion was no longer afraid and believed that she had an important role in the family.

In retrospect, the parents and grandfather did not understand that Marion was working feverishly to communicate her unhappiness about the perceived loss of her mother's affection. When the grandfather, also in The Preacher, endorsed her parents' views, Marion shut down. They were stuck in an intense situation with no resolution. In the interactional roles of The Journalist and The Detective, he explored Marion's needs as expressed by her behaviors during the previous year. This offered Marion the opportunity to "voice" her fears and anger in a safe way. Listening to Marion the grandfather recognized the emotional gap between mother and daughter.

What Interactional Roles Will Give Me Personal Power?

There are a number of interactional roles that you can utilize to replace "The Preacher" allowing you to become less verbally responsive or rigid when emotional situations arise. As The Preacher, you tend to react to any and all emotional situations with aloofness and very authoritative, lecturing, behavior in order to save others from emotional pain or duress. You take complete control of emotional situations by telling others how to behave or not behave from a view from a religious, political, or value-laden perspective. Therefore, you need to practice interactional roles where you can learn to listen, observe, support, remain present, and be less verbally reactive and intellectual toward others. Through the skillful adoption of the alternative interactional roles discussed below, you may change situations which are characterized by chaos, sadness, anger, and hopelessness. The following chart suggests the best interactional roles for you to select from each quadrant:

Table 9 – Alternate Interactional Roles for The Preacher

Quadrant	Roles to Best Try	Roles to Initially Shy Away From
Quadrant I; Need to Intellectualize	The Doctor The Judge The Teacher	The Superman
Quadrant II: Need to Control and Manage Information	The Clown The Construction Worker The Mediator The Peacemaker The Referee	Potato Hot-Head
Quadrant II: Need to Be Curious	The Detective The Journalist	
Quadrant III: Need to Avoid	The Bird Watcher The Recorder The Runaway	
Quadrant IV: Need to Save	The Angel The Savior	The Firefighter

*Please see Chapter 5 for a quick overview of the interactional roles or read Part III, *How Do I learn a New Interactional Role?* Part III will introduce and teach the skills of the new interactional role(s) that you selected from the above chart when you are stuck in the interactional role of The Preacher.

The Risk:

When you want to move out of the interactional role of The Preacher, you must learn to listen to others' belief and value systems without judgment. Your greatest challenge is to demonstrate openness to and acceptance of other philosophical views. Others will need to be able to express their family, political, or religious views without being interrupted. You must work to understand divergent ideas, beliefs, values, and cultural norms. You need to become more approachable, yet remain keenly aware of the actions of others.

The Reflection:

In order to determine if The Preacher is your preferred interactional role in tense situations with others, it would be helpful to ask yourself the following questions:

> **Family:** As a child, was I quick to share my opinions based on my moral or ethical principles and become angry if other family members did not endorse my thoughts?

> **Social Circles:** was I eager to share my opinions based on my moral or ethical principles, then become defensive and ignore friends if they did not support my views? If I actively engaged in social clubs, did I insist that things be done my way? If others in my circle chose a different way, did I respond by getting upset?

> **School Experience:** When I worked on a group project, did I decide what had to be done, how it had to be done, and by whom based on my moral and ethical principles?

> **Co-Workers:** When co-workers speak of their dismay at work do I tell them how they should respond in various situations based on my moral or ethical principles?

> **Spouse or Significant Other:** Do I sometimes talk down to my spouse or significant other by lecturing on how he should or should not respond in a situation?

> **In General:** Am I tolerant of others' views or do I find myself imposing personal moral or ethical principles unto others? Do I often find myself saying, "They need to do things this way...after all it is in their best interest."

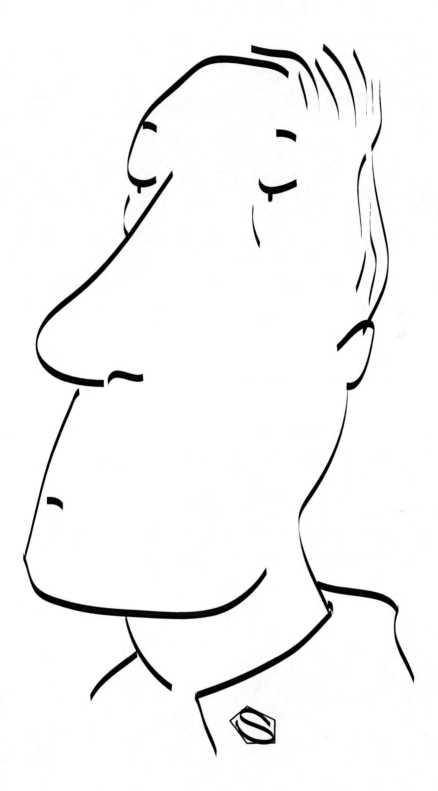

The Superman 67

Chapter Nine

The Superman

"No longer am I just a man. I am Superman....you look at me as just a 'man'...but I know the difference between right and wrong... as I am Superman...." (Superman theme song lyrics, retrieved 2010). As "The Superman" you have an unhealthy sense of responsibility and you believe that others lack the capacity to resolve their own issues successfully, and therefore, need you to "guide" them. You know everything and can be easily identified by the books you collect on your shelf or the degrees that you have acquired and hang on your walls. You are confident in all aspects of a situation regardless of the presenting concerns or differences. Listening to others is not your strength. All communication is directed toward you and others must constantly thank you for the honor of being your spouse, significant other, friend, co-worker or acquaintance. You have advice for all situations and answers for all questions. Furthermore, you frequently share your experiences and tend to engage in "name dropping" of all the important people you know.

How Did I Learn This Role?

As a child, you may have been uncomfortable when others around you appeared to be more competent. As a result you may have brought attention to yourself by telling others of your "gifts and talents". After a while, in order to gain attention and acknowledgment, you focused on yourself and your accomplishments. As an adult, you come to action when others are highly insecure and demonstrate very low self-esteem. You like people who need guidance. They often will look upon you as being a "father or mother "figure for them. Your Key-Relations often place you on a pedestal, and you enjoy the attention and acknowledgment from others. You limit the discussion by others and monopolize the conversation. When you want to "guide" others you use your intellect to control others during an emotionally charged situation.

Is this Interactional Role Ever Good For Me to Use?

In most situations, this interactional role is not beneficial. You take too much responsibility and easily overwhelm those around you. However in very extreme, chaotic, and tense situations this interactional role can help to organize quickly and calm the situation. In this interactional role you give orders and you expect people to follow without questioning.   This interactional role is very powerful as people see you as their leader or guru. However, you become stuck when you habitually use this interactional role rigidly as others; (1) others may become totally dependent on you and you realize you cannot fulfill their needs, or (2) others stop listening to you and are unwilling to obey your orders. At this point your relations with those around you begin to suffer as you feel out-of-control.

EXPAND:

In the next part of this chapter, we reveal to you what happens when this interactional role becomes rigid. We will guide you to other more useful interactional roles.

Help I am Stuck:

When you take the role of "The Superman" people do not learn how to make decisions or resolve problems. Interactions among and between those around you are not encouraged, so others rarely discuss their differences or concerns openly. Your Key-Relations typically fail at decision making as they regularly defer to the superior intelligence of you as the Superman. People in a highly charged emotional situation rarely make progress, because they are not provided with opportunities to grow or learn ways to resolve their own issues. Consequently, you become stuck as there is no change in those around you and you become overly responsible for others.

What Happens Within You:

When tensions or differences arise you begin to feel very uncomfortable, anxious, and have a strong sense of wanting to take control of the situation in order to "guide" others. When people express emotion, you react with authoritarian and disengaged behavior. You emphasize your educational accomplishments in an attempt to disguise your own personal insecurities. In all situations, you need to be in-control and present as "perfect" and "all-knowing", which places a lot of pressure and responsibility on you for the well-being of others.

The Case Scenario:

Sherita and Jackson are newlyweds and seem to have difficulty with differences in gender roles and their expectations of each other. Sherita's father left when she was nine years of age, and she has not had a positive male role model in her life. Jackson had trouble learning in school and barely graduated from high school. They have a mutual older friend, Ronnie. Every time they have a fight they phone him. Ronnie then answers their questions and lectures them on how they should conduct their marriage. Sherita is enthralled by the strength of Ronnie and often brings this up to Jackson when they are fighting. Jackson is intimidated by Ronnie's (Superman) intelligence and the fact that his wife is "enthralled" with him. They are young and do not want to question him, so they do exactly what he says. Gender role differences and expectations continue to be an issue for them and are at the base of their arguments. Yet, each time they attempt to discuss these differences with Ronnie he redirects attention to himself and explains how he, as an older more experienced person, knows what is best for each of them. This response further magnifies the seriousness of Sherita's and Jackson's presenting problems. Sherita and Jackson believe that their marriage will not survive if left on their own without Ronnie's guidance.

Changing of the Interactional Role:

Ronnie became a pseudo parent to them. They feared that they would displease him which was keeping them in a communication exchange that led to little change between them and increased dependence on Ronnie to "guide" their marriage. In order to create change in the case scenario above, Ronnie could shift into the interactional role of The Mediator. In this role, he could invite discussions of differences between Sherita's and Jackson's gender roles from their unique perspectives and explore what they expect from each other in these roles. By switching to the role of The Detective, he could ask questions about Sherita's and Jackson's expectation of their roles when they married. By integrating the roles of The Mediator and The Detective, Sherita and Jackson would learn how to negotiate with each other and come to resolution about their gender differences and expectations. In the interactional role, The Teacher, Ronnie could educate both Sherita and Jackson about their differences, which have stemmed from their family of origin, friends, education, and social contexts. Through these roles, Ronnie would connect with Sherita and Jackson in a humanistic level. He would become a mentor rather than a pseudo parent and abandon the "all knowing" Superman interactional role.

What Interactional Roles Will Give Me Personal Power?

There are a number of interactional roles that you can utilize to replace "The Superman" allowing you to become less reactive when tensions arise. As The Superman you tend to react to any and all emotional situations with extreme aloofness and very authoritative behavior in order to guide others from emotional pain or duress. You take complete control when emotions become too intense. Therefore, you need to practice interactional roles where you can learn to listen, observe, support, remain present, and be less verbally reactive and intellectual toward others. Through the skillful adoption of these alternative interactional roles, you may instill hope into situations which are characterized by chaos, sadness, anger, and hopeless. The following chart suggests the best interactional roles for you to select from each quadrant:

Table 10 – Alternate Interactional Roles for The Superman

Quadrant	Roles to Best Try	Roles to Initially Shy Away From
Quadrant I; Need to Intellectualize	Judge Teacher	Doctor Preacher
Quadrant II: Need to Control and Manage Information	The Clown The Construction Worker The Mediator The Peacemaker The Referee	Mr. Potato Hot Head
Quadrant II: Need to Be Curious	Detective Journalist	
Quadrant III: Need to Avoid	The Bird Watcher The Recorder	The Runaway
Quadrant IV: Need to Save	The Angel The Firefighter The Nurse The Savior	

*Please see Chapter 5 for a quick overview of the interactional roles or read Part III, *How Do I learn a New Interactional Role?* Part III will introduce and teach the skills of the new interactional role(s) that you selected from the above chart, when you are stuck in the interactional role of The Superman.

The Risk:

In order to move out of the interactional role of The Superman, you must practice being a caring human being and demonstrate the ability to listen to others before speaking. Furthermore, you need to believe that others can solve their own issues with minimal guidance, direction, or advice. This is extremely risky for you; as you like to remain aloof from others, and you rely on your extraordinary intellect to help others who seem helpless when in the face of a situation. You must learn how to move away from this "safe" position to one that is open to connection and sensitive to other's input. You must learn to explore the differences or concerns of others, actively seek out enough information, observe the behavior of those present and comprehend how tensions may influence the presenting problem. In this manner, the behaviors, communication, and tensions around issues or differences will surface and change can occur.

The Reflection:

In order to determine if The Superman is your preferred interactional role in tense situations with others, it would be helpful to ask yourself the following questions:

> **Family:** With my family did I attempt to garner attention by talking about my intelligence and accomplishments?

> **Social Circles:** When friends talked about themselves, did I refocus the conversation back to myself and how good I was in so many things? In social clubs, did I need to be the leader because I knew so much more than others?

> **School Experience:** As a student, did I strive to be the best of the best? If other students appeared more knowledgeable, did I "talk myself up" in front of them?

> **Co-Workers:** Do I have a tendency, when co-workers speak of their dismay, to focus attention on myself and do strive to "better" than them?

> **Spouse or Significant Other:** Do I sometimes talk down to my spouse or significant other? Do I tell them about my superiority intellect and become dismissive toward their suggestions?

> **In General:** Do I dominate others by talking about myself and how I know more about an issue than they? Do I often find myself saying, "Due to my knowledge and experience, I know....?

Chapter Ten

The Teacher

"Do you realize that your children are always interrupting you? I think that you need to look at your parenting style and see how you respond to your child. You know your parenting styles are interfering with the way your children act. For example … " In the interactional role of "The Teacher", you tend to reduce all tensions, differences and/ or emotions into a lesson. You espouse to all that knowledge is the cure-all for every situation. When difficulties between Key-Relations arise, as The Teacher you impart knowledge in order to help others grow in a physical, intellectual, and even spiritual level. You often use a lecturing style or suggest books others *should* read in order to help "fix" any and all situations that they are encounter. You possess strong oral and written communication skills and are effective at multi-tasking. Although you demonstrate interest in others' concerns, you rarely display any emotional response. Interaction among Key-relations is neither encouraged nor explored. You believe that others need to be educated about how to be a better parent, spouse, child, etc. You have the knowledge for them and when adopt your knowledge they will live a better life.

How Did I Learn This Role?

You learned early in life that when you shared your knowledge people became impressed by what you shared. You then discovered that you helped them through situations. As result, Key-Relations who present themselves as learners easily engage you into the interactional role of The Teacher. When they question you about some difficulty, you immediately begin to teach them how to make things better. In these situations, it is not uncommon for you to conduct your own research, so you can pass knowledge onto others. You also respond to requests for information by referring Key-Relations to informational websites. You might also provide them with an informational reading list.

Is this Interactional Role Ever Good For Me to Use?

Quite often this interactional role can be beneficial for you to use as your preferred way of responding in various highly charged emotional situations. In this interactional role, you are able to help others to grow as you introduce new understanding about their differences. Your teachings are based on your knowledge and training. This interactional role is very powerful as those around you see you as logical, wise, and smart. However, you become stuck when you habitually use this interactional role rigidly. In this role you remain aloof, which can distance others from you. Furthermore, when others follow through on your ideas that promise to solve all emotional problems and your teachings fail, others become distrustful of you. When they fail, they tend to blame you, and as a result your relations with them begin to suffer.

EXPAND:

In the next part of this chapter, we reveal to you what happens when this interactional role becomes rigid and guide you to other more useful interactional roles.

Help I am Stuck:

When you are eager to help others understand their differences or concerns with another, you tend to rush to "educate". Through the process, you risk getting insufficient information about the presenting concern or its impact on those around you. As a result, people do not learn how to change their relational behaviors for the better. Typically Key-Relations like the fact that you remain aloof and controlled during intense emotional moments. When others have difficulty adjusting to your educational suggestions you may become more rigid, aloof, and insistent about the importance of education being the main solution. If others present you with several new solutions from which to choose, you are afraid to try out one of these solutions if it does not have an educational base. Your desire to only "educate" others can ultimately lead to a bottleneck where no change is made, and differences or conflicts remain.

What Happens Within You:

When others present with expressions of emotion or tensions, you may feel at a loss as to how to appropriately respond. In order to avert discussions of serious concerns or expressions of strong emotions, you resort to presenting information through education, thereby "protecting" yourself from uncomfortable feelings. You tend to disengage from the emotional part by resorting to education. During the process, you take control by becoming intellectual and thinking, which keeps you aloof from others and emotions are not addressed.

The Case Scenario:

When Andrias entered Bijay's office, he did not make eye contact with him. He sat in a slumped position with his eyes cast at the floor and appeared to be exhausted and anxious. Andrias had just been promoted to a managerial position at the store where they both were employed. He was responsible for managing five subordinates and for insuring that each met daily sales quotas specified by the store owner. Andrias told Bijay that he was unhappy in his new position. He shared that he was initially excited about his promotion, but now had "problems" with it. After leaving work, he began to sweat, had difficulty breathing, and felt dizzy. He was even afraid he may have cancer.

Bijay listened to Andrias' concerns and told Andrias that he was sure he was having anxiety issues. Bijay immediately went to the internet and pulled up a webpage on, *Living with Anxiety*. After reading it, he concluded that Andrias had Panic Attacks. He told him that the problem could be "fixed" if he understood how panic attacks developed. Bijay then spent the next 30 minutes looking at web articles on anxiety. He enthusiastically shared his findings with Andrias. Bijay explained that Andrias should not worry about his anxiety attacks. He just needed to follow the instructions on the internet: "inhale and take deep breaths" to stop them.

Six weeks later, Andrias returned to Bijay's office and said that his anxiety attacks had not gotten better. Bijay and Andrias revisited the websites to look for new solutions and Andrias was told to drink tea when he felt overwhelmed. Three weeks later Andrias phoned Bijay to report that his panic attacks were occurring on a daily basis, and were so intense he "felt certain that he was going to die." Bijay suggested that he buy a book on dealing with anxiety.

Changing of the Interactional Role:

In the case scenario above, Bijay had not taken the time to understand the basis for Andrias' anxiety. Instead, he was offering "cookbook" approaches for solving Andrias' issue. Bijay would have been more helpful if he had integrated the interactional roles of The Journalist and The Detective. Through asking questions and listening to Andrias' story, he would have learned when, where, how and why Andrias was becoming anxious. Once he understood the basis for Andrias' concerns or worries he would have been able to help Andrias deal more effectively with the situation, rather than band-aiding the situation.

Andrias met Bijay for lunch a month later and shared that he had seen his general practitioner who referred him to a therapist. The therapist had helped Andrias explore the circumstances (i.e., antecedents, immediate conditions) in which Andrew's anxiety attacks occurred. In particular, what Andrias experienced just prior to these attacks. Andrias shared that he learned that he became most anxious when his supervisor questioned him about the productivity of "his five employees". Andrias then said that he discovered the supervisor reminded him a lot of his father, who was very religious, rigid, and who had very high expectations of him. In a trailing voice, Andrias said that he could never please his father. His supervisor, unconsciously, touched a "very sensitive string" in him. The therapist taught him to realize that his supervisor was much more confident about Andrias' competencies than his father used to be since he promoted him to this job. Also, the therapist taught him how to relax himself in these situations. Even though his anxiety attacks were continuing, they had lessened and he knew how to cope with them better. With his new understanding, Andrias was becoming more self-confident and he was developing effective skills for managing his daily stress.

What Interactional Roles Will Give Me Personal Power?

There are a number of interactional roles that you can utilize to replace "The Teacher" enabling you to become less responsible for educating when differences among others are presented to you. You tend to react to any and all differences with aloofness and knowledge in order to save others from emotional pain, conflict, or duress. You try to take complete control of emotional situations by educating others on what they *should* or *should not* do. You will need to practice interactional roles where they can learn to listen, observe, support, remain present, be curious about situations and open to allowing others to express their differences. Through the skillful adoption of these alternative interactional roles, you may instill hope into situations which are characterized by chaos, sadness, anger, and hopeless. The following chart suggests the best interactional roles for you to select from each quadrant:

Table 11 – Alternative Interactional Roles for The Teacher

Quadrant	Roles to Best Try	Roles to Initially Shy Away From
Quadrant I; Need to Intellectualize		The Doctor The Judge The Preacher The Superman
Quadrant II: Need to Control and Manage Information	The Clown The Mediator The Peacemaker	The Construction Worker The Referee Potato Hot-Head
Quadrant II: Need to Be Curious	The Detective The Journalist	

Table 11 – Alternative Interactional Roles for The Teacher Continued

Quadrant	Roles to Best Try	Roles to Initially Shy Away From
Quadrant III: Need to Avoid	The Bird Watcher The Recorder	The Runaway
Quadrant IV; Need to Save	The Angel The Savior	The Firefighter

*Please see Chapter 5 for a quick overview of the interactional roles or read Part III, *How Do I learn a New Interactional Role?* Part III will introduce and teach the skills of the new interactional role(s) that you selected from the above chart when you are stuck in the interactional role of The Teacher.

The Risk:

When you want to move out of the interactional role of the Teacher, you must be willing to allow tensions to develop between or with others and encourage others to talk about their differences or concerns without wanting to teach. This is extremely risky behavior for you as you are very comfortable in an instructional position. If you try to "teach" before knowing the real basis for the presenting concerns or differences, others may become more comfortable, but they will not be motivated to explore their emotional levels. Consequently, presenting problems or differences cannot be resolved. Simply put, if you truly want to help others, you must allow tensions to rise so that behavior patterns around the presenting concern or differences can be identified through what people say and how they behave. The creation of tension is especially discomforting for you as you like to maintain harmony. Adding to your discomfort is the fact that you may freeze and not know how to respond to others who present strong emotions such as anger, deep sadness, grief, or depression. You will need to learn how to deal with the present moment; staying with the presented affect, and engaging in new interactional roles that will allow others the opportunity to openly discuss their differences, concerns or worries.

The Reflection:

In order to determine if the Teacher is your preferred interactional role in tense situations with others it would be helpful to ask yourself the following questions:

Family: Did I try "educate" family members about appropriate behaviors when conflicted situations arose? Did some family members refer to me as "A know-it all?"

Social Circles: When friends were hesitant to complete a task, did I teach them the best way to approach it? In social clubs, did I assume responsibility for teaching others about the best options for completing an activity?

School Experience: Did I reinforce information provided by the teacher and regularly serve as a tutor to classmates? If other students complained about completing an assigned task, did I attempt to "educate" them about the value of the assignment?

Co-Workers: Do I have a tendency when co-workers are dismayed or confused about something to try to "teach" them about how they should respond, think, or do?

Spouse or Significant Other: Do I try to teach or instruct my spouse or significant other on what they should or should not do in a particular situation? Do I become annoyed if they do not follow my teachings?

In General: Is my gut reaction to educate others? Do I often suggest that others read books or articles on various subjects? Do I often find myself saying, "I need to teach them about...." about my intelligence and accomplishments?

Quadrant II

The Need to Manage and Control Information

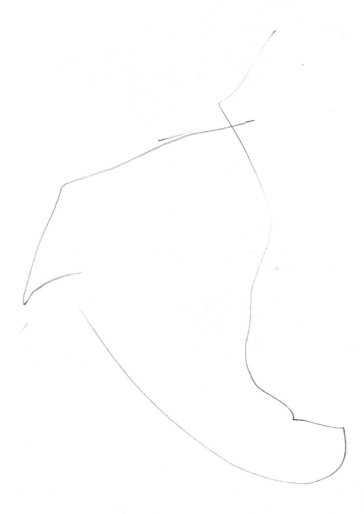

Quadrant II - The Need to Manage and Control Information

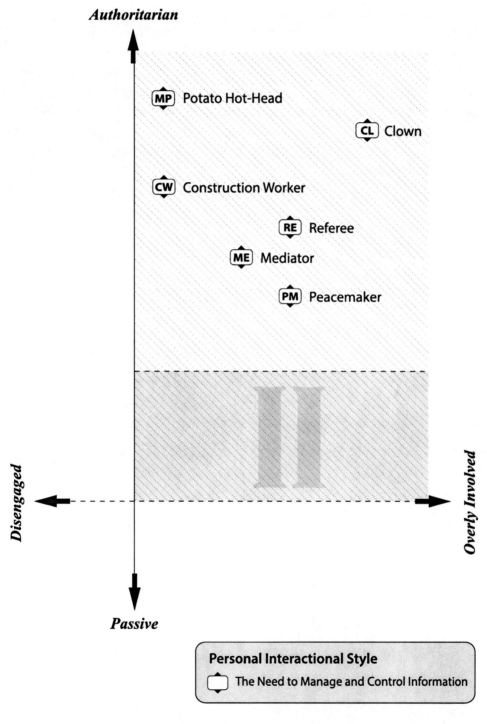

In pondering your interactional roles and style, you discover that you need to control who speaks to whom. Then you make decisions as to how others *should* behave or what actions they *should* take in order to solve a particular situation. Through the communication exchange, you tend to interrupt others. Furthermore, you manage how much information and what type of information will be conveyed during a conversation. You have a tendency to become extremely uncomfortable when confronted with high levels of disagreement or confrontation between others or when too much information at one time is provided. You may respond by over-reacting, becoming angry, or limiting all conversation between and among others. If you find yourself frequently in one of these interactional roles when tensions arise you need begin to read Part Two Quadrant II chapters eleven, twelve, thirteen, fourteen, fifteen and sixteen; the interactional roles of *The Clown, The Construction Worker, The Mediator, The Peacemaker, Potato Hot-Head, and The Referee.*

Chapter Eleven

The Clown

Of all the interactional roles that you can assume, the interactional role of "The Clown" can be one of the most profound and yet at the same time, somewhat confusing interactional roles to others. In this interactional role, you interject humor, laughter, creativity, or playfulness into tense situations in order to create levity and an atmosphere of calmness when tensions escalate between or with your Key-Relations. In such trying circumstances, you find yourself telling jokes, offering humorous comments about the dilemma, or even making exaggerated faces in order to relieve the tension. You may even use humor and creativity to re-define or reframe the differences in and between others into positive connotations. Humor helps you to address very painful emotions and problems can be looked at more realistically.

In the interactional role of The Clown, you display a good sense of timing and balance and are able to monitor conflicts between others. You tend to be creative, witty, and able to improvise quickly when necessary. Your strongest quality is that you can help others look at their world views from a less destructive perspective. Through creating lightheartedness, you tend to control the impact of communication between others. As a result, you work very hard and are very engaged with others to insure that intense conflict is addressed in a productive, lighter way. The Clown believes that no matter what others differences may be, he can help them to see things from a different, less serious, perspective and show them that there is always hope.

How Did I Learn This Role?

As a child, you may have accidentally interjected humor when parents or family members argued or disagreed resulting in a highly emotionally charged atmosphere, which was somber but became neutralized. You began to discover that humor could lower the tension and pain caused by differences between those around you and that they began to be more open to varying viewpoints. Eventually, you began to interject humor with friends especially when they displayed emotional pain, "stuckness", or depression.

Even though humor can lighten the atmosphere, you must use humor appropriately or there is a risk of not being taken seriously resulting in a loss of respect from those around you. Stephen Sondheim's lyrics (1993) *Send in the Clowns* aptly capture inappropriate "Clown humor" when he writes, "Isn't it rich? Are we a pair? Me here at last on the ground, you in mid-air. Send in the Clowns." These lyrics symbolize the pain that emerges in an estranged relationship when one person decides to leave after a prolonged experience with conflicted feelings. Sondheim's lyrics highlight the cynics that such a situation evokes. Because the couple's relationship has mirrored the ups and downs of a circus, they sarcastically ask for the Clowns to interject humor. In a situation where one friend is estranged from another, such humor would not only be inappropriate but would also likely severely irritate others.

Is this Interactional Role Ever Good For Me to Use?

Quite often this interactional role can be one of the most beneficial for you to use as your preferred way of responding in various highly charged emotional situations. This unique interactional role, which uses humor, allows others to look at their problems and value system from a surprising new perspective. Playing this role for a short time allows you to create a situation that enables you to step into another interactional role in order to keep the momentum of change forward. This interactional role is very powerful as you balance humor, seriousness and timing at key moments within a stressful environment. However, if this interactional role is used rigidly, too long, or too extensively others may stop taking you seriously and you become stuck. Also, you risk being perceived as making snide comments, rude, or inappropriate by others. At this point, your relations with those around you begin to suffer.

EXPAND:

In the next part of this chapter, we reveal what happens when this interactional role becomes rigid. We then guide you to other more useful interactional roles.

Help I am Stuck:

Feeling pressured to protect others from emotional pain you try to make those around you laugh in a humorous way so they can rethink their positions from a different perspective. If you try to interject humor every time when differences or problems are discussed, people around you will be prevented from authentically exploring their problems, differences, or relationship. Although everybody seems to be laughing, you may feel stuck because the root of the problem is neither allowed to surface nor explored in depth. The tension in and between those around you only begins to deepen. Through haste and wanting to "guide" others from pain, a productive resolution to differences may never be found. When too much humor is interjected, your Key-

Relations may feel as if their situation is not taken seriously, becoming angry with you or simply choosing not to include you in their discussions. These result in your feeling stuck.

What Happens Within You:

When tensions arise with or between others you have a tendency to become anxious, nervous, and may feel overwhelmed by the pressure of the disagreement. In order to relieve the pressure, you interject humor to try and help others to relax and be willing to look at differences from several angles. As people relax, you become calmer and feel more in control of the situation.

The Case Scenario:

Emily is quite concerned about her daughter Kim and her son- in- law Adrian, who have recently adopted a young boy of four from Russia. She shared with her friend Irene that when she is around her daughter, who lives out-of-state, she becomes very nervous and anxious. When Emily's husband John, an alcoholic, is there, the situation becomes extremely tense. John and Kim argue constantly over his drinking and Kim's parenting styles. She shared with Irene that John speaks his mind openly and when under influence she never knows what he may say. Emily shared that she can "deal more effectively with the situation when she is alone with her daughter." She stated that her daughter was very strict and often yells at their adopted grandson. In addition, her daughter worked long hours and was rarely home till late at night leaving her husband to care for the child. Kim's husband, Adrian, was a very good man and often spoke about the situation in a complacent manner saying, "That is how life is." Emily described a situation over Thanksgiving that was extremely tense and uncomfortable to Irene. The disagreement between John and Kim could have ruined the entire holiday weekend. Emily and John stayed at Kim and Adrian's home together with Adrian's parents for three days.

On Thanksgiving Day, Kim had been nonstop yelling at the four-year-old child about his manners and how he responded to any of the activities they were doing. Finally, Emily's husband, John exploded. He and Kim went into the office and closed the door. The others could hear John and Kim yelling at each other. John was calling Kim an inept mother of which she was denying and she called him nothing but a, "flat out drunk." The rest of them including, her daughter's husband Adrian, sat quietly in the living room, staring at the floor, listening to the argument. No one said a word and her stomach felt sick, the tension was so intense. Her daughter's in-laws finally said,

"Maybe we should leave and go back home to Pennsylvania." At this point, her son-in-law Adrian laughed and said, "What? You want to miss this side show? Now that the temperature in the house is warmer lets' bring out the turkey to eat, I love hot turkey." Those in the room laughed, and there was a fresh of breath air. Emily shared that the laughter brought a halt to the yelling, and soon things returned to normal.

Changing of the Interactional Role:

In the case scenario presented above, the father and daughter had created a scenario where those sitting in the living room had become frozen with fear and anxiety. The mother was embarrassed and felt helpless. The family members were hesitant to intervene as they were concerned the anger may escalate and further interrupt the holiday. When the husband Adrian interjected humor into the situation, the laughter which erupted in the living room surprised the father and daughter who became curious about what was happening, and the argument instantly stopped. Even though the root of the problem was not further addressed nor did people speak of their reactions toward the situation, the holiday proceeded without further interruptions. Emily stated, "Thank God for my son-in-law, he put levity back in our lives and I got through the weekend."

What Interactional Roles Can I Try To Give Me Personal Power?

There are a number of interactional roles that you can utilize to replace "The Clown" in order to become powerful in a different way when tensions arise. Through interjecting humor, you are able to control and manage information as well as change the atmosphere. However, when you constantly (over) use this approach, it will lose its effectiveness, and you will be viewed more as The Jester, one who makes snide, rude, inappropriate comments, rather than The Clown. So you will need to practice interactional roles where you can still manage information, be more open to encouraging communication, and allow tensions to rise between others so that the root of their differences can be resolved. The following chart is an overview of the best interactional roles for you to try initially from each quadrant:

Table 12 – Alternative Interachional Roles for The Clown

Quadrant	Roles to Best Try	Roles to Initially Shy Away From
Quadrant I; Need to Intellectualize	The Judge	The Doctor The Teacher The Preacher The Superman
Quadrant II: Need to Control and Manage Information	The Mediator The Peacemaker The Referee	The Construction Worker Potato Hot-Head
Quadrant II: Need to Be Curious	The Detective The Journalist	
Quadrant III: Need to Avoid	The Recorder	The Runaway The Bird Watcher
Quadrant IV: Need to Save	The Angel The Firefighter The Savior	

Please see Chapter 5 for a quick overview of the interactional roles or read Part III, *How Do I learn a New Interactional Role?* Part III will introduce and teach the skills of the new interactional role(s) that you selected from the above chart when you are stuck in the interactional role of The Clown.

The Risk:

In order to move out of the interactional role of The Clown, you must listen carefully to others' with concern and compassion. This is extremely risky as you tend to interject humor when tension builds or use humor to create different but more acceptable viewpoints. Even though you desire an atmosphere that is light and tension free, you must learn to demonstrate comfort with, and openness to, expressions of conflict that emerge with others so that differences can be discussed and resolved. You may fear that if you do not use humor, you will freeze and not know how to respond to those who present anger, pain, grief, sadness, or depression. You must practice dealing with the present moment, and help others to productively engage in new conversations. You need to accept that conflicts and tension between others are inevitable, but necessary so differences can be resolved. You need to productively balance and use humor to touch in a very sensitive way, the very painful areas within those around you. When you use the role of The Clown, you must be aware that you have to shift into another effective interactional role after the humor has created a good momentum in the way people address each other. You must take advantage of this moment to take a more serious interactional role and help others look at their differences in a more productive way. In other words: you should not use humor to avoid tension but rather *use* humor to manage, control, and confront tensions so that others are able to gain a new perspective on their presenting issues.

The Reflection:

In order to determine if The Clown is your preferred interactional role in tense situations with others, it would be helpful to ask yourself the following questions:

Family: Did I use humor to deflate or minimize tensions in your family? Was I able in this way, to help my family look at problems from a different perspective?

Social Circles: When with friends, did I work hard to make everyone laugh when conflict emerged or tension escalated? In clubs or social organizations, was I the person consistently working to make others laugh? Did I re-define relational behavior in a "Comedian" way?

School Experience: As a student, was I referred to as the class clown? Would I re-define presenting problems creating moments of silence and then a shift in thinking?

Co-Workers: Do I have a tendency to interject humor when co-workers speak of their dismay or concerns about the workplace environment or issues with the management?

Spouse or Significant Other: Am I quick to interject humor when my spouse or significant other tries to express intense emotion or issues, not allowing them to discuss their differences, concerns, worries or fears openly with me?

In General: How much humor do I interject when around others? My Key-Relation's get annoyed when I joke? Am I able to create fruitful chaos in the system? Can I redefine situations in a playful manner so the others feel surprised, forcing them and are forced to look at their perspectives from a different angle? Do I often say, " "This situation needs some humor?"

Chapter Twelve

The Construction Worker

"What? Stop it! We have talked enough about it." The Construction Worker metaphorically lays brick after brick and pounds nail after nail to create structure in and between others. As The Construction Worker you assume an active role with others. When you provide structure, you block out erroneous information so that Key-Relations can communicate more clearly with each other about what to do. So, you work hard to limit discussions and initiate action so a fix can be created for the differences of those around him.

How Did I Learn This Role?

As a child, you most likely became extremely nervous or frightened when parents of family members disagreed or had intense differences. At first you probably interrupted with a stern, "Stop it" and discovered that you could control the flow and tempo of communication through blocking of communication among and between others. When friends started to argue or disagree you did a similar pattern and discovered that you were effective in stopping intense arguments between those around you. You were able to get others to shift into action. As an adult, you are engaged into action by others who engage in disruptive communication patterns and want a "fix".

Is this Interactional Role Ever Good For Me to Use?

Quite often this interactional role can be very beneficial for you to use as your preferred way of responding in various highly charged emotional situations. In this interactional role, you rely more on constructive action rather than useless quarreling. This interactional role is very powerful as those around you see you as very strong and in control. However, you become stuck when you habitually use this interactional role rigidly as sometimes there is so much structure that you thwart the natural interactional styles and communication in and between others. When you prescribe how much information is shared by others, and presenting conflicts are only briefly discussed, others are unable to fully examine their differences. When this happens you inadvertently become part of the chaotic interactional pattern by blocking and structuring the flow of conversations. In the process, you create a climate in which discussions about conflicts are suppressed, and you unconsciously conspire with those present to avoid examinations of their

personal issues or concerns. Not surprisingly, you may jump into action before exactly knowing what the problem is resulting in a feeling of stuckness with you and those around you.

EXPAND:

In the next part of this chapter, we reveal to you what happens when this interactional role becomes rigid and guide you to other more useful interactional roles.

Help I am Stuck:

During intense moments of conflict you may feel overwhelmed, out-of-control and respond by interrupting others. You feel a strong need to implement action. You are quick to create walls and you focus on building a quick solution based on changing behavior. You have a tendency to intervene to the point where those around you become silent and engage in action. Key-Relations may describe their experiences with you as being annoying as their emotions, feelings or reactions to a situation cannot be expressed, and they may even pull away from you. They may become angry, and their respect in you may be diminished. The action based solutions offered by you only serve as a band-aide for the presenting issues. In these situations you become stuck as through the process key information about the presenting concerns become marginalized or avoided.

What Happens Within You:

When tensions arise with or between others you become anxious, nervous, afraid, and feel out-of-control. You want to get into control by guiding others into actions rather than discussing emotional concerns. Your action with others is more of a way to reduce your anxiety than an effective solution for the problem.

The Case Scenario:

Fourteen-year-old Alison has been experimenting with drugs and Judy, her mother, found marijuana under her mattress while cleaning her room today. Judy is the first to bring up the topic of Alison's drug use during dinner. She shared with Alison that she was worried and believes she is using drugs because … when she is abruptly interrupted by her husband, Gary, who asks her to pass the potatoes and inquires how Alison's day was at school. Alison looks down at her plate and says nothing. Her mother begins to tell Alison that she has a serious problem … Gary raises his voice and says, "I do not want to hear about it." Judy states, "We need to talk about it as the counselor from school phoned and shared that Alison is now failing three classes, and she skipped school today." Again, Alison is asked a question about school by her mother and she responds by throwing her fork in her food, tipping her chair over and running to her bedroom. At this point, Judy tries again to bring up the issue of drugs to her husband when he interrupts her and states, "Let's stop talking and take the damn marijuana out of her room!" He then goes to Alison's room and asks her to hand the marijuana to him. She remorsefully takes marijuana from under her mattress and gives it to her father. Her father tells her never to buy marijuana again; Alison agrees. A week later, Judy finds marijuana in Alison's cupboard, again.

Changing of the Interactional Role:

In the above case scenario, Gary, the father, in the interactional role of The Construction Worker did not resolve the problems of his daughter. Throughout the conversation Alison's drug use, poor school performance, and behaviors were never discussed. The father blocked his wife from speaking with him and Alison about her concerns. Rather Gary jumped immediately into action. A combination of The Detective coupled with The Journalist interactional roles would have been best for him to use. In these interactional roles, he would piece together the history and story surrounding his daughter's current behaviors, especially with regard to her drug usage. These interactional roles would then allow his wife space to speak. Judy would be able to share with Gary and Alison what she had discovered. She could also share what the counselor conveyed so that as a family they could compromise on the best approach to help Alison. In addition, he could come to understand from Alison why she was using drugs. By adopting the interactional role of The Doctor he could remain disengaged from the situation; yet attuned to her drug usage behavior and how the drugs may impact her emotional and physical well-being. Furthermore, a drug assessment could be suggested.

What Interactional Roles Will Give Me Personal Power?

There are a number of interactional roles that you can utilize to replace "The Construction Worker" in order to become less afraid of discussions and gathering of information when tensions arise. You need to practice interactional roles where you can manage information but be less action-oriented. Thereby allowing more open communication between others so that the root of their differences can be resolved. The owing chart suggests the best interactional role for you to select from each quadrant:

Table 13 – Alternative Interactional Roles for The Construction Worker

Quadrant	Roles to Best Try	Roles to Initially Shy Away From
Quadrant I; Need to Intellectualize	The Doctor The Teacher	The Judge The Preacher The Superman
Quadrant II: Need to Control and Manage Information	The Clown The Mediator The Peacemaker	Potato Hot-Head The Referee
Quadrant II: Need to Be Curious	The Detective The Journalist	
Quadrant III: Need to Avoid	The Bird Watcher The Recorder	The Runaway
Quadrant IV: Need to Save	The Angel	The Firefighter The Savior

*Please see Chapter 5 or a quick overview of the interactional roles or read Part III, How Do I learn a New Interactional Role? Part III will introduce and teach the skills of the new interactional role(s) that you selected from the above chart when you are stuck in the interactional role of The Construction Worker.

The Risk:

If you want to leave the interactional role of The Construction Worker, you need to practice allowing and encouraging those around you to speak directly to each other. This is extremely risky for you as you are used to jumping into action. In order to achieve this goal, you may need to become more silent and less reactive to conversations or tense moments. The biggest risk for you will be to slow down, trust that others can resolve their own differences, and avoid interrupting or the offering quick action.

The Reflection:

In order to determine if The Construction Worker is your preferred interactional role in tense situations with others, it would be helpful to ask yourself the following questions:

Family: Was I the person in the family that would try to stop family members from quarreling with each other when tensions escalated by telling them to come to action.

Social Circles: When friends argued would I interrupt them and draw their attention to action-based solutions? In social clubs, did I stop brainstorming sessions and tried to get people to become task-oriented?

School Experience: As a student, was I the one in the classroom who would get annoyed with long discussions and intervene by getting my peers to come to a quick solution?

Co-Workers: Do I have a tendency to interrupt others when they speak of their dismay or concerns about the workplace environment or issues with the management and try to tell them to do something about their issues?

Spouse or Significant Other: Do I interrupt my spouse or significant other when they discuss their differences, concerns, worries, or fears and do I tell them to do something?

In General: Do I interrupt others when they attempt to share information and suggest action? Do I often find myself saying, "NO...NO...NO.... we do not need more information, we must do something!"

Chapter Thirteen

The Mediator

"After listening to both of you, I think that you should consider going to the beach as Raymond suggested and then drive home through the mountains as Abbie suggested. In that way, both of you will have your preferences at least partially met." As The Mediator, you present as a non-biased negotiator for everyone involved in the presenting issues. You rely primarily on problem-solving skills to help opposing parties come to an equitable agreement. Through the process, you adopt a neutral position, listen, and then calmly try to explain each person's position, with the hope that this knowledge will lead to a mutually agreeable problem resolution. Each person offers his/her position, without interruption, on a presenting issue or dynamic. Information presented is taken at face value. You do not analyze this information, but use it only to help everyone in the conflict understand each other's desires. You then reframe this information into a positive perspective with the goal of insuring that everyone's expectations are at least partially met making those around content and satisfied.

How Did I Learn This Role?

As a child, you may have become quite anxious when those around you disagreed. At first you would watch and listen to each person's concern and then you may have interjected a solution that made everyone happy. Unconsciously this interactional style became your preferred way of handling the conflicts of others. Eventually you began to use this with your friends and found the process helpful and others may have begun to look at you for problem resolution. As an adult, you are engaged into action by those who quarrel frequently and who are unable to take others' perspectives. You adopt The Mediator interactional role when others around you display poor insight, linear thinking, and they lack the ability to negotiate solutions to common personal or family problems. By listening carefully to all the perspectives, you make a decision designed to make everyone happy and that meets everyone's personal desires,

Is this Interactional Role Ever Good For Me to Use?

Quite often this interactional role can be very beneficial for you to use as your preferred way of responding in various highly charged emotional situations. In this interactional role, you use negotiation skills to mediate and find a positive outcome for differences.

You intently listen to differences and create solutions so that all present become satisfied that they "got their way". This interactional role is very powerful as those around you see you as being fair and as having good problem-solving ability. However, you become stuck when you habitually use this interactional role rigidly as others may become dependent on you to resolve their differences. At this point, you become overburdened by the demands of others. But if you step back and stop being The Mediator the relations with others begin to suffer as they become angry with you.

EXPAND:

In the next part of this chapter, we reveal to you what happens when this interactional role becomes rigid. We will guide you to other more useful interactional roles.

Help I am Stuck:

As The Mediator you are the decision maker. As a result, those around you fail to learn effective decision-making solution skills, so the interactional and communication patterns of those in conflict do not change. When you intervene to control and manage information, everyone involved in the conflict experiences temporary reductions in the tensions, but they fail to learn how to resolve their own problems. Key-Relations become highly dependent on you to make decisions or resolve their differences. Through the process, a lot of responsibility is placed on you by others, and you may find that you become exhausted by the demands of this interactional role, the failures of others to resolve their problems, and the sense of being stuck as communicative and interactional patterns of others remain unchanged.

What Happens Within You:

When others present with conflict and obvious tensions you may become quite anxious, worried, and overwhelmed by the turmoil. In order to avert discussions of serious concerns or expressions of strong emotions, you resort to making decisions for others that result in everyone being happy. Through the process tensions are lowered and your mediation skills protect you from experiencing uncomfortable feelings. You take control of and manage information but remain aloof from others.

The Case Scenario:

Connie and Mary have been co-sharing a position for six months at work. At first the co-share job was working well and both women enjoyed working part time. Carlo's desk was located in the same area. Carlo began to notice that Connie and Mary had begun to complain about how certain tasks were not being completed by the other person and that each person blamed the other for not doing "their assigned work". At first Carlo ignored the bickering and just listened to each of the women complain. As their shared cubical, along with his, had a combined responsibility for weekly output, Carlo began to realize that their bickering could have a negative impact on his job performance and eventual salary increase. Being uncomfortable with the situation, he called a luncheon meeting where both ladies were present, and he listened intently to each woman's concerns. He realized that Connie and Mary were not clearly communicating with each other regarding the daily tasks that needed to be completed and just "assumed" that the other person would complete the assigned work. He suggested that together they make a daily list of tasks that needed to be completed. Then to initial those tasks that they believed could be accomplished successfully in the time they were at work. That way they would know what each other was expected to do. Connie and Mary liked this suggestion, and for a week it worked quite well. Soon, the women started complaining about the other's work output and again Carlo became the negotiator and decision maker. On a daily basis, he began to listen to each woman's concerns and actively began to offer resolution and advice. Connie and Mary had even begun to phone him at home on a daily basis when they had problems. These exchanges burdened him to the point where his productivity was dropping, and he was not sleeping well at night.

Changing of the Interactional Role:

In the above case scenario Carlo realized that Connie and Mary had become dependent on him and were not taking the initiative to solve their own differences. Carlo decided that he needed to teach (The Teacher) both women how to negotiate and compromise. So he asked them to make a list of their expectations of each other and how they viewed their job sharing duties (The Mediator). He began to ask questions (The Detective) about their ideas on how to make the position work better for each of them, so they could be happier. Carlo asked them first, to try and resolve their differences by writing concerns down and then meeting over lunch in a public arena (The Peacemaker) to discuss their differences face-to-face. He interrupted ineffective communication patterns (The Construction Worker) and moved Connie and Mary to action when needed. Through the process, he would teach various decision-making skills and conflict resolution skills (The Teacher). In the end, Connie and Mary learned new negotiation skills and were able to resolve most of their differences without Carlo.

What Interactional Roles Will Give Me Personal Power?

There are a number of interactional roles that you can utilize to replace that of "The Mediator", in order to become less responsible for making decisions for others. As The Mediator, you take complete control of emotional situations by offering solutions that make everyone happy. You need to practice interactional roles where you can learn to listen, observe, support, remain present, be curious about situations and open to allowing others to express their differences. Through the skillful adoption of the alternative interactional roles described below, you may instill hope into situations which are characterized by arguing and unhappiness by encouraging others to create resolutions for their differences. The following chart suggests the best interactional roles for you to select from each quadrant:

Table 14 – Alternative Interactional Roles for The Mediator

Quadrant	Roles to Best Try	Roles to Initially Shy Away From
Quadrant I; Need to Intellectualize	The Judge The Teacher	The Doctor The Preacher The Superman
Quadrant II: Need to Control and Manage Information	The Clown The Construction Worker The Peacemaker The Referee	Potato Hot-Head
Quadrant II: Need to Be Curious	The Detective The Journalist	
Quadrant III: Need to Avoid	The Bird Watcher The Recorder The Runaway	
Quadrant IV: Need to Save	The Angel The Firefighter The Savior	

*Please see Chapter 5 for a quick overview of the interactional roles or read Part III, *How Do I learn a New Interactional Role?* Part III will introduce and teach the skills of the new interactional role(s) that you selected from the above chart when you are stuck in the interactional role of The Mediator.

The Risk:

In order to move out of the interactional role of The Mediator you must increase your comfort level when tensions rise in those around you. The biggest risk for you is to practice allowing differences to surface, which will permit those around you to negotiate solutions to their own problems. You must learn to model and teach negotiation techniques rather than make decisions for others. You must encourage those around you to listen to each other and be open to alternative perspectives. You will need to practice being curious and asking questions about the issues that exacerbate presenting concerns. By assuming a) less responsibility, b) teaching negotiation skills, and c) creating realistic expectations, decisions can be agreed upon by others, thus leading to problem resolution and effective change in those around you. However, there are situations where you need to become more active and solution directed (e.g., people become aggressive towards each other and mediation is not effective), you may need to become The Firefighter, The Judge or The Construction Worker). These interactional roles while require that you have the courage to engage yourself in a higher level of responsibility, activity, and involvement.

The Reflection:

In order to determine if The Mediator is your preferred interactional role in tense situations with others, it would be helpful to ask yourself the following questions:

Family: When your family members argued, did I try to mediate by creating a solution that would make everyone happy?

Social Circles: When friends argued, did I try to make everyone happy by attempting to blend everyone's wishes and desires? In social clubs, did I listen to all sides of an issue and then make decisions designed to please everyone?

School Experience: Was I the student who listened to classmates argue about the best way to complete a group assignment and then present solutions that would please all?

Co-Workers: Do I offer solutions to make everyone content when co-workers speak of their concerns about the workplace environment, issues with the management?

Spouse or Significant Other: When in an argument or disagreement do I listen and then try to offer suggestions to help my spouse or significant other feel like they "got their way"? Do I quickly want to help my spouse or significant other understand the position of others by offering solutions so that everyone involved in the situation feels like a winner?

In General: When those around me begin to argue do I listen to each side of the story then suggest a solution that will please all? Do I often find myself saying, "Wait... you can do this and then try this...."

Chapter Fourteen

The Peacemaker

"Now I think it would be best if we all got along and stopped this talk about what type of car to buy. What does it really matter anyway?" As The Peacemaker, you present as being very sensitive, accepting, unassuming, and laid-back. You are perceived by others as humble, easygoing, and approachable. You avoid conflict at any level as you adopt a neutral position. You listen to and then try to create an atmosphere where all present are content and harmonious. You observe and interpret the nonverbal body language of others quite astutely and then work hard to maintain peace so that no one is upset. You quickly reframe emotionally charged information into a positive perspective with the goal of insuring a calm atmosphere. Key-Relations are never allowed to express negative emotions in front of you.

How Did I Learn This Role?

As a child, you may have discovered that when those around you disagreed or criticized you at any level, you noticed that you became quite anxious, upset, and afraid. You may have made the following statements to yourself whenever tensions arose between yourself and another:

- "I know she will get angry at me."
- "Maybe he will leave me."
- "He will never speak to me again, if I upset him."
- "I will end up getting hurt as always."
- "I will be blamed and told it is my fault."
- "Whatever I do, I can't win."
- "I will end up in life completely alone."

Emotion displayed at any level, was very painful and uncomfortable for you. At first you would watch and listen to each person's concern but soon realized that in order to remain calm, you had to stop all negative discussions so that harmony could once again be set forth. You consciously avoided being drawn into conflict. As a result you would minimize anything that was upsetting to you. Unconsciously this interactional style became your preferred way of handling conflicts with those around you. Eventually, you began to use this interactional role with your friends and found the process helpful as it stopped any and all conflict. As an adult, you are engaged into action by those who appear upset at any level. Because you are highly empathetic, you need to create an atmosphere where the people around can feel relaxed in order for you to be able to remain relaxed and calm.

Is this Interactional Role Ever Good For Me to Use?

Quite often this interactional role can be very beneficial for you to use as your preferred way of responding in various highly charged emotional situations. In this interactional role, you create an atmosphere of simplicity, peace, and harmony. This interactional role can be extremely powerful as it provides protection for those that are near you. You come across to others as very caring and agreeable. People like being with you as you go along with others and never disagree. However you become stuck when you habitually use this interactional role in order to be appreciated by those around you. In this interactional role, you never express your true self or feelings and those around you are unable discuss differences fully. As presenting concerns in and between others remain unresolved and the anger around a situation tends to become buried differences surface in another way and at another time. Therefore, in reality you are often not at peace as you are on pins and needles waiting for the next "upset" to surface.

EXPAND:

In the next part of this chapter, we reveal to you what happens when this interactional role becomes rigid and guide you to other more useful interactional roles.

Help I am Stuck:

As The Peacemaker you work hard to maintain harmony at any cost and sometimes issues are not resolved with and between your Key-Relations. You prevent those involved in the conflict to express any negative emotions, so they fail to learn how handle these emotions or how to negotiate and resolve their own problems. Through the process, a lot of responsibility is placed on you, and you become exhausted by the demands of this interactional role, which is to keep the peace at any cost. Because you silence your own wants as well as the needs of others, you may never feel satisfied. You feel stuck as you do not go after what you truly want in life, which can eventually result in a high level of resentment towards others.

What Happens Within You:

When others present with conflict and obvious tensions you may become anxious, upset, worried, overwhelmed, you are scared by the turmoil. In order to avert discussions of serious concerns, or expressions of strong negative emotions you avoid conflict, complications, and you do not judge other people. You are petrified of being shut down, overlooked, rejected, or not included by others. Your biggest fear is being unloved by others. Through the process tensions are lowered and your peacemaking skills protect you from experiencing uncomfortable feelings. You take control of and manage information, but you do not deal with any issues nor allow others to deal with anything unless it can be done in a peaceful way. Paradoxically, your avoidance of anger and conflict only lead to more conflict, which results in a feeling of entrapment and being stuck.

The Case Scenario:

Claire sat doing her homework and was feeling overwhelmed as she had three tests in school the next day. Kenny her brother entered the kitchen and began to swear because their older sister, Marijke had not done the dishes and he knew he would get blamed for it. When Marijke walked in the kitchen, Kenny began to yell at her. Claire immediately looked up from her studying and said, "Don't worry, I will gladly do the dishes," and with that Kenny and Marijke left with a smile on their face. Claire knew she had to do the dishes before her mother got home in order to keep her happy, but she had basketball practice and needed to get her studying done. As she was leaving the house, to go practice, Marijke was all out-of-sorts as she could not find the iron and she needed a dress ironed in order to go out on a date. Marijke and her mother started to bicker as her mother was saying she needed better time management skills so this would not happen. In order to keep them calm, Claire ran upstairs and began to iron Marijke's dress before she went to practice. When Claire arrived at practice she was late, and her coach started to yell at her. Claire began to cry as she said she lost her earring in the parking lot, so the coach sent one of the girls out to help her look. Claire knew this was not true, but she hated that her coach was upset and this stopped him from yelling. On the way home, Kenny phoned Claire and asked her to pick up a pizza as he was hungry. Claire knew she had to study before she went to bed; she was already tired but agreed to do it so that Kenny could watch his favorite TV show. By the time she had gotten home it was almost 10:30 pm, and she knew she had little time to study. Kenny and her father had started to argue, as Kenny did not fill the gas tank as he was supposed to after taking the car to his friend's house. Their voices began to rise, and they were interrupting each other. Claire's stomach immediately began to feel queasy as she became very nervous when her brother and father fought; as once they came to blows. Claire immediately started to talk about her basketball practice and told her father she needed his help with her jump shot, which stopped the two of them bickering. She also said she would gladly take the car and fill it with gas when she woke up in the morning, before her father went to work. So there was no need to worry. By then it was 11:15 pm and Claire was too tired to study her math material. Claire went to bed feeling resentment towards her siblings and worried about school as she was not prepared for her math test, she knew that she had to study in the am, but now she did not have time as she had to fill the car with gas. Claire knew she would fail the exam, which would upset her parents. She was in a no-win situation.

Changing of the Interactional Role:

In the above case scenario, Claire was taking responsibility to keep peace and harmony within the home. She was placing her own needs in the background while she attended to the needs and requests of her family. Claire needs to learn how to say, "No" as well as develop negotiation skills. As The Mediator, she could have helped her brother and sister decide whose turn it was to do the dishes. When her mother and sister argued she could have become The Runaway left the situation and let them resolve the ironing details. When her brother requested the pizza, she could have switched into the interactional role of The Clown and made some humor about his priority (TV watching) versus her test and then said, "No". When her father and brother began to argue she could have served The Construction worker determining who would speak and when. As The Referee, she would be able to block their attempts of interruption. This would have helped to calm the atmosphere and both family members would be able to express their viewpoints or concerns without infuriating the other by interrupting. As The Construction Worker, she could have helped them resolve the issue by suggesting her brother could fill up the car before he left for work in the morning.

What Interactional Roles Will Give Me Personal Power?

There are a number of interactional roles that you can utilize to replace "The Peacemaker" and to become less responsible for keeping the peace when around others. You tend to react to any and all differences with a high level of control by blocking any level of differences believing that you are saving others from emotional pain, conflict, or duress, but in reality you are only saving yourself. You need to practice interactional roles where you can learn to listen, observe, support, remain present, be curious about situations and open to allowing others to express their differences. Through the skillful adoption of the alternative interactional roles listed below, you may instill calmness into situations which are characterized by tension.

The following chart suggests the best interactional roles for you to select from each quadrant:

Table 15 – Alternative Interactional Roles for The Peacemaker

Quadrant	Roles to Best Try	Roles to Initially Shy Away From
Quadrant I; Need to Intellectualize	The Teacher	The Doctor The Judge The Preacher
Quadrant II: Need to Control and Manage Information	The Clown The Construction Worker The Referee	Potato Hot-Head
Quadrant II: Need to Be Curious	The Detective The Journalist	
Quadrant III: Need to Avoid	The Bird Watcher The Runaway The Recorder	
Quadrant IV: Need to Save	The Angel The Firefighter The Savior	

*Please see Chapter 5 for a quick overview of the interactional roles or read Part III, *How Do I learn a New Interactional Role?* Part III will introduce and teach the skills of the new interactional role(s) that you selected from the above chart when you are stuck in the interactional role of The Peacemaker.

The Risk:

In order to move out of the interactional role of The Peacemaker you must learn to increase your comfort level when tensions rise in those around you. The biggest risk for you is to practice taking a less active role, allowing differences to surface, which will permit those around you to negotiate solutions to their own problems without being blocked. You must learn to model and teach negotiation techniques rather than shutting people off from expressing their dismay with one another. You must teach those around you to listen to each other and be open to alternative perspectives on the problem. You must learn how to reflect the desires and wishes of those present and demonstrate flexibility in thought and action in order to negotiate a solution acceptable to all. You will need to practice being curious and asking questions about the issues that exacerbate presenting concerns. By assuming less responsibility for keeping the peace, you will be able to express your true emotions, be more open and receptive, which will allow you to more easily relate to others. By allowing others to discuss their concerns openly, decisions can be agreed upon which will lead to problem resolution and effective change in those around you.

The Reflection:

In order to determine if The Peacemaker is your preferred interactional role in tense situations with others, it would be helpful to ask yourself the following questions:

Family: When your family members argued, did I try to keep the peace by cutting people off when speaking and taking on their responsibility for making them happy? Was I uncomfortable expressing anger, sadness, or disappointment at any level?

Social Circles: When friends argued, did I try to change the subject or take on additional tasks in order to make others content? In social clubs, did I intervene when tensions rose and block the expression of anger until the tension subsided? Did I take on the responsibilities of others?

School Experience: Did I listen to classmates argue about the best way to complete a group assignment and then took on the project myself in order to make others more content?

Co-Workers: When co-workers speak of their concerns about the workplace environment, issues with the management or others, do I have a tendency to minimize their concerns and reassure them that all will be okay? Do I find myself completing their work, so they are not unhappy?

Spouse or Significant Other: When my spouse or significant other tries to discuss concerns, do I avoid or change the subject? Do I take on my extra responsibilities around the house so that my spouse or significant other is happier in life and feels less stressed?

In General: When those around me begin to argue do I quickly try to squelch the tension by minimizing the concern or cutting people off from speaking? Do I often find myself saying, "I do not like this … I do not like this … I must stop the fighting now! I will do their work!"

Chapter Fifteen

Potato Hot-Head

Face red, eyes bulging, "What the hell do you think you are doing? I told you that you cannot go now shut-up, or I will need to teach you a lesson." As Potato Hot-Head, you have a low tolerance for any kind of emotional pain or tension. When something very emotional happens you react with some level of abuse (verbally or physically) to those around you. You have a strong need to control and manage information in a very authoritative way. In order to remove yourself from the emotional content, the following behaviors are often displayed:

- Yelling, screaming, or using degrading and/or demeaning language

- Shutting down and not talking or responding to others when problems are presented

- Hanging up the telephone or other social media contact

- Withholding of affection, financial help or anything else you think would punish others

- Becoming physically assaultive (e.g., hitting, shoving, punching, or kicking others)

- Partaking in drinking, use of drugs and/or other addictive behaviors

In the interactional role of Potato Hot-Head, you present to those around you as angry. You are an expert at blaming others rather than assuming any responsibility for a situation. Also, when a situation occurs, you tend to tell the other person that, "They need to change." You rarely listen to others and only see your perspective in a disagreement. You may use strong non-verbal behaviors (e.g., pointing of finger, red face etc.) to further intimidate others. People around you often report they are on "egg shells" and try carefully not to be the victim of your anger. Through the process, everyone becomes frustrated and emotions are rarely resolved. Key-Relations provide only minimal information, which is taken at face value by Potato Hot-Head who then minimizes and dismisses any and all concerns.

Note: In this section we are speaking about individuals who display a *pattern* of bullying, demeaning, intimidating, and threatening behaviors. They are coercive, manipulative, and/or very controlling towards others. It is true that all people experience anger and rage on some level, but here we address people who consistently display this type of responding when under emotional duress.

How Did I Learn This Role?

As a child, you may have become quite anxious when those around you disagreed. You felt extremely helpless and overwhelmed by fear. Overtime you began to display behaviors of anger, disrespect, or abuse towards others. You found that when you presented these behaviors you were reinforced as others became intimidated, would immediately respond to your requests, and went out of their way not to "upset' you. Unconsciously this interactional style became your preferred way of handling conflicts by those around you. Eventually, you began to use this pattern of behavior with your friends and found the process powerful as others were careful not to disagree with you. As an adult, you are engaged into action by those who present to you situations that are upsetting or have an emotional base to them.

Is this Interactional Role Ever Good For Me to Use?

This is the only interactional role in this book which is not beneficial for you to use as your preferred way of responding in any situation. In this interactional role, you tend to intimidate and distance others from you. Even though this is an extremely powerful interactional role for controlling and managing the information which is imparted by Key-Relations, as Potato Hot-Head you demean other people, which results in others not trusting you. You become stuck when you habitually use this interactional role as others fear and even dislike you. At this point, your relations with those around you severely suffer as often others will end the relationship with you or begin to lie to you so as not to upset you.

EXPAND:

In the next part of this chapter, we reveal to you what happens when this interactional role becomes rigid. We will guide you to other more useful interactional roles.

Help I am Stuck:

As people tend to "walk on egg shells" when around you, eventually they begin to withhold information from you or they stop communicating with you. As a result, you do not learn decision-making, negotiation, or conflict resolution skills. So, the communication between you and others does not change. When you become angry, everyone involved in the conflict is shut down. Therefore, your Key-Relations become highly dependent on you to make any and all decisions, so you do not become angry. Through the process, a lot of responsibility is placed on you by others, and you may find that you become exhausted and even more irritated by the demands of this interactional role, the failures of others to resolve their problems, feeling overly over- responsible and the sense of being stuck.

What Happens Within You:

When others present with conflict and tensions you may become quite anxious, irritated, and overwhelmed by the turmoil; you may even feel out-of-control. In order to avert discussions of serious concerns or expressions of strong emotions, you use anger to control others and stop all forms of communication. Instead of looking inward, and trying to figure out why you are experiencing such negative emotions you bury the pain, live in denial of it, and distort the reality of other's behaviors.

The Case Scenario:

Heide had just lost her mother and was very emotional whenever she received any news from her extended family about her mother's assets. Her family had started arguing over the estate and out-of-the blue an individual was claiming that she was the "daughter" of the now deceased mother. Heide knew of this person during her childhood years but had no idea that she could be a "step-sister". Heide was very upset with this latest development and phoned her husband who was at work for support. As she began to explain to him what had occurred he listened for a few minutes and then responded in front of his secretary, "When you get your head out of your ass phone me back". Heide was quite shocked that he responded in this manner and called him back immediately. She told him that she needed his support and understanding. Her husband ignored her words, her plea for him to just listen to her, and also her embarrassment for what he said in front of his secretary. Again he stated, "Get your head out of your ass," and hung the phone up. At noon her husband came home for lunch, and Heide told him that she was emotionally off balance, as it had only been two weeks since her mother died and she needed his support; she just needed him to listen and reassure her that it was all going to be "okay". Her husband responded by being angry, making nonverbal gestures of dismay, mocking her, belittling her, calling her "crazy" and again stated that she needed to "get her head out of her ass." In utter disbelief, Heide left the room, angry, confused, and misunderstood. She realized that she could not rely on her husband for any level of emotional support during this time and vowed not to speak to him again about any of her concerns related to the loss of her mother. She picked up the phone to call a male friend who was there. He listened to her and offered comfort.

Changing of the Interactional Role:

In the above case scenario Heide's husband was rude and insensitive. His behavior was clearly that of a Potato Hot-Head. The use of yelling, belittling, and degrading did not help Heide to feel understood. By hanging up the phone, he cut off the communication in mid-air. This was a good way for him not to have to deal with Heide's strong emotions. His abusive behavior created an emotional wedge between them, to which Heide was not open to forgiving. Furthermore, Heide's reaching out to another male friend for comfort could put the marriage at risk. In this case, the husband would have been more effective if he had tried to be The Bird Watcher. When someone is in grief or shock, they need to be heard. As Detective, he could have shown curiosity about the "sister". These interactional roles would have allowed Heide to share her confusion with him.

What Interactional Roles Will Give Me Personal Power?

There are a number of interactional roles that you can utilize to replace "Potato Hot-Head" in order to become less emotionally reactive when highly charged emotional situations are presented. You need to practice interactional roles where you can learn to listen, observe, support, remain present, be curious about situations and open to allowing others to express their differences. Through the skillful adoption of the alternative interactional roles described below, you may become less authoritarian and more in control when face-to-face with emotional situations characterized by chaos, sadness, anger, and hopelessness. The following chart suggests the best interactional roles for you to select from each quadrant:

Table 16 – Alternative Interachional Roles for Potato Hot-Head

Quadrant	Roles to Best Try	Roles to Initially Shy Away From
Quadrant I; Need to Intellectualize	The Teacher	The Doctor The Judge The Preacher The Superman

Table 16 – Alternative Interactional Roles for Potato Hot-Head Continued

Quadrant	Roles to Best Try	Roles to Initially Shy Away From
Quadrant II: Need to Control and Manage Information	The Clown The Construction Worker The Peacemaker The Referee	
Quadrant II: Need to Be Curious	The Detective The Journalist	
Quadrant III: Need to Avoid	The Bird Watcher The Recorder The Runaway	
Quadrant IV: Need to Save	The Angel The Firefighter	The Savior

*Please see Chapter 5 for a quick overview of the interactional roles or read Part III, *How Do I learn a New Interactional Role?* Part III will introduce and teach the skills of the new interactional role(s) that you selected from the above chart when you are stuck in the interactional role of Potato Hot-Head.

The Risk:

In order to move out of the interactional role of Potato Hot-Head you must increase your comfort level when tensions rise in those around you. The biggest risk for you is to practice taking a less reactive role and allowing differences to surface, which will permit those around you to discuss their problems without interjection of anger. You must learn to show curiosity and interest rather than respond with an abusive tone or nonverbal actions.

The Reflection:

In order to determine if Potato Hot-Head is your preferred interactional role in tense situations with others, it would be helpful to ask yourself the following questions:

Family: When my family members argued, did I try to stop all communication by yelling, displaying of tantrums or being disrespectful?

Social Circles: When friends argued, would I threaten or attempt to bully them?

In social clubs, did I take control by yelling at others and refusing to let others speak?

School Experience: Do I bully others in an attempt to intimidate?

Co-Workers: When co-workers speak of their concerns, do I have a tendency to become angry and shut down all levels of communication in and between others? Is it hard for co-workers to talk with me without feeling intimidated?

Spouse or Significant Other: When in an argument or disagreement do I yell and put the other person down? Do I intimidate to the point where my spouse or significant others tries not to upset me? Do I shut off all communication and refuse to speak?

In General: When those around me begin to argue do I yell, intimidate, use strong nonverbal language? Do I often find myself saying, "They need to … now"!

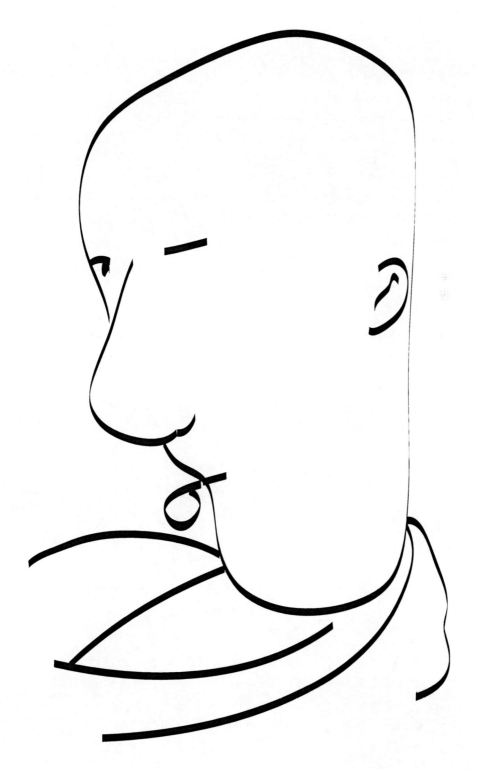

The Referee   129

Chapter Sixteen

The Referee

The whistle blows, action stops, and those around you freeze… all focus their attention and eyes on you. The Referee is about to make a decision regarding the rules of engagement. As The Referee, you operate from a rigid set of internal rules that apply to everyone. You assume responsibility for determining who speaks to whom, when, for how long, and in what way. Through this process, tensions may be moderated as all present get a turn to speak. You have the ability to handle very stressful, highly charged situations and are not hesitant to structure communication in ways that will result in limiting the expression of anger by others.

How Did I Learn This Role?

As a child, you may have become quite anxious when those around you disagreed. You particularly became upset when others interrupted each other or began to speak for each other. At first you would watch and listen to the chaos unfold, but then you began to take a very active role by blocking who spoke to whom, when they spoke, and how much information they could share unconsciously this interactional style became your preferred way of handling conflicts with those around you. Eventually, you began to use this approach with your friends and found the process helpful as the tensions among and between friends was reduced. As an adult, you are engaged into action by those who quarrel frequently and when there is confusion, chaos, and people interrupt each other. When those around you are unable to control their inappropriate behaviors, you set rules and limitations as to how their differences can be discussed.

Is this Interactional Role Ever Good For Me to Use?

Quite often this interactional role can be beneficial for you to use as your preferred way of responding in various highly charged emotional situations. In this interactional role, you introduce the rules around when others speak and how. This interactional role can be powerful as it provides direction and guidance in very chaotic situations especially when people interrupt each other. However, you become stuck when you habitually use this interactional role rigidly and with high levels of control. As the Referee, you can unintentionally stifle the natural rhythms of communications and interactions of those around you to the point that others do not speak or act without your permission. When information imparted by others is shortened or blocked, meaningful resolutions may not be reached and you become stuck, as the root of the differences between others is never revealed.

EXPAND:
In the next part of this chapter, we reveal to you what happens when this interactional role becomes rigid and guide you to other more useful interactional roles.

Help I am Stuck:

Chaotic patterns presented by those around you are often intensified by their conflicting messages to you (e.g., "Help me but don't help me"). Let us say that your co-workers may communicate desires for you to monitor their unruly, disruptive interactions and help them discuss their differences easier with each other; yet when you set the rules around when they speak they simultaneously challenge or even sabotage your efforts to do so by ignoring your guidance. Through the process of setting rules and limitations, you may have success in reducing the anxiety levels of others. The problem is not the limited discussions as The Referee you can allow for very long and detailed discussions rather through managing how information is imparted others do not learn how to communicate properly so when differences arise between them again, they will need a referee to help them. You get stuck as others become highly dependent on you to control them when they fail to learn effective communication skills. Appropriate boundaries may also break down when you are not present to set the structure. As the Referee, you often feel exhausted from the energy required to control the structure and flow of the discussions.

What Happens Within You:

When others present with conflict, chaos, disorderly behaviors toward each other, and highly charged emotions, you may become quite anxious, confused, and overwhelmed by the turmoil. In order to avert expressions of strong emotions, you resort to setting rules of engagement which helps to calm an intense atmosphere as each person present can have a voice without interruptions. Through the process tensions are lowered and your rules protect you from experiencing uncomfortable feelings.

The Case Scenario:

While visiting his cousin, Ken notices that the family is upset. Anna, the youngest daughter, has a boyfriend and some family members do not like him. The mother, Cynthia, supports Anna's choice while Scott, the father and the older sister, Rebecca oppose. Strong coalitions are apparent between Cynthia and Anna and Scott and Rebecca. When Cynthia speaks, Rebecca makes gasping sounds and Scott turns his body away from her. When Anna begins to yell at Rebecca, Scott steps in to protect her. In response, Cynthia and Anna look at each other and both roll their eyes. Ken attempts to intervene, but the family goes on with their interactions as if the he does not exist. Ken becomes exasperated, and his anxiety begins to rise as the family members attempt to speak for each other and as both daughters consistently interrupt their parents' communications.

In an effort to create some structure for his cousins, Ken firmly speaks with a raised voice and the whole family looks at him in with a stunned expression. He takes the risk and proposes a communication plan that specifies the circumstances in which each family member is permitted to discuss the issue, the amount of time provided for this discussion.   He states that everyone else must be silent when someone is speaking. As he implements this plan, both daughters attempt to interrupt their parents' conversation by sighing deeply and shaking their heads. Ken responds by stringently monitoring and reminding them that this type of behavior must stop. Eventually this process seems to lower the anger present among his cousins, and they are able to come to some resolution about the boyfriend.

A few weeks later, Scott phoned his cousin, Ken and shared that Anna had continued her relationship with her boyfriend despite his strong objections and dismay. Ken suggested that maybe the parents needed to discuss their differences. Scott phoned back to share that they tried to discuss their parenting styles, but both daughters demonstrated highly disruptive behaviors that diverted attention from this critical issue. He asked if Ken could come back to help them hold a discussion and stop the disruption by the daughters.

Changing of the Interactional Role:

In the case scenario above Ken realized that his cousins had become dependent on him to resolve their differences around Anna's boyfriend. He revisited his cousins a few days later and decided to adopt the interactional role of The Mediator. He asked the parents to sit directly across the table from each other. The daughters sat near the parents with pen and paper in hand. Ken asked the parents to discuss their concerns about Anna's boyfriend and the positive aspects of the relationship. During this discussion, Ken instructed the daughters to remain silent, but they could record (The Recorder) their reactions on a sheet of paper.

When the parents finished their discussions, Ken asked the girls to collaborate, creating two lists: a list of parental concerns about the boyfriend and list of positive elements of the relationship identified by their parents. He further directed that he would return in a week for another meeting. The daughters had to present their combined written list to their parents. A week later, the daughters read their list to the parents. While reading their lists, Anna and Rebecca exhibited no reactive behaviors and remained silent while their parents discussed their reactions to the listed items.

At that point, Ken shifted into the professional therapeutic roles of The Journalist. In this role, he explored each parent's up-bringing related to values, beliefs, and gender roles. The parents described similarities and differences between the boyfriend's culture and those of their families of origin. They began to see that their differences about Anna's boyfriend were based on their own upbringings. The boyfriend's culture appeared to mirror that of the mother's family of origin. As the father's culture had been vastly different in values, he distrusted the boyfriend. Ken shifted into three interactional roles and asked the daughters to use the role of The Recorder. In this way, Ken was able to help his cousins improve their communication skills. Through the process, Scott discovered he was being unfair to the boyfriend. Scott agreed to get to know the boyfriend and later accepted him with warmth into his home.

What Interactional Roles Will Give Me Personal Power?

There are a number of interactional roles that you can utilize to replace "The Referee" in order to become less controlling of others during highly intense emotional situations. As the Referee, you tend to react to any and all differences by controlling the flow of information between others. You need to practice interactional roles where you can learn to listen, observe, support, remain present, and be curious about situations. You may teach negotiation skills to others so that differences can be fully explored. The following chart suggests the best interactional roles for you to select from each quadrant:

Table 17 – Alternative Interactional Roles for The Referee

Quadrant	Roles to Best Try	Roles to Initially Shy Away From
Quadrant I; Need to Intellectualize	The Doctor The Judge The Preacher The Teacher	The Superman
Quadrant II: Need to Control and Manage Information	The Clown The Construction Worker The Peacemaker	Potato Hot-Head
Quadrant II: Need to Be Curious	The Detective The Journalist	
Quadrant III: Need to Avoid	The Bird Watcher The Runaway The Recorder	
Quadrant IV: Need to Save	The Firefighter	The Angel The Savior

*Please see Chaper 5 for a quick overview of the interactional roles or read Part III, *How Do I learn a New Interactional Role?* Part III will introduce and teach the skills of the new interactional role(s) that you selected from the above chart when you are stuck in the interactional role of The Referee.

The Risk:

In order to shift out of the interactional role of The Referee, you must demonstrate the abilities to carefully observe and analyze the issues that create an enmeshed situation among those present. You need to learn how to watch, listen, follow conversations, show curiosity and even take the risk to block disruptive behaviors of others without setting of rules. You need to help those around you analyze the roots of their problem and how to negotiate about their differences so that true change can be made.

The Reflection:

In order to determine if The Referee is your preferred interactional role in tense situations with others, it would be helpful to ask yourself the following questions:

Family: When family members argued did I intervene by trying to control who spoke and when? Did I often feel exhausted after a family argument as I needed to set the rules of engagement?

Social Circles: When friends fought, did I "step in" and try to stop the arguing by saying who could speak and when? In social clubs, did I attempt to allay others' social fears by controlling communications (e.g., determining who spoke to whom) when things appeared chaotic?

School Experience: Did I take charge of group assignments by determining who would complete specific tasks and establish deadlines for their completion? If other students spoke at once, did I try to regulate interactions?

Co-Workers: Do I have a tendency when co-workers speak of their concerns about the workplace environment, issues with the management or others, do I "step in" and control how much communication is imparted? In meetings do I try to control communications (e.g., determining who spoke to whom) when things appear frenzied?

Spouse or Significant Other: When in an argument or disagreement do I try to control how much information is imparted by my spouse or significant other? If my spouse or significant other should interrupt when I am speaking do I silence them from speaking until I tell them they may continue?

In General: Am I uncomfortable when those around me interrupt each other? Do I sometimes feel compelled to determine who speaks to whom, when, and for how long? Do I say to myself, "Do something, Do something" when constant interruptions and rude nonverbal behaviors result in rising tensions between others?

Quadrant II

Need to Be Curious

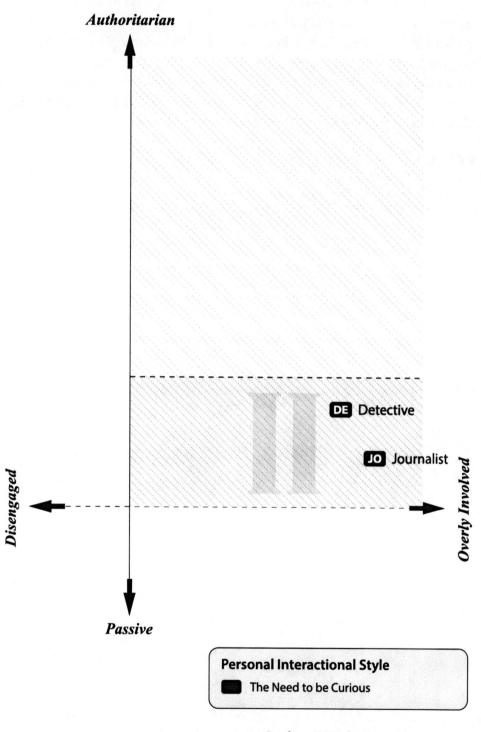

Figure Six

Quadrant II - The Need to be Curious

In pondering your interactional roles and style, you discover that tension makes you very uncomfortable, so you try to control or manage information shared by others by being curious and asking questions. You may believe that the most important aspects of your interactions with others have been to help them understand, without emotion, the underlying causes of their presenting problems. Through the process, you have a tendency to ask questions when others are speaking. You may also try to piece information together from a logical viewpoint as others tell their stories. If your interactional style involves the need to be curious consider reading Part 2 Quadrant II chapters seventeen and eighteen: *The Detective and The Journalist.*

Chapter Seventeen

The Detective

"I spy something very curious, let me look closer!" In the interactional role of The Detective, you might spend considerable energy exploring minute details of others' lives. No stone is left unturned while looking for clues to help others understand their differences. As The Detective, you spend most of your time looking for details or a "guilty" party. Someone must change his behavior because it is deemed as *detrimental* for other people. You are highly focused on "stated" words and observing the behaviors of others. You adopt a linear approach when analyzing information communicated by Key-Relations. You believe that something is "hidden" behind the issues, which needs to be discovered before the problem can be "fixed." Like, The Journalist, you have developed the art of asking questions that are used to create hypotheses about the origin of problems. Therefore, all conversation is directed toward you. You develop and present one hypothesis and one solution, and then attempt to convince those around you that your solution is "correct" by revealing "uncovered facts." In this process, all other points of view and hypotheses are rejected. You believe that only *you* have the ability to put clues together that will lead to the truth so that real changes in others can happen.

How Did I Learn This Role?

As a child, you were probably very curious and tended to ask questions when people displayed presenting concerns or differences. In the quest to identify "one" reason for presenting concerns, you tended to utilize a connect-the-dot approach in looking for answers to highly charged situations. You worked very hard by presenting endless questions about each detail that was presented by your Key-relations. As an adult you tend to enact The Detective role when others around you discuss their issues, are confused by their situations, and display a linear style of thinking in relation to their presenting concerns or differences.

Is this Interactional Role Ever Good For Me to Use?

The Detective is one of the most beneficial interactional roles to select as your preferred way of responding in various highly charged emotional situations. In this interactional role, you help others to explore the basis for their disagreements by uncovering through questioning key information that is hidden. This interactional role can be extremely powerful, as it provides direction for helping to resolve conflicts and determine appropriate interventions that can lead to lasting change. However, you become stuck when you habitually use this interactional role very rigidly as it can result in a barrage of questions that lead nowhere. When others are exposed to useless and excessive questioning, your relations with those around you begin to suffer, as people will distance from you.

EXPAND:

In the next part of this chapter, we reveal to you what happens when this interactional role becomes rigid. We will guide you to other more useful interactional roles.

Help I am Stuck:

In your desire to help others, you laboriously examine clues surrounding differences or presenting problems. Every word or action presented by others is overly analyzed and/or discussed (to the point of boredom). Yet, you treat every detail as critical because you believe that following the trail of clues will lead to answers and, ultimately, a resolution for the tension and differences which are present. When this occurs, the tension between others remains unexposed as endless questioning depletes energy and limits expressions of strong emotions such as anger. This approach creates a structured but sterile atmosphere that provides limited opportunities for problem resolution. Even when you become successful in analyzing clues and present your hypothesis to others, there is a substantial risk that one person related to the situation will ultimately be blamed for the development and maintenance of the concerns or differences. This results in one or more of your connections being alienated from you. You become stuck as differences or concerns with others do not change. Furthermore, your Key-Relations may become bored with the endless questioning and will walk or away or stop discussing their concerns with you.

What Happens Within You:

As information is presented you appear to be analytical, carefully weighing out all the feasible options. You are astute to details and plan everything in advance. When tensions arise with or between others you may have a tendency to become uncomfortable and feel overwhelmed by the expression of emotion being displayed. Due to the unexpected nature of the differences you may feel out-of-control. You ask analytical questions in order to relieve your painful feelings and try to control the emotions by engaging others in a logical and systematic approach of the conflict. When you try to explain why others cannot resolve their differences you over-rely on your sensing, thinking, and judgment skills.

The Case Scenario:

Kathy had received some news at work and she was quite shaken by the fact that she may lose her job. She immediately called her husband, Peter, to share her concerns. Kathy told Peter that she had just met with Linda.... when he asked, "Now who is Linda?" Kathy replied, "The women who sits next to me in my office." She continued by saying that her department may be downsized... when Peter interjected, "And how long has Linda been with the company?" Kathy responded, "What difference does that make?" Peter said, "Well it is nice to know whom the information is coming from." Kathy, replied, "But what I heard is more important, and that some of us may be laid off..." "Who is Linda's source of information?" Peter asked again. "She has a very good friend who works in the president's office." "Has this friend worked long for the president?" At this point Kathy's anger was rising as her husband continued to ask questions, "Will you listen to me and what I heard?" "Well I think we need to figure out whom this friend is and how long they have been friends," replied Peter. At this point, Kathy started to yell into the phone and told her husband to, "Stop it." Peter responded, "I think you are over reacting, now can you find out the name of Linda's friend?" At this point, in a furry, Kathy hung up the phone without saying, "Good-bye" leaving her husband in a bewildered state.

Changing of the Interactional Role:

In the case scenario above, the husband's barrage of questioning was blocking his wife's ability to share her fears and worries about being terminated from her job. Rather than asking questions, the husband needed to connect with and offer reassurance, understanding, and hope in order to calm Kathy. The interactional roles of The Angel or The Firefighter would have served this purpose. The husband may have wanted to join with his wife by moving into the interactional role of The Journalist, which would have allowed her to report her story. Then, after hearing the story in full, move into The Detective roll for clarification of information shared. Through using the interactional roles described above, the husband could have clarified information, remained analytical, while remaining in a supporting role which would have lessened his wife's level of emotion. Through the process, the husband would have stayed in control of the affect, the information being shared, and remain in a place where he felt more comfortable with his wife's anxiety. Kathy's worries would have been attended to and reassured.

What Interactional Roles Will Give Me Personal Power?

There are a number of interactional roles that you can utilize to replace "The Detective" in order to become less analytical when tensions arise. You will need to practice interactional roles where you can manage information and be more open to encouraging communication by creating an atmosphere where people feel free to express their thoughts, thereby resolving the root of their differences. Through the skillful adoption of the alternative interactional roles described below, you will be able to continue manage and analyze information from a systemic viewpoint rather than a linear one. The following chart suggests the best interactional roles for you to select from each quadrant:

Table 18 – Alternative Interachional Roles for The Dectective

Quadrant	Roles to Best Try	Roles to Initially Shy Away From
Quadrant I; Need to Intellectualize	The Judge The Teacher	The Doctor The Preacher The Superman
Quadrant II: Need to Control and Manage Information	The Mediator The Peacemaker The Referee	The Clown The Construction Worker Potato Hot-Head
Quadrant II: Need to Be Curious	The Journalist	
Quadrant III: Need to Avoid	The Bird Watcher The Recorder	The Runaway
Quadrant IV: Need to Save	The Angel The Firefighter The Savior	

*Please see Chapter 5 for a quick overview of the interactional roles or read Part III, *How Do I learn a New Interactional Role?* Part III will introduce and teach the skills of the new interactional role(s) that you selected from the above chart when you are stuck in the interactional role of The Detective.

The Risk:

In order to move out of the interactional role of The Detective, you will
need to refine your questioning of others. You must listen to the concerns and then
analyze information for the purpose of determining its relevance for further exploration.
You must be able to explore the full range of issues, dynamics, and environmental
contexts surrounding differences. This is risky behavior because it requires you to take
less control of what information is shared by others. You must also learn to use received
information to generate several ideas for helping others understand what is maintaining
their differences. By asking fewer questions, the risk of assigning blame will be lessened,
and a safer atmosphere will be created for people to talk. Though you may not be
comfortable, you must also learn to allow others to share information that may be more
ambiguous and less detailed.

The Reflection:

In order to determine if The Detective is your preferred interactional role in tense
situations with others, it would be helpful to ask yourself the following questions:

> **Family:** Was I the person in the family who asked questions about every
> concern that arose in your family to the point where people became angry at
> me?

> **Social Circles:** When friends disagreed, would I pester them with questions
> about the details of their thinking? In social clubs, did I interrupt business by
> constantly interjecting questions?

> **School Experience:** As a student was I the one in the classroom that would
> ask too many questions of the teacher about a task or homework assignment? If
> other students presented an idea, would I persistently question them about it?

> **Co-Workers:** Do I have a tendency to ask detailed questions when co-workers
> speak of their dismay or concerns about the workplace environment or issues
> with the management?

> **Spouse or Significant Other:** Am I quick to formulate questions when my
> spouse or significant is trying to convey their concerns, worries, or fears about a
> situation which does not allow for open discussion?

In General: Do I find myself asking the question after question without looking at the total aspects of the presenting concerns? Do I often find myself saying, "Ahh… clues, I need more information!"

Chapter Eighteen

The Journalist

"I do not understand, you and your son were so close. Can you tell me the story of what you use to do together?" The Journalist assumes a role of wanting to get to the root of the problem by helping others present their experiences in a clear and engaging style. The Journalist likes to collect information about current family events, family interactions, trends, and situations around the presenting issues. The Journalist is curious about others and how their differences developed overtime. The Journalist's use of detailed questions permits all aspects of the interactions around the concerns to be revealed. The Journalist attempts to gather as many points of view from as many different sources as possible. Throughout this process, The Journalist maintains a neutral posture and does not judge others as information is collected.

As The Journalist, you relate effectively to all kinds of people. You communicate interest in and respect for those around you, while efficiently absorbing large amounts of information which is communicated. You are comfortable in allowing tensions to develop and are able to remain cool under the resulting pressure. You actively suppress or lower tensions experienced by others through the skillful use of your questions. Through the process, you manage and control the flow and tempo of communication. You are not afraid to ask tough questions when necessary, and you intentionally direct communications away from yourself. Through this process, interactions and communication of others are encouraged. You work hard to help others understand their differences and you allow Key-Relations to work in a collaborative fashion with you in selecting the solution to the "presenting" problem.

How Did I Learn This Role?

As a child, you may have enjoyed listening to others speak about their life experiences. As you listened to these stories you probably became curious and began asking questions, and soon you discovered through helping people speak about their differences from a historical perspective you helped them work through difficult situations. Later in life you used this approach with friends and found it very effective and they were able to resolve their problems through guided reflection. As an adult, Key-Relations who are in conflicted state engage you into the interactional role of The Journalist. When others pose difficulties or differences, you immediately begin to investigate by asking them to share their stories around the differences and then use the information shared to work collaboratively to come up with solutions for their differences.

Is this Interactional Role Ever Good For Me to Use?

The Journalist is the most beneficial interactional role for you to use as your preferred way of responding in various highly charged emotional situations. In this interactional role, you are able to connect well with all kinds of people. By listening to the stories behind the differences of others, you are able to get to the root of differences. This interactional role is extremely powerful as hearing the history of differences can result in understanding and lasting resolutions can be developed in a collaborative fashion with others. True change in your relations with others is possible with this interactional role. However, you become stuck when you habitually use this interactional role very rigidly. You may be viewed as an annoyance and your relations with others may suffer.

EXPAND:

In the next part of this chapter, we reveal to you what happens when this interactional role becomes rigid. We will guide you to other, more useful interactional roles.

Help I am Stuck:

Typically you are very successful with most persons and in most situations especially when those around you experience panic or helplessness in various life circumstances. However when those around present as cut off from each other or silent you have difficulty knowing what to do next. If you attempt to demonstrate curiosity or ask questions about concerns that you see, those present may ignore you and persist in their detached and under-reactive response style. Any attempts you make to create a dialogue by asking additional questions or probing into aspects of their family or work environment, may be met with more silence and emotional distancing. Continuing to ask probing questions may only irritate to the point of producing a complete breach in the communication process. In such circumstances, discussion is avoided, and you may feel trapped in a double bind as those around you may request help but refuse to talk or answer questions. If you try to persist in asking questions your relations will suffer, as people may distance, close off, or even break the connection with you.

What Happens Within You:

When others present with expressions of emotion or obvious tensions you may feel as if you need to take control of the tense atmosphere by asking others to share their differences through stories. In order to avert discussions of serious concerns or expressions of strong emotions, you resort to analyzing and probing deeper into situations thereby "protecting" yourself from uncomfortable feelings. During the process, you take control of what information is presented, how much information is shared, and the way in which the information is presented. You use questioning to calm differences and control the tempo and type of information being conveyed.

The Case Scenario:

Gail, a long-time neighbor, was invited to tea, and she began to speak to Jessie about her younger son, Chip as he was extremely withdrawn and she was worried as he rarely interacted with anyone. She shared that her other three sons were fine, but Chip really agitated his stepfather David (Gail's present husband). At first, Gail was anxious to speak about the situation, but when Jessie began to ask probing questions about Chip and his relationship with his stepfather, Gail became quite uncomfortable and began to silence or give one-word responses. In order to try to understand Gail's concerns, Jesse began to ask more detailed questions but all of her probes were met with stony silence. Without warning, Gail quickly got up from the table without finishing her tea, and said she needed to "hurry" home. The next day Jesse walked over to Gail's home to invite her for another cup of tea. Even though Gail was at home she did not open the door.

Changing of the Interactional Role:

In the above case scenario Jessie could have created a safe environment and promoted Gail's trust by simply acknowledging how difficult it must be for her to have a son who is withdrawn. When Gail stopped answering her questions, Jessie needed to understand that she was fearful of something, and at this point Jessie needed to display empathy and to listen without interruption. If Jessie had shifted into the interactional role of The Bird Watcher, she would have been able to listen and observe Gail's nonverbal behavior which could have helped uncover her fear. Another interactional role that would have been useful would have been the interactional role of The Angel. This interactional role would have provided opportunities to communicate empathy, share emotional responses nonverbally, and reduce the probability of Gail's resistance. As Gail shared her story, Jessie could have interjected some hope into Gail's situation, which would have encouraged her to share more information, without concern or fear.

What Interactional Roles Will Give Me Personal Power?

There are a number of interactional roles that you can utilize to replace "The Journalist" with to become less reactive and more open to listening to others when they are resistant to share their stories. When people have difficulties you want them to provide you with the history of how these difficulties developed. You try to take control of emotional situations by managing how information is gathered and shared by others. You will need to practice interactional roles where you can learn to listen, observe, support, remain present, be curious about situations and instill hope into others. The following chart suggests the best interactional roles for you to select from each quadrant:

Table 19 – Alternative Interactional Roles for The Journalist

Quadrant	Roles to Best Try	Roles to Initially Shy Away From
Quadrant I; Need to Intellectualize	The Doctor The Teacher	The Judge The Preacher The Superman
Quadrant II: Need to Control and Manage Information	The Clown The Construction Worker The Mediator The Peacemaker The Referee	Potato Hot-Head
Quadrant II: Need to Be Curious	The Detective	
Quadrant III: Need to Avoid	The Bird Watcher The Recorder	The Runaway
Quadrant IV: Need to Save	The Angel The Firefighter The Savior	

*Please see Chapter 5 for a quick overview of the interactional roles or read Part III, *How Do I learn a New Interactional Role?* Part III will introduce and teach the skills of the new interactional role(s) that you selected from the above chart when you are stuck in the interactional role of The Journalist.

The Risk:

In order to move out of interactional role of The Journalist you must practice patience. You need to learn how to demonstrate respect, empathy, and a concern for others, and refrain from asking people to share their stories until a safe environment has been created. You must learn that moving slowly, and listening will create the conditions necessary to establishing rapport with others. This will be challenging for you as you have developed your craft by asking people to tell their stories behind underlying causes. You must learn to resist your immediate impulse to get "their story" and instead, adopt an accommodating and tracking approach especially when those around you become silent.

The Reflection:

In order to determine if The Journalist is your preferred interactional role in tense situations with others it would be helpful to ask yourself the following questions:

> **Family:** Did I regularly ask family members tell their stories around their differences with others in order to understand their perspectives or thoughts? Did those around me become silent?

> **Social Circles:** Did I ask friends to tell their stories in order to help them understand their problems? In social clubs, did I create opportunities for extensive discussions so that information could be analyzed and issues resolved?

> **School Experience:** Was I the student who regularly wanted more information in an attempt to analyze events that occurred in the classroom, at recess, and in relationships?

> **Co-Workers:** Do I have a tendency to ask co-workers who are dismayed or confused about something to share their stories from the beginning? Do I try to analyze employee relations issues by getting as much detail around the issues as possible? Do I encourage others to listen and collaborate in coming up with resolutions? Do others become silent around me?

> **Spouse or Significant Other:** Did I regularly ask my spouse or significant other to start at the "beginning" in order to understand their perspectives or thoughts? Is there silence or anger when I want too much information?

In General: Do I regularly ask others to share their stories and probe for information from those around me? Do I provide space for others to share their stories? Do you find yourself saying, "I wonder about…" and request more information from Key-Relations when tensions rise or strong emotions are expressed?

Quadrant III

The Need to Avoid

Quadrant III - The Need to Avoid

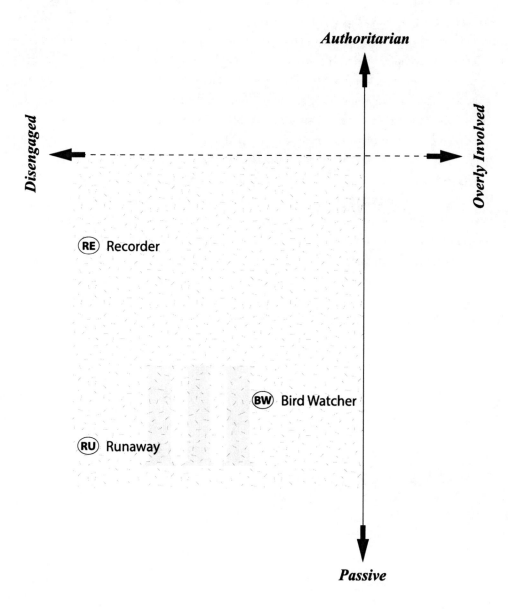

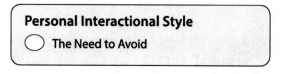

Personal Interactional Style
○ The Need to Avoid

In pondering your interactional roles and style, you discover that tension make you very uncomfortable. So you try to avoid the situation by becoming silent often observing others, recording, or writing down your struggles for later analysis. You may even panic when confronted with high levels of disagreement or confrontation between others or when too much information at one time is provided, and you may either under-react, or over-react by wanting to escape the situation. As you read the interactional roles within this quadrant, you will notice they are quite similar in the description of how you *take* information in (e.g., observe and say little). What makes each interactional role unique is how you handle information once you leave a highly charged situation. In other words, it is what you do, or the action associated with the stress. For example; after leaving a tense situation: (a) if you tend to think about the situation **mentally in your head** and that is where things stop you are the Bird Watcher, (b) if you immediately **write** your thoughts and reactions down in a journal, diary etc. and use your writings for reflection you are The Recorder. While (c) if you **engage in avoidant behaviors** such as drugs, drinking, work etc. or totally leave without returning home, you are The Runaway. If your interactional style involves the need to a need to avoid, escape, or become silent, consider reading Part 2 Quadrant III chapters nineteen through twenty-one: *The Bird Watcher, The Recorder,* and *The Runaway.*

Chapter Nineteen

The Bird Watcher

Barely a sound is uttered, but The Bird Watcher's eyes are open wide and intently focused on others, watching every move, every sigh, and every action. Periodically, as The Bird Watcher, you utter a sound, a statement or a question, allowing others to continue their disagreements or tense situation. Through minimal utterances and brief comments, you acknowledge Key-Relations' communication and interactions, but share little with them. The focus of your interactions during a time of stress is to listen to the presenting information and note all nonverbal behaviors and communication within and between those in your presence. You are inactive in the situations and others present initiate all discussions. You watch and record copious mental notes about the differences of others in your head. These mental notes are basically for your recall and analysis at a later time. Rarely do you share your observations, gathered information, or thoughts with others.

How Did I Learn This Role?

The Bird Watcher interactional role is often activated when others around you present highly complex, intense and confusing communication or behavior patterns. As a child when you experienced highly complex emotional situations, you may have become overwhelmed by the complexity of the presenting issues and did not know what to say or do. Therefore, you became silent and watched as others engaged in their highly enmeshed behaviors or communication. Those around you may even have discussed a wealth of relevant and irrelevant topics in lively, intimidating ways as if you are not even present. As they spoke, you noticed that they frequently interrupted and spoke for each other when tempers flared, and their behaviors become quite animated. You learned early on, that if you offered an opinion others ignored you or they tried to pull you into the conflict by becoming angry at you. As you progressed into adulthood, you learned that you were most comfortable watching others as they engage in highly complex and emotional issues, so you remain silent and do not express your own thoughts and opinions.

Is this Interactional Role Ever Good For Me to Use?

Quite often this interactional role can be very beneficial for you to use as your preferred way of responding in various highly charged emotional situations. In this interactional role, your silence allows you to step out of the emotion, remain neutral, observe, and then have time to reflect on the situation before taking action or no action. This interactional role can be extremely powerful as it helps to keep you from being pulled into the conflict of others. However, you become stuck when you habitually use this interactional role very rigidly as others come to believe you are useless in times of stress. At this point, your relations with those around you begin to suffer as people may stop confiding or associating with you.

EXPAND:

In the next part of this chapter, we reveal to you what happens when this interactional role becomes rigid and guide you to other more useful interactional roles.

Help I am Stuck:

During intense moments as described above you may feel overwhelmed, helpless and uncertain as to how to respond. Some of the communications may even be directed toward you. If you should interject a comment, those present may ignore you, proceed with their typical form of communication and leave you feeling totally invalidated. They can also bring you in to the conflict by becoming angry with you. So you listen and say nothing more than a few words here and there. You are afraid to intervene with any ideas you may have about how to rectify a problem or situation for fear of rejection. Key-Relations may describe their experiences with you as being totally "useless" and they may even pull away from you. At the same time, their trust and respect in you may be diminished.

What Happens Within You:

When tensions arise with or between others you become anxious, nervous, afraid, and have feelings of being helpless. You believe that even if you interject something others may invalidate what you share, or they may turn and use their anger toward you. You become afraid to intervene or say anything for fear of rejection, looking foolish, or being belittled. So you elect to remain silent and as a result, issues and problems with others do not get resolved or are only partially resolved. You may even notice that you experience feelings of hopelessness after conflict that lead to sadness, anger and even depression.

The Case Scenario:

Dale has been married for nearly 30 years to a man who is an alcoholic. Through the years, she has learned to protect him and does not share details with others about his addiction and what her life is really like. They have one married daughter who no longer wants to hear about her mother's "complaints" about her father and has pulled away from her. Dale feels completely alone and does not know how to help her husband. In the past when she has tried to intervene he has yelled, belittled, and denied anything that she might have shared with others. So overtime, Dale has become a Bird Watcher and is afraid to intervene with her husband at any level. Dale has begun to see a therapist. On this particular day, she entered a session wound up like a rubber band. She shared that "it" happened again. Her husband, who has COPD from years of smoking, was to start rehabilitation at a local hospital. Dale was hopeful that the rehabilitation would help him feel better, and that he would become more active and engaged in life. She had been out to lunch with some friends and decided to stop at home before going to her volunteer job. She shared as she drove down the street she got a sick feeling when she saw her husband's car in the driveway. She knew! When she entered the home, he was on the couch, and she did not ask him why he was not dressed for rehab. She could smell the alcohol which confirmed her suspicions that he had been drinking. She said she felt disappointed with him especially when he responded he was slurring his words. She left, went to her job, and then returned about 8 pm. When she entered the house, her husband was on the couch, alcohol bottles around him, and she did not say a word to him. Instead, she grabbed a book and went into the other room and began to read. She was on the edge on her seat, listening to her husband's every groan and movement. Eventually her husband started up the stairs, and she heard him fall down what she imagined to be about 6-8 steps. She did not move from her chair, and she said he lay at the bottom of the stairs for several minutes, he made no sounds, and she did not know if he blacked out, but she thought so. After five to ten minutes, she heard him arouse, groan, whine, and she heard him crawl up the stairs. Again, she did not say anything or get up to assist. When he got to his room he fell again, and she heard a table fall over. She continued to read her book. After 30 minutes, she went upstairs and peeked quietly into his room. He was on the floor passed out. She got a blanket and threw it over the top of him and then left him where he was. She went back to reading and about 2 am she went to sleep in her bedroom, which was separate from his. Dale had no idea if he was awake, if he was hurt, or if he needed her. She was afraid to approach him or say anything to him, so she remained silent. The next morning, she noticed he was holding his back and appeared to be hurt. She did not mention the drinking, what she observed, or the fact that he appeared injured. Instead, she served him breakfast and quietly read the newspaper.

Changing of the Interactional Role:

As illustrated in the case scenario, Dale's previous encounters with her husband and daughter had seduced into the role of The Bird Watcher. After hearing her story, her therapist, asked her if she was courageous enough to change her interactional role with others, and if so, was she willing to do what the therapist would suggest. Dale hesitantly agreed to comply with the suggestion of the therapist because she felt overwhelmed, alone, and uncertain of how to help her husband. The therapist suggested that she may want to take on the interactional roles of The Savior and The Teacher with her husband. The interactional role of The Savior would allow her, without conveying judgment, to become involved with her husband's well-being and to check if he had hurt himself. Through this role, she could offer compassion, kindness, and yet be able to assess his situation up close rather than silently observing from a distance. By acting as The Savior, Dale would be able to engage in conversations that would allow her to assess his injuries and level of drinking. After she assessed his status she could then move into the interactional role of The Teacher. This would allow her to offer suggestions that could help him, without coming across as judgmental, controlling, or overwhelming. This would help Dale to become more active and involved in her husband's drinking habits without being confrontational.

In order to engage her daughter, it would be helpful for Dale to phone her and explain, in the interactional role of The Recorder, her written list of concerns. She needed to share that her father was not well as he had fallen down the stairs and report his injuries. This would keep her daughter informed of her father's status and allow her to ask questions without Dale being perceived as a complainer. This interactional role would keep her daughter involved at some level in the family.

At the next session, Dale reported that she did as she was asked and she felt stronger and more engaged with her family members; not as helpless. She reported that through the interactional role of The Savior, she was able to connect with her husband for the first time in years, he did not belittle her and no longer defensive. She learned he had injured his back and was having problems breathing. He was afraid to tell her because he thought she did not care and he knew he had been drinking "some." He shared that he did not remember falling or being on the floor in his bedroom. He accepted her suggestion that he should see a doctor, get an X-Ray, and even let her go to the appointment with him so she could help him get better. He reported to the doctor that he had tripped over some shoes and fell down the stairs. Dale did not confront her husband's story and felt disappointed that she could not reveal the "family secret" to the doctor. Dale and her husband learned from the doctor that in the fall, he had broken three ribs, cracked a disc, and he might need surgery. Dale recorded his injuries as described by the doctor.

After seeing the doctor, Dale phoned her daughter and reported the written concerns of the Doctor without mentioning the drinking of her husband. To her surprise, her daughter was very responsive and through asking questions, had learned of her father's drinking and concluded that his drinking was now out-of-control. Together, Dale and her daughter began to talk about steps that could be taken to get treatment for his drinking. They agreed the drinking could no longer be a "family" secret, and that for his well-being they needed outside support. Dale shared that she was pleased by her daughter's willingness to speak about the issue. She felt more in control and hopeful that finally something positive might change in her life. She did "not feel so alone" or "afraid."

In the above scenario, Dale had learned overtime that to try to intervene with her husband's drinking only resulted in verbal abuse and alienation from her daughter. So, to cope she became silent but her anxiety, worry, and fear had escalated to the point where she was losing weight and had trouble sleeping due to the daily duress and stress of her husband's drinking. She felt alone and needed to protect the "family" secret at all cost. Together, Dale and her daughter need to consult with experts and to educate themselves as to how alcohol addiction was impacting their life. Dale was just beginning the stages of change, but through expanding into the interactional roles of The Savior, The Teacher, and The Recorder she stepped out of her helplessness and had begun to release her power from within which will turn activate true change within herself and her family.

What Interactional Roles Will Give Me Personal Power?

There are a number of interactional roles that you can utilize to replace "The Bird Watcher" with to become more active and involved when tensions arise. In most conflicted situations, you appear to be very passive and disengaged from others as you typically fail to demonstrate expression of your feelings or thoughts. So, you need to learn how to express your thoughts openly during times of stress. You will need to practice those interactional roles which are more involved, can help to assist other's decision-making, or intervene when other's interactions are escalating differences rather than helping. The following chart suggests the best interactional roles for you to select from each quadrant:

Table 20 – Alternative Interactional Roles for The Bird Watcher

Quadrant	Roles to Best Try	Roles to Initially Shy Away From
Quadrant I; Need to Intellectualize	The Teacher	The Doctor The Judge The Preacher The Superman
Quadrant II: Need to Control and Manage Information	The Mediator The Peacemaker The Referee	The Clown The Construction Worker Potato Hot-Head
Quadrant II: Need to Be Curious	The Detective The Journalist	
Quadrant III: Need to Avoid	The Recorder	The Runaway
Quadrant IV: Need to Save	The Angel The Firefighter The Savior	

*Please Chapter 5 for a quick overview of the interactional roles or read Part III, *How Do I learn a New Interactional Role?* Part III will introduce and teach the skills of the new interactional role(s) that you selected from the above chart when you are stuck in the interactional role of The Bird Watcher.

The Risk:

A fundamental learning goal for you will be to take a more active role with others. You must learn ways to become more assertive and involved when tensions arise. You will need to practice taking a risk by speaking, acting, or responding in situations which are uncomfortable rather than remaining silent. Perhaps the greatest risk for you, as The Bird Watcher, is learning how to respond when you feel overwhelmed by a deluge of words or dysfunctional behaviors by others. In such circumstances, you must find the courage to act in the face of uncertainty and risk that others may get angry or ignore you. You must believe that they will not cut you off or reject you.

The Reflection:

In order to determine if The Bird Watcher is your preferred interactional role in tense situations with others, it would be helpful to ask yourself the following questions:

Family: When family conflict developed, did I become quiet, sit back, and observe family members in action? Was I afraid if I said anything I would be rejected?

Social Circles: When friends or co-workers argued or when tensions rose in personal relationships, did I pull back, watch, not saying a word? If I was actively engaged in social clubs, was I the person who would sit back and observe other members speak, not saying a word about the process?

School Experience: As a student, was I the one who observed class member's, activities being completed, not a saying a word or trying to help at any level?

Co-Workers: When co-workers disagree do I observe and say nothing?

Spouse or Significant Other: When my spouse or significant other shows dismay, concern, or worry, do I listen and basically not respond?

In General: When conflict or tension arises with others, do I find myself sitting back, observing and not responding to the interactions? Do I freeze or become silent in the face of tension? Do I say to myself, "If I speak they will reject me or become angry!"

Chapter Twenty

The Recorder

Paper in hand… pencil at the ready… others speak, and the Recorder devotedly mentally records the flood of ensuing communications and behaviors displayed by Key-Relations. During intense, highly charged situations, as the Recorder, you say little but later you write in your diary, journal, or even on Twitter. You use a secret name, reflecting on your emotions and estranged relationships with others. Through silence, you assume an interpersonal posture of being aloof and passive. You are typically skilled in multi-tasking (e.g. listening, mentally recording, and later writing, etc.). You believe it is safer for you to write down your emotions when upset, rather than to express your feelings openly toward others.

How Did I Learn This Role?

As a child you may have watched as others around you, especially parents or other family members, engaged into actions that were enmeshed. During intense emotional moments, (e.g., disrupted communications, blaming, yelling) you were afraid to express your thoughts, reactions, or ideas as when you did; others may have turned their anger or frustrations toward you. In order to protect yourself you wrote your thoughts and emotional reactions into a journal or diary. This way you were safe as the journal or diary could not speak back to you. You often re-read your writings in order to analyze and think about how you wanted to respond. Also with friends you learned it was safer to write in a diary than to share openly your thoughts or opinions about them directly. This way did they not get angry and reject you. Again you used your writings for self-reflection. As an adult, you may discover that you continue to journal or write about those feelings, which are not "safe" to openly express to others. You find that through writing you have learned the skill of self-reflection and the ability to analyze emotionally charged situations more clearly. Your recording of events allows you to think about how you want to respond in future discussions with Key-Relations.

Is this Interactional Role Ever Good For Me to Use?

Quite often this interactional role can be beneficial for you to use as your preferred way of responding in various highly charged emotional situations. In this interactional role you are able to mentally record, write openly about your emotions, and determine a course of action after analyzing your recordings. Using social media with a fake name is perfect for you as in a non-direct, safe way you are able to express your thoughts and emotions during highly charged situations. This way others do not know who you are and cannot get angry or reject you. This interactional role is very powerful as you can logically and safely review and reflect upon your written recordings which keep you from responding impulsively. However, you become stuck when you habitually use this interactional role rigidly. Since you do not verbally respond to conflicts, Key-Relations may question your motives in a particular situation. Your relationships may suffer as people fail to understand you or your wishes.

EXPAND:

In the next part of this chapter, we reveal to you what happens when this interactional role becomes rigid and guide you to other more useful interactional roles.

Help I am Stuck:

When you become silent and only observe what is happening in an intense situation, your conflicted feelings never surface and you do not discuss your concerns with others. Although you become astute at observing the communications and reactions of others, you find they pay little to no attention to you because you fail to express your opinions or thoughts openly. You become stuck because emotionally charged situations of difference are often not resolved; your emotions are never expressed, so people do not know how to please you or what you are thinking. Through recording, you become reinforced by safely hiding behind a diary, journal, or written lists. As you rarely, if ever, openly express your thoughts or differences to others you may discover that keep your anger inside, consequently, you become depressed and feel like no one understands you.

What Happens Within You:

When tensions arise with or between others you become anxious, nervous, and/or afraid. You may even notice that you become, sad, or develop feelings of hopelessness. During tense situations you do not intervene or say anything for fear of rejection, looking foolish, or being belittled. So you elect to remain silent, watch, mentally record what people are saying or doing and then later will write your thoughts or feelings down in a diary, notebook, journal, or through social media. The latter is already a step forward to expressing yourself towards others, As a result, issues and problems with others do not get resolved, and you only present to others a superficial, happy or neutral face.

The Case Scenario:

Fourteen-year-old Maria watched as her parents engage in a heated discussion over the money that her mother was spending without first speaking to her father. As they argued, her older brother, Jared interrupted. Her parents then yelled at Jared who became very angry. Maria began to feel afraid, and her stomach hurt as she had seen this fighting in the past. Maria's father begins to call her mother names and belittles her. Maria's mother cries and Jared begins to argue with his father who then pushes him up against a wall. Maria filled with fear, runs to her room, and grabs her diary, that she keeps which under her mattress.

She begins to write:

> *Dear Diary:*
> *My family is fighting again, and I am so scared. They are arguing over money*
> *and I am wondering if we are going to lose our home. I am worried that my*
> *father might hit my brother or that my mother might leave. I am very scared,*
> *but I cannot tell my mother as she does not listen to me. She calls me, "Stupid"*
> *and my brother only laughs at me. What can I do? I am so scared. I have trouble*
> *sleeping at night, and I feel sick to my stomach. This all makes me so sad. You*
> *are my only friend, Maria.*

Changing of the Interactional Role:

In the case scenario above, Maria was afraid to speak out for fear of rejection or belittlement from her family members so she kept quiet. In reality, being fourteen, it would be difficult for her to try to intervene by managing or controlling the information of her family when in a heated situation. So, she might want to stay in the interactional role of The Recorder until the situation becomes calmer. After journaling her thoughts, probably the safest interactional role with her family would be The Detective. Through this interactional role, she could ask her mother and father individually if they were in financial trouble and were they going to lose their home? She could also try to gain an understanding from her sibling as to why their father angers so quickly. Furthermore, she could find out if her mother was thinking of leaving the family and if so what would happen to her. To show her family how fearful she becomes when her parents argue; she may risk sharing her writings, since she is afraid to speak to them directly. In the interactional role of The Savior, she could ask her parents how she could help to earn money so that the family finances would be better.

Note of Caution:

Children/adolescents must be more cautious than adults when attempting to engage in new interactional roles, as they are responding to authority figures. In the case above, the interactional roles of The Detective, The Birdwatcher, and The Recorder in combination would appear respectful towards other and less likely to meet with resistance, anger, or back lashing.

What Interactional Roles Will Give Me Personal Power?

There are a number of interactional roles that you can utilize to replace The Recorder" with to become more active and involved with others when tensions arise. In most emotional situations, you become very disengaged from others and passive when differences surface. So the risk is to become more engaged and practice verbally expressing your thoughts and opinions openly to others. The following chart suggests the best interactional roles for you to select from each quadrant:

Table 21 – Alternative Interactional Roles for The Recorder

Quadrant	Roles to Best Try	Roles to Initially Shy Away From
Quadrant I; Need to Intellectualize	The Teacher The Doctor	The Judge The Preacher The Superman
Quadrant II: Need to Control and Manage Information	The Mediator The Peacemaker The Referee	The Clown The Construction Worker Potato Hot-Head
Quadrant II: Need to Be Curious	The Detective The Journalist	
Quadrant III: Need to Avoid		The Bird Watcher The Runaway
Quadrant IV: Need to Save	The Angel The Firefighter The Savior	

*Please see Chapter 5 for a quick overview of the interactional roles or read Part III, *How Do I learn a New Interactional Role?* Part III will introduce and teach the skills of the new interactional role(s) that you selected from the above chart when you are stuck in the interactional role of The Recorder.

The Risk:

In order to move out of the interactional role of The Recorder, you must allow yourself to be fully present (i.e., physically, psychologically, emotionally, relationally, spiritually) and trust that others will not reject you. This is extremely risky behavior for you, as you feel safe in an aloof position and you know that your recordings will not turn on you. You must learn how to be yourself in front of others, working to create stronger relationships by expressing your thoughts and feelings when differences occur. You will need to listen to what is being said or done in the conflicts of Key-Relations in order to decide how to respond. You will need to learn how to ask questions, query presented stories and learn how to block others when they begin to get out-of-control. You need to be more of yourself and verbally express your true reactions and feelings to others. The Clown could be an important role, but you must have the special skills needed for this role.

The Reflection:

In order to determine if The Recorder is your preferred interactional role in tense situations with others, it would be helpful to ask yourself the following questions:

> **Family:** Did I keep track of family members' arguments, tensions and differences by writing in a diary or making a written list?

> **Social Circles:** When friends shared a wealth of information, did I keep a diary to make sure I remembered what they said? In social clubs, did I volunteer to take notes so I did not need to say anything during the meetings?

> **School Experience:** Did I take copious class notes in order to remember information presented by the teacher? If other students complained about taking notes, did I provide a copy of my notes? Did I write about things that happened in school in a diary or journal?

> **Co-Workers:** When co-workers disagree do I have a tendency to observe and say nothing and later make written notes about what was said or actions taken?

> **Spouse or Significant Other:** When my significant becomes upset, do I become quiet, say little or nothing and later write my thoughts and feelings in a journal or diary?

In General: Am I likely to keep a journal or diary to reflect on things as an adult? When others argue or disagree do I say to myself, "I am afraid to say anything but I will write it down in my journal or diary?"

Chapter Twenty-One

The Runaway

"I don't want you to cry on my shoulder. I don't want to hear about your unhappiness. I must get away, far, far away, I must run away." As The Runaway, it is not uncommon for you to feel overwhelmed when others bicker, argue, fight, or present highly charged emotional conflicts. In these circumstances, you may panic, not know what to say, or what to do in order to calm the situation. When this happens you may engage in a number of behaviors which can include; (a) displacement activities rather than dealing with a problem (e.g., you put your energy into something totally unrelated such as organizing your home, work, hobbies, sports, socializing, travel, or volunteer activities), (b) Turning to destructive behavior (e.g., drugs, alcohol, reckless gambling), (c) Physically running away such as moving to another location (e.g. changing jobs, running away from home), (d) Changing relationships in search of a new one that doesn't have any problems, or (e) Blaming others for your problems as you believe that if someone else has caused the problem then you do not need to put energy into changing, taking responsibility, or fixing it. In intense emotional situations, you respond by becoming silent, appearing lost, and are unable to solve the situation. You believe that you are in a helpless position, and the further you can get away from the problem, the less likely Key-Relations will ask you to "fix" the problem.

How Did I Learn This Role?

The Runaway interactional role is often activated when others around you present highly complex, intense, and confusing communication or behavior patterns. As a child when your parents or other members of your family fought or argued you may have felt very helpless, scared, and would hide in your room or leave your house. During these family encounters, you may be overwhelmed by the complexity of the presenting issues. Overtime, you learned that by leaving or avoiding a highly charged emotional situation you felt more in control and had less anxiety. So, at an early age you discovered that avoiding problems or situations was more comforting for you than facing the fear, confronting others, or dealing with the anxiety within you. As an adult, you discover that when tensions build with Key-Relations you have a tendency to remove yourself from the situation quickly, engage in substance abuse, become unavailable to others or leave the situation or relationship altogether.

Is this Interactional Role Ever Good For Me to Use?

Quite often this interactional role can be one very beneficial for you to use as your preferred way of responding in various highly charged emotional situations, especially if you feel panicked or your anger is rising to a point of no control. This unique interactional role allows you to remove yourself from a heated situation until you can gain your composure and have time to reflect on the best way to respond rationally. Playing this role for a short time helps you think things over logically. This interactional role is very powerful as you it is a way to initiate and maintain self-control. However, if you use this interactional role rigidly, too long, or too extensively where you consistently run, use drugs or bury yourself in a hobby or work you will learn to avoid issues and resolutions will not be forthcoming. At this point, your relations with those around you begin to suffer. Key-Relations become annoyed and perceive you as uncaring, insensitive, and useless. The more you hide from situations and do not express your feelings openly to others the more likely you are to develop depression.

EXPAND:

In the next part of this chapter, we will reveal to you what happens when this interactional role becomes rigid and guide you to other more useful interactional roles.

Help I am Stuck:

Others who bicker, quarrel, fight, nag, constantly complain, yell, or are abusive engage you into action. Feeling overwhelmed by others who present with highly charged emotion or emotional distress, you respond by removing yourself from the situation. As a consequence, the differences are rarely analyzed, and others may become annoyed and view you as uncaring, insensitive, and useless. Worse, they do not understand you and may totally ignore you failing to take into account your reactions, thoughts or feelings. Through the process of leaving, you fail to gather sufficient information that can help you resolve differences. When you fail to express your emotions and engage in self-destructive or avoiding behaviors you can become extremely depressed and/or suicidal.

What Happens Within You:

It is not uncommon especially if you have a physical or verbally abusive history that you become overwhelmed with fear and anxiety when face-to-face stressful or highly charged emotional situations develop. When tension or anger is present in others you may have a tendency to become, silent, afraid to express your thoughts due to perceived or real rejection, or worry that others may perceive you as a "mean" person. You may become so overwhelmed that you feel incapacitated. So you elect to remain silent and avoid the painful situation by leaving or becoming involved in distancing behaviors. By virtue of your own emotional distress and behaviors, you may actually create more tension and conflict with those around you. Your silence often results in escalating others' vulnerabilities and possible depression in you.

The Case Scenario:

Octavia and Romaine have been in a long-term relationship for approximately one-year. Octavia is upset as Romaine is out-of-town and has not e-mailed her in about a week. She is certain that he no longer loves her, she therefore writes a long e-mail sharing that she wants to break-up. When Romaine reads the e-mail he becomes visibly upset, angry, and when they speak on the phone he lashes out at her in total frustration. They quickly regress into arguing and blaming each other for the lack of intimacy, connection, and distance between them. Romaine has taken a new job which requires him to travel and Octavia has issues with him not being home. Octavia begins to cry and shares how much she loves him. Romaine uncertain of how to handle or respond to Octavia's "craziness" decides he has had enough of the relationship and suggested that they need to part ways. He hates fighting as it reminds him of his parents. Neither wants to end the relationship, but they don't how to make the changes so they fight less. Romaine shared that he would be moving out when he returned home.

Changing of the Interactional Role:

In the case scenario above Octavia had brought insecurities from her past relationships into her current relationship. Especially, coming from parents who were divorced, and a father who did not make much time for her. Her lack of trust in former Key-relations was impacting her relationship with Romaine. She had a hard time believing that Romaine would not leave her. As a result, she was trying to push him away. Romaine had grown up in a home where there was constant bickering and fighting between his parents. Whenever they would begin to bicker, Romaine would leave the house and go across the street to his friend's home. As soon he was eighteen, he moved out of his family's home. So when Octavia accuses him of cheating or wanting to leave he has a hard time expressing his thoughts. Immediately he jumps back into his memories and remembers his parent's unhappy marriage. Rather than listening to Octavia's fears he quickly reverts back to his anger with his parents and wants to leave the situation.

Neither Octavia nor Romaine wants the relationship to end, but they are at a loss as to how to save their relationship. In this particular situation, it would be helpful for Octavia and Romaine to go to a couple's therapist so they can learn how their childhood and past experiences were negatively playing out and blocking their ability to move past their prior hurt and fears. Romaine, however, could take the risk to stop and listen to Octavia through the integrated roles of The Journalist and The Detective. Through these roles, he could hear and understand her stories as to why she feels so insecure in their relationship. This action by Romaine would help Octavia to feel more connected to him. Romaine could learn ways to reassure and help her when she does become insecure. When Octavia does act "crazy", Romaine could shift into the interactional role of The Firefighter in order to put out the emotional crisis and reassure her that he is there for her. Later he could shift into the interactional roles of The Peacemaker and The Angel to calm the emotional situation. Romaine could then offer Octavia hope, by sharing that he has no plans of leaving her. These interactional roles would serve to reassure and help Octavia become more trusting and help to build a stronger relationship between them. Also, Romaine would not feel helpless and have a desire to leave the relationship.

What Interactional Roles Will Give Me Personal Power?

There are a number of interactional roles that you can utilize to replace "The Runaway" with to become more active, involved, and openly willing to express your feelings or thoughts to others. Rather than leaving an emotional situation you will need to learn how to help calm a situation down, by blocking arguments that are not helping a situation and more actively work towards helping to resolve differences. The risk for you is to stay and assist in emotionally charged situations rather than leave. However, a note of caution is offered: *If you are involved in a highly abusive (physical or emotional) situation you must be very careful as to how you respond to the person inflicting the abuse. We, as experienced therapists, highly encourage you to seek out therapeutic help from others and guidance as to how to handle the abusive situation, so you do not put yourself in further physical or emotional harm (See Part 5 Chapter 27).* The following chart overviews the best interactional roles for you to try initially, from each quadrant:

Table 22 – Alternative Interactional Roles for The Runaway

Quadrant	Roles to Best Try	Roles to Initially Shy Away From
Quadrant I; Need to Intellectualize	The Teacher	The Doctor The Judge The Preacher The Superman
Quadrant II: Need to Control and Manage Information	The Construction Worker The Mediator The Peacemaker The Referee	The Clown Potato Hot-Head
Quadrant II: Need to Be Curious	The Detective The Journalist	
Quadrant III: Need to Avoid		The Bird Watcher The Recorder
Quadrant IV: Need to Save	The Angel The Firefighter The Savior	

*Please see Chapter 5 for a quick overview of the interactional roles or read Part III, *How Do I learn a New Interactional Role?* Part III will introduce and teach the skills of the new interactional role(s) that you selected from the above chart when you are stuck in the interactional role of The Runaway.

The Risk:

In order to move out of the interactional role of The Runaway you must learn how to block insults by others gently, so that you can be heard. You will need to learn to engage in thoughtful explorations of presenting concerns by asking questions. You will need to learn how to interject hope and peace into an intense situation. Most importantly, you need to become more confident that you can share your thoughts and not be rejected by others. These behaviors are quite risky, as you may make others annoyed or upset with you, something you have spent your life trying to avoid.

The Reflection:

In order to determine if The Runaway is your preferred interactional role in tense situations with others, it would be helpful to ask yourself the following questions:

Family: When tensions rose among family members, did I say nothing? Hide in my room? Suffer in silence? Or run away from home?

Social Circles: When friends argued, did I withdraw and remain silent? In social clubs, was I intimated by members' emotional expressions and respond by saying nothing or quitting the club?

School Experience: Did I rarely speak in class? If other students complained, did I sit quietly, listen, and say nothing?

Co-Workers: When co-workers disagree do I have a tendency to remain silent, say nothing, and/or walk away?

Spouse or Significant Other: When my significant other shows dismay, concern, or worry do I argue, leave the house, bury myself into work, hide on the computer, drink? Do I threaten to end the relationship?

In General: When conflict or tension arises with others, do I walk away? Do I seek out activities or hobbies that I can immerse myself in? Do I feel panicked and sick to my stomach? Do I find myself saying, "I need to get out of here now!"

Quadrant IV

The Need to Save Others

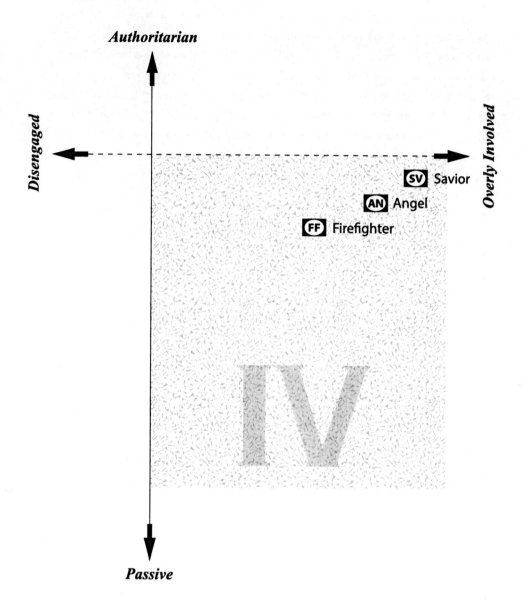

Figure Eight

Quadrant IV - The Need to Save Others

Authoritarian

Disengaged

Overly Involved

SV Savior

AN Angel

FF Firefighter

IV

Passive

Personal Interactional Style

⬤ The Need to Save Others

In pondering your interactional roles and style, you become aware that the most important aspect of your interactions with others has been to guide, strengthen, assist, and encourage them. You also believe that you want to resolve a desperate or intense situation for them. You have a strong need to take care of or protect others, be highly involved in other's lives, and your goal is to make them happy or comfortable. You try to relieve all pain or discomfort for others. By adopting this interactional style, you have worked hard to provide for, protect and deliver others from their losses, fears, anxiety, depression, and emotional wounds. You have a strong tendency to assist and reassure others that you can and will save them. Often you sacrifice your own needs, desires and wants for others. If your interactional style involves the need to save others consider reading Part 2, Quadrant IV chapters twenty-two, twenty-three and twenty-four: *The Angel, The Firefighter,* and *The Savior.*

The Angel   189

Chapter Twenty-Two

The Angel

Ah, The Angel, the interjector of hope, the person who relieves all pain, hurt, and sadness in others. As The Angel, you assume a role of wanting to please everyone in the world especially your family members. Throughout all situations, especially when tensions arise, you guide, protect, reveal positive insight, strengthen and encourage those around you. You are viewed by others as being a kind and lovable person. You personify goodness, purity, and selflessness. Others describe you as being gentle, sweet, charming, a good listener, empathetic and polite. You display little emotion, rarely make a fuss, and are always there to help others. You are the closest thing to perfection that one can get.

How Did I learn This Role?

As a child, you learned early on that your main existence in life was to inject hope into the lives of others. You have spent countless hours doing for, helping, and assisting others. Whenever tension arose, you would find the "good" no matter how bad the situation was. You became extremely anxious if others around you experienced any discomfort, pain, or sadness. As an adolescent, you were quick to want to "cheer-up" your friends and reassure them that their life was good. As an adult, you are engaged into action by others who appear helpless or have lost hope in life.

Is this Interactional Role Ever Good For Me to Use?

Quite often this interactional role can be very beneficial for you to use as your preferred way of responding in various highly charged emotional situations. This unique interactional role, gives you much personal power and contentment as you instill hope and worth into the lives others. Playing this role for a short time helps you to create a situation that enables others to get stronger. This interactional role is unconsciously powerful as it provides for you an atmosphere of control, power, and manipulation as you are able to limit the social context and interactions around you so that other's may remain protected and happier. Although you breathe perpetual hope and comfort into conflicts, your behavior unconsciously can contribute to inducing more pain and emotional distance in and between people. If you use this interactional role rigidly too extensively, others will never resolve their differences and may perceive you as an interference. You become stuck as others may become angry at you and your relationships become very superficial.

EXPAND:
In the next part of this chapter we will reveal to you what happens when this interactional role becomes rigid and guide you to other more useful interactional roles.

Help I am Stuck:

During moments when conflicts are avoided you do not allow the true concerns around differences to surface. Consequently, the underlying cause of the presenting issues between you and others is not uncovered. Although all people around you seem pleased with avoiding the source of the disagreement or conflict, especially you, differences remain unresolved because the root of the problem, concerns, or annoyance is not discussed. The interjection of hope encourages a level of calmness and false happiness in and between others. In the end, you must continue to work hard to maintain this serenity, which places a lot of pressure on you, to make sure everyone remains happy, so that they can continue in a superficial relationship without discussing of pain, anger, sadness, or disappointment.

What Happens Within You:

When tensions are present, you may experience feelings of being scared, nervous, or anxious, have feelings of insecurities, or possibly thoughts of being abandoned or rejected by others. Your biggest fear is that someone may become upset with you, criticize, or dislike you. By being The Angel, you place yourself in an important position with others as you need to be needed and they like having you around. You do not complain, and you always see the positive side to every situation. Within this interactional role, you present a very superficial person to others as your true emotions, thoughts, feelings or cognitions are buried within; which can result in a deep level of unhappiness. You also experience a lot of pressure when trying to keep other's happy. You must be careful as this interactional role gives you a feeling of false security. It can temporarily fill the emptiness or lessen the fear of abandonment within you.

The Case Scenario:

Sherita is a 54 year-old woman who has spent her life trying to make other people happy, especially her mother and paternal grandmother. In various therapy sessions when asked why she would sacrifice her needs for others she would often state, "But this is what everyone expects." When asked about her own feelings, thoughts, or reactions she would say, "What does it matter, it is not about me." When Sherita married a lover of many years, she refused to tell her mother or wear a wedding ring as she knew her mother would become upset. So rather than having the wedding of her dreams, being openly happy, she went to a Justice of the Peace and quietly got married, not even telling her two daughters.

Sherita's new husband, Eduardo, has Huntington's disease and is at the point where he cannot walk, take care of himself, go down stairs, eat, or lift himself on the toilet. Sherita spends her entire day, waiting on him, doing his finances, and attending to his every need in order to, "Make him happy." Recently her husband has been thinking of a former girlfriend and has now dubbed Sherita, the former girlfriend's name of Lucy. He refers to Lucy a lot, which hurts Sherita deeply, but she will not openly tell her husband of her hurt. In the last session, Sherita had hired a detective to locate Lucy and phoned her to let her know that her husband still thinks of her. Lucy is a nurse and now divorced, shared that if Eduardo personally phoned her she would come to him. Sherita believes that this will make her husband happy and complete, so she is spending all of her energies to make this reunion occur. When asked why she would sacrifice her marriage to do this, she replied, "Because it is not about me, it is what he wants and he needs to be happy." When asked where she would go, what would she do, she stated, "What does it matter? All that matters is that he is happy." When asked if she was happy in her marriage, she replied, "Sure, but it is not about me, it is about my husband and what he wants." She even shared that she would teach Lucy all about Eduardo's needs so she could take care of him and she would give all her financial assets from her marriage to Lucy as this would make Lucy and her husband, who is very wealthy, "happy."

Changing of the Interactional Role:

As illustrated in the case scenario Sherita has spent a lifetime devoted to making others happy. She learned from an early age that her role in life was to please her mother and grandmother. Whenever she expressed her emotions, she was severely punished. Eventually, she learned it was safer not to express herself openly, and she buried all emotion, thoughts, and reactions to situations deep within her. Her therapist recognized that she needed to move slowly and that Sherita was being reactive to her husband's thoughts, which could be related to cognition decline or fantasy related to the illness, and not a true search for a lost love.

The first thing Sherita was requested to do was to change her interactional role to The Doctor. She was encouraged to read as much as possible about those with

Huntington's disease. To learn about the cognitive decline and hallucinations that may result from neurological changes or medication. The second thing she was asked to do was to become The Recorder and journal about her reactions, hurt, fear of rejection and pain from her husband's actions and words. She was asked not analyze just write and bring the journal back to the next session. She was also temporarily to become The Construction Worker and STOP trying to connect her husband and Lucy. Before she proceeded, she needed to stop, think, analyze and assess the situation and learn about the progression of the disease before she pursued in impulsive behavior. Her desire and belief system of having Lucy reunite with her husband may only result in undue duress for her husband, herself, and Lucy.

Sherita came to the next session carrying her journal. She shared that she had temporarily stopped trying to connect Lucy and her husband. Even though he still used Lucy's name now and then, the frequency had lesson. She had read on the cognitive concerns related to medication and Huntington's disease and agreed that some of her husband's fantasies could be contributed to his medication, but she was not 100% convinced. She still believed he wanted Lucy in his life, not her to be truly happy.

The biggest insights for Sherita occurred when her journal was reviewed. She wrote a lot about her sadness as a child and her fear of being rejected. She believed that her brother was deeply loved by her mother and grandmother, but that she was not. The only way to get their attention was by taking care of their every need and making them "happy." She realized how angry she was at her mother, who is still alive and she waits on her daily in addition to her husband, and how she continues not to express her own needs or desires for fear of her mother's rejecting behavior toward her. Sherita rarely speaks to her brother, and she was beginning to have an insight that her anger towards her brother was more jealousy than hate. She realized that she had transferred some of her feelings toward her sibling onto Lucy and that she was truly jealous of Lucy. She had to sacrifice her own desires to be the "perfect" one, as she was the "black sheep" in the family. She also wrote about how her husband put her down constantly and how imperfect she was in his "eyes" (just like the eyes of her grandmother and mother). She realized she was living the same life and fears as a child, now as an adult.

Sherita was not ready to take any direct action about confronting her husband or mother. By journaling her emotions, thoughts, and responses to current situations, she was beginning to release the power from within as she connected how she had never grown past her childhood experiences or emotions; and how she had transferred them to her encounters with significant others as an adult.

What Interactional Roles Will Give Me Personal Power?

There are a number of interactional roles that you can utilize to replace "The Angel" with to become more engaged and active allowing others to experience pain when highly charged emotions are present. You will need to practice interactional roles where you can feel like you are helping others while not being responsible for creating other's happiness. In addition, these roles will help you to become more attentive to your own needs, desires, and wishes when tensions arise. Through the skillful adoption of these alternative interactional roles, you may instill hope into situations which are characterized by chaos, sadness, anger, and hopelessness. The following chart suggests the best interactional roles for you to select from each quadrant:

Table 23 – Alternative Interactional Roles for The Angel

Quadrant	Roles to Best Try	Roles to Initially Shy Away From
Quadrant I; Need to Intellectualize	The Doctor The Teacher	The Judge The Preacher The Superman
Quadrant II: Need to Control and Manage Information	The Clown The Construction Worker The Mediator The Peacemaker The Referee	Potato Hot-Head
Quadrant II: Need to Be Curious	The Detective The Journalist	
Quadrant III: Need to Avoid	The Bird Watcher The Recorder The Runaway	
Quadrant IV: Need to Save	The Firefighter	The Savior

*Please see Chapter 5 for a quick overview of the interactional roles or read Part III, *How Do I learn a New Interactional Role?* Part III will introduce and teach the skills of the new interactional role(s) that you selected from the above chart when you are stuck in the interactional role of The Angel.

The Risk:

If you find yourself enacting the interactional role of The Angel, it may be necessary to practice allowing others to be *un*comfortable. This is extremely risky, because you are always eager to please everyone. You will need to let tensions rise in various social contexts so that the real underlying issues between and among people can be openly discussed. Keep in mind that because you desire peace and happiness for all especially your family members, allowing tensions to surface will be quite scary and unsettling for you. In addition, you may freeze out of fear and not know how to respond to others who present anger, pain, grief, sadness or depression which may make you feel out of control of the situation rendering you helpless.

The Reflection:

In order to determine if The Angel is your preferred interactional role in tense situations with others, it would be helpful to ask yourself the following questions:

> **Family:** Was I the interjector of hope into my family system? Did I re-interpret tense family situations into hopeful scenarios?

> **Social Circles:** When friends or co-workers fought, was I the person that they sought out to relieve their inner turmoil? If I was actively engaged in social clubs, was I the person trying to allay others' social fears by rephrasing language, watching other's actions, and immediately translating nonverbal cues into more palatable interpretations?

> **School Experience:** As a student, did I exhibit happiness regardless of the assigned task? If other students complained, would I offer them comfort regarding the work ahead?

> **Co-Workers:** Do I have a tendency when co-workers speak of their concerns about the workplace environment, issues with the management or others, to reframe and point out the positive aspects of their jobs?

> **Spouse or Significant Other:** When in an argument or disagreement do I give in to make my partner happy? When my spouse or significant other displays negative emotions do I comfort, reassure, and try to make them happy?

In General: Am I uncomfortable with the necessary conflict and tension that arise with others? Do I want to develop resolution quickly, so that others are happier? Am I afraid of being rejected or that not everyone will love me? Do I say, "I need to make them happy"?

Chapter Twenty-Three

The Firefighter

"Watch out! Watch out! Let me in, I am here to help!" The interactional role of The Firefighter requires you to adopt a crisis-oriented approach as you are typically engaged with others "putting out fires." As The Firefighter, you are quick to respond to emergency situations and work quickly to rescue Key-Relations from all types of emotional disasters. You are able to assess situations and decide immediately on a course of action for those around you. You are able to respond to unforeseen circumstances as they emerge. Typically, you will collect only minimal information about the situation or differences before moving into action to resolve the issue. You usually accept and do not challenge how the issue is presented. Through the process, you become highly reactive in order to save the "victim" from further distress. As The Firefighter, you work hard to help those in the situation return to a level of "normalcy." You strive to create a sense of emotional safety for others by minimizing the distress, emotional suffering, and/or tensions caused by the crisis. You tend to become overly involved in a situation in order to save others and will go out of your way to connect with outside agencies to assist. Typically, all communication is directed towards you.

How Did I Learn This Role?

As a child when people in your family or parents became very explosive, emotionally reactive, helpless, or presented in crisis you learned that you were able to calm them by taking charge and making decisions. With friends, you noticed that you were able to display a similar response when they were in crisis. Overtime, others would actively seek you out to solve their crises based on previous experiences with you. Key-Relations learned to lean on your ability to react quickly to any and all situations and resolve them. Individuals may contact you at all hours of the day or night to assist them with solving the crisis of the moment. You began to feel very important and liked being held in high esteem by others. So you work hard to "protect" and make others "safe" from further distress.

Is this Interactional Role Ever Good For Me to Use?

Quite often this interactional role can be very beneficial for you to use as your preferred way of responding in various highly charged emotional situations. In this interactional role, you are able to remain calm, think quickly, and respond well in all crisis situations. This interactional role is very powerful as those around you see you as having good problem-solving ability and the ability to keep them safe. However, you become stuck when you habitually use this interactional role rigidly as others may become overly dependent on you to resolve their differences, especially in times of crisis. At this point, you become overburdened by the demands of others. Your relations with others begin to suffer as you become overly responsible and they become more helpless.

EXPAND:

In the next part of this chapter we will reveal to you what happens when this interactional role becomes rigid. We will guide you to other more useful interactional roles.

Help I am Stuck:

Feeling compelled to resolve the presenting crisis and emotional distress for others as quickly possible, you may respond with "band aid" solutions and block others from developing resources for themselves. You tend to collect only enough information to get a basic understanding the crisis before acting. As a consequence, the problem is rarely sufficiently analyzed, and others tend to become dependent on you. Never allowing those around you the chance to learn how they contribute to the crisis or how to resolve their own issues. You can easily become overwhelmed. If you try to step back and be less helpful when differences arise, others may become angry if you do not react quickly enough to their demands or block their attempts to contact you. Once others become dependent on you for guidance they typically remain much attached.

What Happens Within You:

When tensions or differences arise you may begin to feel uncomfortable, anxious, and have a strong sense of responsibility towards others. When people are in crisis you react quickly to resolve the situation by becoming overly involved. You may even contact outside agencies for them or take them to appointments. Through the process, you develop an exaggerated sense of responsibility for the actions of others and may confuse love with being needed. You may have a strong need for approval and recognition. To fill this need, you have a tendency to do more than your share in order to help others around you. You tend to have a strong personality and are quick to analyze situations. Your confidence and level of control in time of crisis allows other to trust and lean on you. Because others tend to become overly reliant, their high level of expectations may overwhelm you.

The Case Scenario:

Belinda calls her friend, Dot, in a panic as she and her husband had another fight. This is the fourth fight this month. In tears, she asks Dot, to come and get her again as her husband took the car and she did not want to be left home alone. Dot quickly complies. She leaves her job early and drives to Belinda's house. When Dot arrives, Belinda is on the door step, and she runs to the car. Dot smells alcohol on her breath and she remembers that when she had picked up Belinda after the other fights, she had also been drinking. Belinda says that she is not sleeping well because she was worried about her fights with her husband. Dot reassures her that all is ok, and she can spend the night at her house. Tomorrow, Dot will call her boss and report that she is sick, so that she could take Belinda to the doctor to get a sleeping pill. When they reached Dot's home, Belinda is talking nonstop about how much she "hates" her husband and that she wants to leave him. Dot shares that she thinks Belinda has a good point. Tomorrow she will call various attorneys and inquire about how Belinda can obtain papers to file for a divorce. At this point, Belinda seems to calm down, and shares she feels much better. She then asks Dot if she would like to go out and get a drink.

Changing of the Interactional Role:

Based on information provided in the case scenario above, Dot, as The Fire Fighter, quickly reacted to Belinda's every wish and desires before finding out what was the cause of the fight. She did not ask how Belinda had reacted during the fights and where her husband had gone. By siding with Belinda and encouraging her to proceed with a divorce, Dot may make Belinda become even more dependent on her. Dot even took on the responsibility of contacting attorneys for Belinda. Of utmost importance to address was Belinda's odor of alcohol, and desire to go out for a drink. Even though Dot was aware of her drinking, she did not investigate how the alcohol was related to the problem. Did it cause the fight or a was it simply a coping reaction to the fight? Was Belinda's drinking becoming an issue between her and her husband? Dot would have had more power had taken on the interactional role of The Detective, which could have helped her analyze the current situation in depth. Appropriate action could be taken and Dot could then guide Belinda in a manner so that she could take more control of her life (e.g. suggestion of a therapist). As The Peacemaker, Dot could have spoken to the husband to obtain his perspective on the situation, and share that Belinda was safe at her home. Belinda's drinking might have been broached by speaking to the husband, and Dot could suggest contacting a treatment center if Belinda's drinking was an issue between them.

What Interactional Roles Will Give Me Personal Power?

As written above, there are a number of interactional roles that you can utilize to replace "The Firefighter" in order to allow others to experience pain when highly charged emotions are present, especially when faced with a crisis, without making snap judgments. You will need to practice interactional roles where you can feel as though you are helping others, while being less reactive and responsible for resolving issues. In addition, you will need to become more attentive to your own needs, desires, and wishes when tensions arise. Through the skillful adoption of the alternative interactional roles described below, you can learn to guide others into taking action and responding with less emotion when faced with situations which are characterized by chaos, sadness, anger, and hopelessness. The following chart suggests the best interactional roles for you to select from each quadrant:

Table 24 – Alternative Interactional Roles for The Firefighter

Quadrant	Roles to Best Try	Roles to Initially Shy Away From
Quadrant I; Need to Intellectualize	The Doctor The Judge The Teacher	The Preacher The Superman
Quadrant II: Need to Control and Manage Information	The Clown The Construction Worker The Mediator The Peacemaker The Referee	Potato Hot-Head
Quadrant II: Need to Be Curious	The Detective The Journalist	
Quadrant III: Need to Avoid	The Bird Watcher The Recorder	The Runaway

Table 24 – Alternative Interactional Roles for The Firefighter Continued

Quadrant	Roles to Best Try	Roles to Initially Shy Away From
Quadrant IV: Need to Save	The Angel	The Savior

Please see Chapter 5 for a quick overview of the interactional roles or read Part III, *How Do I learn a New Interactional Role?* Part III will introduce and teach the skills of the new interactional role(s) that you selected from the above chart when you are stuck in the interactional role of The Firefighter.

The Risk:

In order to move out of the interactional role of The Firefighter you must learn to be less reactive to other's concerns. You will need to learn how to slow down, think, and resist the desire to develop a quick response for resolving the presenting issue. You will need to learn how to ask questions so you can analyze the situation better before acting. You must watch that others do not share erroneous information propelling you into quick action. You will need to develop good listening and observation skills so that you can share what you see with others, teaching them how to respond in helpful ways.

The Reflection:

In order to determine if The Firefighter is your preferred interactional role in tense situations with others, it would be helpful to ask yourself the following questions:

Family: Was I the person in my family who became reactive when disagreements surfaced, and family members argued? Did I react to these situations by developing strategies designed to reduce tensions?

Social Circles: When friends argued or behaved in an erratic way, did I try to help by intervening immediately? In social clubs, did I quickly intervene to diffuse mounting tensions among club members?

School Experience: Was I the class member who reacted quickly if other students became annoyed with a situation?

Co-Workers: When co-workers speak of their dismay or concerns about the workplace environment or issues with the management, do I have a tendency to intervene quickly, and take on the responsibility of solving the situation?

Spouse or Significant Other: Am I quick to want to rescue my spouse or significant other when they become emotionally upset in various situations?

In General: Do I react quickly when others are in trouble? When a friend, co-worker or acquaintance phones late at night or on the weekend to discuss a concern, do I immediately react and intervene? Do I often find myself saying, "I need to do something now to fix the situation and they need me"?

Chapter Twenty-Four

The Savior

"Help me! Help me!" cries a friend. "I have no money and need a beer. To the victim's aid the Savior runs, "I am here! I am here! and, I will save you. I promise." As a Savior, you have a strong tendency to seek out people who desperately need help and will assist them, often sacrificing your own personal needs for Key-Relations. As a result, you are highly involved with others, work very hard, and take responsibility for making everyone happy. The Savior believes "saving" Key-Relations is very noble and makes you feel needed and wanted by others. There may be times when you try to save the perceived "victim" from vicious family members and heartless governmental agencies that intentionally deprive people of required resources. Consequently, you may spend hours or days trying to resolve a problem for someone else. You respond to tensions and conflicts by trying to subdue them. Communication is often directed toward you and issues will only be addressed until the victim is "saved." You will often stop discussions between others if the discussion causes distress to the victim. You do not challenge the victim's perceptions of the problem but accepts the problem at face-value.

How Did I Learn This Role?

The Savior role can actually be somewhat narcissistic, as it leads to self-fulfillment, inflation of importance to others, and feelings of being needed or wanted. Somewhere early in life you learned that when you helped other people they became dependent on you which gave you a sense of self-value. Through the process, you became addicted to helping others, and ended up being as dependent on the need to "save" other people as much as people became dependent on you.

Is this Interactional Role Ever Good For Me to Use?

Quite often this interactional role can be very beneficial for you to use as your preferred way of responding in various highly charged emotional situations, especially if you feel someone is a "victim." This unique interactional role allows you to remove yourself from a heated situation until you can gain composure, and have time to be highly involved in the life of others. This interactional role is very powerful, as others will seek you out and will become highly dependent on you. This gives you a feeling of self-importance. However, if you use this interactional role too rigidly or too extensively and you overlook your own personal needs for the sake of another, you may become conflicted and resentful, feeling bitter, frustrated, and used by the victim. At this point you become stuck, and your relations with others become suffer as you harbor resentment and unspoken anger.

EXPAND:

In the next part of this chapter, we will reveal to you what happens when this interactional role becomes rigid and guide you to other more useful interactional roles.

Help I am Stuck:

Early in life you may have developed insecurities, strong fears of rejection and needed adornment by Key-Relations. Early in life, to fulfill these, needs you learned to be a "pleaser" so those around you needed you. When you see pain in others, these fears are activated. In your rush to aid others, you rarely collect enough information to assess or understand the differences between those around you accurately. Consequently, the real issues that maintain the problems are never revealed and responsibilities for what are causing the problem and why it is not being resolved is never explored. Through your knee-jerk reaction to "save" the world, you may keep others from learning new skills or creating bridges to required resources. When this happens, people become dependent on you, feel entitled, and are often unappreciative as they come to "expect" you to "do" for them, no matter what they ask. When you assume too much responsibility for the problems of others, you foster dependency and helplessness. When this occurs, your judgment and relationship boundaries with others become blurred. As a result, you feel overwhelmed and disenfranchised, having assumed these excessive responsibilities. You discover that the tensions between people remain unchanged. Key-Relations remain happy with you as you do their work for them. However, you feel trapped in a system of your own making; Key-Relations never learn to take responsibility for their lives.

What Happens Within You:

When tension, sadness, pain or anger engulfs another you are quick to intervene and try to "save" them. You are especially attracted to needy people such as; drug addicts, alcoholics, criminals, sex addicts, mentally ill, physically ill adults or troubled children. In your discomfort, you have a strong need to take care of others who are in trouble. As a child, adolescent and adult you might be highly involved in church charities and fundraisers. When you see pain in others you become nervous, anxious, and overwhelmed with the feeling of "need to do." Through the process of helping others, you have developed co-dependency habits and may never feel satisfied. As a result, you become angry, controlling, preachy, blaming, hard to talk to, and subtly manipulative. You display to others an amorphous personality, but are generally miserable. In your attempt to "save" others, you become a martyr and ignore your own life, which may crumble into bitterness, despair, guilt, and hopelessness.

The Case Scenario:

Wendy is married and has four children ages 12, 10, 8, and 5. She is married to a well-off man and even though she has a Ph.D. in business she has decided not to work. Wendy has sought out the church and has become highly active in taking on projects to "save" others. She will spend as many as ten hours a day assisting someone who she perceives is in need. The projects are time consuming, and she has begun to ignore the needs of her children and husband. When her husband tries to speak to her about her over involvement with others she becomes very angry, says he is a very selfish man and does not know how she ever married such an uncaring person. Their marriage has begun to suffer and the children are basically left on their own after school as Wendy is never home. Recently, Wendy has begun to give money to people. Every day she is approached by someone in need and she thinks nothing of handing them a hundred dollar bill. In order to stop this destructive behavior, her husband has placed a hold on their savings and checking account. This has infuriated Wendy as when she is unable to give cash to another, they become annoyed or angry. They even reject her which causes her to become depressed and she thinks about how her parents neglected and rejected her as a child. Her husband, overwhelmed with dismay feels totally helpless and has begun divorce proceedings and request for full custody of the children.

Changing of the Interactional Role:

The case scenario above is quite complex, as Wendy is seeking out ways to fulfill an emptiness within her that began as a child. Her parents had neglected, physically abused, and threatened to "give her away" if she made them unhappy. As a result, Wendy seeks satisfaction in "doing" for others. In the case scenario above, Wendy had assumed excessive responsibility in her attempts to help others to the point where she was neglecting her family and children. Wendy had a strong need to be needed and wanted by others. She even tried to buy other's affection. What Wendy did not realize is that her behaviors were resulting in her family (especially her children) being neglected and she was forcing her husband to place controls on her behavior (stopping the accounts). In this particular case, family therapy might be quite useful, as Wendy needs to work on her fears of abandonment and neglect. The question comes to mind as to why her family and husband were not fulfilling her needs and why she would resort to others to fulfill her needs. Obviously the marriage is at risk and Wendy is creating a scenario to be rejected by her family. At the onset, Wendy may need to practice the roles of The Angel where she could interject hope to others but not be overly responsible to help them. Also, the role of The Firefighter would allow her to become involved in the "caring" of others during a crisis, but then step out once calmness had been restored. Through the interactional role of The Recorder, Wendy could journal about, reflect, and her reactions and needs of wanting to "save" others.

What you must remember is that when you operate in the interactional role of The Savior, you can cause significant harm to yourself and others despite your best intentions. When you adopt a new interactional role, you will be able to redress personal needs for control coupled with self-worth. By helping others learn self-sufficiency, you will truly "save" others as you will teach them self-awareness, independence, responsibility, and self-value.

What Interactional Roles Will Give Me Personal Power?

There are a number of interactional roles that you can utilize to replace "The Savior" with to become more attentive to their own needs, desires, and wishes when tensions arise. Your sole purpose in life has been to sacrifice your own happiness and needs for the happiness of others. So you need to practice interactional roles which are less re-active, and involved, and can assist other's decision-making without assuming responsibility for action. Through the skillful adoption of these alternative interactional roles listed below, you will still be able to instill hope into situations which are characterized by chaos, sadness, anger, and hopelessness. The following chart overviews the best interactional roles for you to try initially, from each quadrant:

Table 25 – Alternative Interactional Roles for The Savior

Quadrant	Roles to Best Try	Roles to Initially Shy Away From
Quadrant I; Need to Intellectualize	The Doctor The Teacher	The Judge The Preacher The Superman

Table 25 – Alternative Interactional Roles for The Savior Continued

Quadrant	Roles to Best Try	Roles to Initially Shy Away From
Quadrant II: Need to Control and Manage Information	The Clown The Construction Worker The Mediator The Peacemaker The Referee	Potato Hot-Head
Quadrant II: Need to Be Curious	The Detective The Journalist	
Quadrant III: Need to Avoid	The Bird Watcher The Recorder The Runaway	
Quadrant IV: Need to Save	The Firefighter	The Angel

*Please see Chapter 5 or a quick overview of the interactional roles or read Part III, *How Do I learn a New Interactional Role?* Part III will introduce and teach the skills of the new interactional role(s) that you selected from the above chart when you are stuck in the interactional role of The Savior.

The Risk:

In order to move out of interactional role of The Savior, you must take time to learn the basis for someone's difficulties. You will need to develop strategies to suppress your reactive, "saving" impulses, reduce the need for control, and grow comfortable with helping others take responsibility for their own life. When other's express pain or need you to demonstrate curiosity, and try to understand why a person may present as helpless, lacking assertiveness, and has difficulty with solving their own problems. You must learn to listen carefully, objectively, and with a "third ear" for distortions of their problems and concerns. You must further adopt a less re-active posture and demonstrate abilities to facilitate their decision-making without assuming responsibility for action. These are extremely risky behaviors for you believe that your self-value is connected to saving Key-Relations from their plight.

The Reflection:

In order to determine if The Savior is your preferred interactional role in tense situations with others, it would be helpful to ask yourself the following questions:

Family: In my family of origin, did I play the role of martyr and assume responsibility for everyone else's behavior? Did I try to make others happy by sacrificing my own needs?

Social Circles: When friends were hesitant to complete a task, did they rely on me to complete it for them? When engaged in social clubs, did I assume responsibility for completing unfinished jobs when members' follow-through failed?

School Experience: Did I assume primary responsibilities for completing group assignments and allow other students to take credit for your work? If other students complained about completing an assigned task, did I react by doing the work myself? Did I become resentful when they also obtained a good grade on "your" work?

Co-Workers: Do I assume primary responsibilities for completing co-workers' tasks and allow them to take credit for your work? If co-workers complained about completing an assigned task, did I react by doing the work myself? Do I find myself angry at my co-workers but never express my dismay for completing their work?

Spouse or Significant Other: When my spouse or significant other has trouble with drinking, gambling, pornography or other difficult issues do I make excuses for them? If they miss work, do I lie for them?

In General: Am I quick to take on the responsibilities of others? Do I often say, "I am overwhelmed, I am overwhelmed" and become quietly resentful when I assume responsibilities for other's behaviors?

PART THREE

How Do I Learn A New Interactional Role?

Chapter Twenty-Five

EXPANSION

Learning of a new interactional role will take some time and practice. The first thing you need to do is be open to taking a risk and trying to respond differently in a highly intense emotionally charged situation. This is not easy as you may want to resort back to the interactional role which made you most comfortable and helped to lessen your anxieties, fears, or worries. We discuss below each interactional role, teach you how to practice these roles, and when you can best engage each role in various situations. This knowledge will allow you to EXPAND and help you to alter your interactional roles with others which will help you remain calm in periods of intense stress, and assist those around you in resolving issues with the most hope for lasting change.

The Angel

Steps to Becoming The Angel:

1. Listen to the concerns of others.
2. Acknowledge and repeat their concerns to them.
3. Take their issues at face-value.
4. Practice contradicting what others are saying and reframe any and all issues into a positive light.
5. Change negative views to positive by adding stem words like; *however, wait I see, but, I am confused …* to shift the thinking forward with hope.
6. Practicing instilling hope into all situations.
7. Be available to talk with, comfort, and reassure others.

Situation Example:

Mary and Sally have been friends for a long time. Mary shares with Sally over a cup of coffee her concerns with her son, Tommy and her fear she is an ineffective parent. Sally moves into the interactional role of **The Angel** in order to help her and interject hope.

> Mary: "Tommy is so bad I just want to walk away and give up."
> Sally: "Share with me what is the most difficult thing with your Tommy."

Mary: "He is always arguing, never listens, and resist helping me at home."

Sally: "That would be tiring and I can see why you want to give up."

Mary: "It would be easiest to let his father deal with him."

Sally: "You may be right, *however,* the other day I noticed when you spoke to him you asked him to bring you a glass of water. He stopped his game and got you a drink, so I think he wants to please you."

Mary: "I don't remember that. Do you really think he wants to please me?"

Sally: "Yes, let us look at times when he listened to you and see if we can figure out why he is not listening now…."

Practice:

Listen, repeating back what someone says until they offer a glimmer of information that contradicts what they are saying, then change their view by adding stem words like; *however, wait, I see, but, I am confused*… to shift the thinking forward with hope.

When Should I Use This Interactional Role?

The interactional role of The Angel is best to use when conflict is high, and confrontation is present in and between others. This interactional role would help to introduce hope, calmness, and peace into a situation so that Key-Relations can begin to relate to each other in a calmer manner. The Angel helps others to examine positive aspects of their relationships or situations, so that individuals are more willing to look at different side to a conflict or disagreement.

The Bird Watcher

Steps to Becoming The Birdwatcher:

1. Remain calm during intense emotional situations.
2. Listen carefully to others as they speak.
3. Observe the nonverbal behaviors in others.
4. Share as little as possible with others about your thoughts, reactions, or what you observe.
5. Make mental notes in your head about what you see and hear.
6. Use these mental notes to analyze at a later time and how you might respond to the tensions in the future.

Situation Example:

Jose and Rodrigues are in a highly heated exchange over differences in regards to workload. Roberto, a co-worker, observes the exchange in silence. Roberto moves into the interactional role of **The Bird Watcher** first to get an understanding of the differences before sharing his thoughts and suggestions.

> Jose: (Face is quite red and in a loud voice),
> "What the hell do you know, I've worked here longer?"
> Rodrigues: (Sweat pouring down face responds in a slightly shaking voice), "I know Jose, but I am thinking if we each work 6 hour shifts instead of 8 hours people will not be laid off from work."
> Jose: "Why the hell should I care about you or anyone else, I earn more money and can give three craps about anyone else."
> Rodrigues: (Hands tightening into a fist), "This job is not just about you, we all have tasks to do and expertise in different areas, if we do not give into the boss's wishes we will all be out a job."
> Roberto: Does not say a word, watches the nonverbal and realizes that the situation could come to blows at any minute. He thinks about what is happening and decides not to intervene. Later he reflects on the discussion of his colleagues and decides to take the role of The Mediator when they quarrel.

Practice:

Learn to become silent. Pretend you are watching a movie and step back from the emotion. Observe what people do (actions) and mentally record what they say. Then reflect on what you observed and heard. Think about how, or if you want to intervene.

When Should I Use This Interactional Role?

The interactional role of The Bird watcher would be very useful when heavy tension or disagreements are present in or between others. This interactional role is especially helpful when Key-Relations have difficulty verbalizing information, but convey interactional communication messages via nonverbal behaviors. The Bird Watcher can register the nonverbal interactions and share with others their personal observations. Another intentional use of The Bird Watcher role occurs when others try to seduce you into taking control of a situation, when you do not want the responsibility. In these cases, it is more productive for you to remain silent, observe, and then offer your suggestions at a later time. Also, when two people are in an extremely intense situation, imposing your ideas and thoughts might only escalate the situation.

The Clown

Steps to Becoming the Clown:

1. Practice thinking quickly on your feet.
2. Think of creative solutions "outside of the box."
3. Balance seriousness with humor and playfulness.
4. Practice the right timing in the use of humor in order to introduce flexibility into rigid situations.
5. Remain calm in intense situations.
6. Practice being in the moment when differences surfaces between others.
7. Redefine their differences using humor.
8. Once humor and flexibility are interjected into an intense situation practice shifting into another more serious interactional role to further help people identify solutions for their differences.
9. Rehearse displaying empathy, warmth, and respect to others.

Situation Example:

Friends were in a heated conversation and they ask Ronald to make some decisions for them as they had three options and could not agree on how to spend some inherited money from an older aunt. Ronald knew if he chose one option over another one, two of his friends would be slighted. Ronald moves into the interactional role of **The Clown** in order to bring levity into the situation.

Diane: "What do you mean you think we should buy a car, I told you time and time again that any extra money that we obtain would be used to fix the bathroom."

Tommy: "Well, I think fixing the bathroom is a waste of time; we need a new car and it is about time that we look into which is the best one."

Danny: (Looking puzzled). "I thought we were going to buy a jet ski that is

> what you have been promising me for over a year. How can you now change your mind?"

Diane: "But a bathroom would be a good way to spend the extra money."

Tommy: "No, first a car then we will consider other ideas."

Danny: "I do not believe you lied to me."

At this point, Ronald (a long term friend of the family) walks into the kitchen and they explain their dilemma to him, asking what he thinks they should do. Knowing he was in a "no-win" situation Ronald said, "Very well I can easily solve this problem for you" and picked up some dice.

> Ronald: "The first throw would be for Tommy's choice, the second throw for Diane's choice and the third throw for Danny's choice." His friends look stupefied.
>
> Diane: (Bewildered) "Why would you handle our dilemma like this? We are serious."
>
> Ronald: (Laughing): "I know, if I made a choice, two of you would be mad at me, so throwing the dice was my best option. I cannot take the risk of making you angry."
>
> His friends: (Starring and then laughing): "You are right, we have to solve this ourselves."

Practice:

Begin by listening to the flow of conversation and observing of the nonverbal behaviors (actions) between those present. Try to understand the content of what is being said and how intense the emotion is between those who are present. Exaggerate and EXPAND their point of dissension. Redefine the impossible problem in a humorous way. Reassure them there are other ways to think about their situation. Your goal is to practice bringing lightness, not sarcasm, into a heavy situation.

When should I Use This Interactional Role?

The interactional role of The Clown can be quite useful in many situations. This interactional role is best to use when others appear to be very rigid, authoritarian-like, or when they are very serious about a given issue. Simply stated, the interactional role of The Clown helps others to look at situations through a different and less serious lens. The interactional role of The Clown when used with balance and precision, can yield both immediate relief in tense situations and help others to be able to relate in a better way so that resolutions can be created for their differences.

The Construction Worker

Steps to Becoming The Construction Worker:

1. You need to listen and follow the flow of conversation.
2. You need to practice interrupting the conversations of others when you believe the information being shared is not helpful to the problem.
3. You need to balance between information gathering and coming to action.
4. You need to be comfortable guiding others into action.
5. You need to rehearse being firm with others.

Situation Example:

Carol's family is in a heated argument about missing money that was on a table and were interrupting each other. One family member is even dominating the conversation, ignoring others' comments, and refusing to let others' speak. Carol moves into the interactional role of **The Construction Worker** in order to calm the atmosphere.

> Cassandra: (Crying) "That is not true I never said he took…"
> Frank: "Yes you did stop lying, you are really pissing me off…"
> Joe: "What the hell do any of you know about anything…I told each of you…."
> Cassandra: (Gasping for breath) "Stop… cutting me… off you jerk."
> Frank: "I will cut you off when I …."
> Joe: "Damn it, shut-up each of you! I will make the decisions here and let me remind you, if you do not stop this crap neither of you will do anything. I will make sure that you are both grounded and will have no TV and your iPad…."
> Carol: "Stop it! All of you! Enough! I do not want to hear any more."
> Cassandra: (Sniffling) "But, Frank…."
> Carol: "Enough I said!"

Practice:

Begin listening to the flow of conversation and observing the nonverbal behavior (actions) between those present. Once you have a feel of the flow of the conversation and interactions (verbal and nonverbal), emphatically stop all conversation. Practice taking control by stopping or halting conversations until normalcy can be resumed among those present.

When Should I Use This Interactional Role?

The interactional role of The Construction Worker is best to use when others around you share so much information about their concerns or disagreements that structure is needed for it to make sense. In chaotic situations, Key-Relations may interrupt each other's communications, attempt to speak for each other, or a single member may speak without pause for lengthy periods to the exclusion of input by others. In such circumstances, The Construction Worker can intervene by blocking irrelevant information and structuring the communication with the goal of making it safe for each person to be heard. Providing a space to talk, lessening tensions between others. The Construction Worker can encourage others to respond in less reactive ways, and through the process demonstrate respect for all those present.

The Detective

Steps to Becoming The Detective:

1. You need to like exploring minute details and looking for clues.
2. You must remain calm when others present differences to you.
3. You must practice becoming highly focused on the "stated" words and observed nonverbal interactions of others.
4. As others present their concerns ask probing questions in order to get more details.
5. Practice asking open questions.
6. Rehearse analyzing information as it is presented.
7. Use your judgment and piece information together to create a hypothesis as to why the differences are occurring.
8. Need to practice convincing others that your facts and hypothesis are right by producing facts.

Situation Example:

Kathy has called her sister, Danielle to see if she can drive her to the airport as she needs to go out-of-town unexpectedly for about a month and gives Danielle no other information. Danielle moves into the interactional role of **The Detective** to try and understand why Judy was leaving on a trip so suddenly.

> Danielle: "So when did you decide to go to South Carolina?"
> Kathy: "About a week ago."
> Danielle: "South Carolina is quite a distance from Michigan, can you share what you will be doing there?"
> Kathy: "I may have a new job offer and I am considering the offer seriously."
> Danielle: (Surprised). "That is exciting! Can you share what the offer entails?"
> Kathy: "Not sure yet of everything but a slight pay raise, office management, a new area to explore, finally, a chance to leave Michigan."
> Danielle: (Confused). "I did not know you were unhappy here in Michigan. In what way has Michigan grown old on you?"
> Kathy: (Eyes down). "I have been unhappy here for a long time. I feel it is a dead-end place to live. I need something new, something more alive."
> Danielle: "You look sad and your voice sounds hopeless. A dead-end?"

Practice:

Listen to what others say, ask open-ended questions after each statement which will gather more information. Pay attention to small details. Repeat keywords stated in a question form. Watch the nonverbal behaviors (actions) of those present, listen to their tone of voice. Develop your hypotheses (or thoughts) about why the differences are occurring. Share your thoughts with other sharing the information that you collected as you observed them.

When should I Use This Interactional Role?

The interactional role of The Detective is best to use when others present concerns or differences which are highly complex. This role allows you to help narrow presenting options when opposing viewpoints are provided simultaneously. The interactional role of The Detective can also be used productively when you strongly believe that a hidden dynamic (e.g., a family secret) exists and which serves to maintain the presenting concern. The revealing of critical information being withheld can lead to the development of insights and strategies for addressing presenting problems.

The Doctor

Steps to Become The Doctor:

1. You need to have sufficient knowledge and resources available to you about somatic and psychological concerns.
2. You need to enjoy doing research.
3. You need to like learning about a number of subjects especially related to medical and/or psychological conditions.
4. You need to be knowledgeable of how to use the internet to locate information about somatic or psychological issues quickly.
5. You need to practice listening to others about their psychological or medical concerns and ask open-ended questions to gather more details.
6. You need to be able to create medical or psychological hypotheses about presented information or someone's observed nonverbal behavior.
7. You need to be comfortable with using labels in regards to the somatic or psychological concerns of others.
8. You need to be willing to guide others with somatic or psycho logical concerns to the proper medical or mental health personnel to provide treatment.
9. You need to be able to remain sufficiently aloof from the situation to be able to make a reasonable diagnosis.

Situation Example:

Aliza's husband was recently in a minor car accident and she notices that he is irritable, tends to be forgetting things she asks of him, is slurring his words and seems to have a short fuse. She complains to her long time neighbor that he is, "lazy and depressed." Aliza fails to understand the relationship between the car accident and her husband's behavior could be related to a mild head injury. The neighbor moves into the interactional role of **The Doctor**, to help Aliza understand that the changes she observes in her husband might be related to his accident.

> Neighbor: "Wow that is the first time I have ever heard you say Antoine depressed."
>
> Aliza: "Yeah he is so irritable and gets frustrated easily over the smallest of things."
>
> Neighbor: "Has he always had a poor memory? I have never heard him slur his words in my life."
>
> Aliza: "Usually his memory is sharp that is what is odd. Maybe he is drinking, and that is why he is slurring his words. If he is drinking I shall divorce him. You know his Dad was an alcoholic."
>
> Neighbor: "I would be shocked if Antoine was drinking at neighborhood parties, I have only seen him drink ice tea. When did these concerns develop, they seem rather sudden or new?"
>
> Aliza: "About a month ago."
>
> Neighbor: "That is around the time of his car accident. Maybe his accident has something to do with his behavior. Maybe he hit his head? I think he has a minor head injury. Why do you not call your doctor and tell him what you see?"

Practice:

Read and research medical and psychological topics. Be keen to various medical and psychological diagnosis or uses of medication with its symptoms. Listen to what others say, ask an open-ended question after each statement which will gather more information about their "illness" or concerns around someone else's health. Apply your "medical and psychological" knowledge to social, medical, emotional, or behavioral concerns of others in order to Key-Relations spring into action or gain deeper insight into the situation they face.

When Should I Use This Interactional Role?

The interactional role of The Doctor is best used when a somatic concern influences not only the individual, but also the mental health and well-being of other family members. Adopting the interactional role of The Doctor is appropriate when others are unable to comprehend the somatic concerns, and claim that the individual of concern only wants sympathy or is avoiding responsibility.

The Firefighter

Steps to Becoming The Firefighter:

1. You need to be able to assess situations quickly.
2. You need to practice remaining calm and neutral in intense situations.
3. Listen to the concerns of others.
4. Collect minimal information and base reaction on logical thinking.
5. Accept the concerns of others at face-value.
6. Practices having others follow your advice without questioning.
7. You need to be able to create an atmosphere of emotional or physical safety for others.
8. You need to be open to contacting agencies, mental health providers or medical personnel to assist others if necessary.
9. You need to like being highly involved in the problems of other people.

Situation Example:

Ada's mother, Adair, started dating a man approximately six months ago. Ada and her mother are extremely close but now that a new man is in the picture Adair has little time for Ada. Adair has just discovered that approximately six months ago Ada began cutting herself on her upper thigh. In a panic, she phones her sister Eamon for help. Eamon moves into the interactional role of **The Firefighter** in order to help her panicked sister.

> Adair: (Sobbing uncontrollably) "I... really do not ...know what to do, she has never done anything like this before!"
>
> Eamon: "Settle down, it is upsetting, but we will get through this. Where is Ada now?"
>
> Adair: "She is up in her room, very upset that I know of her secret."
>
> Eamon: "Have you checked her room for any knives or scissors and removed all from the home temporarily?"
>
> Adair: "No, I did not think of that."
>
> Eamon: "Okay, please go upstairs and ask her for any sharp objects and remove them from her room. Sit with her until I arrive which will be about 20 minutes. At that point together we will take her to the emergency room to have her evaluated by a

psychologist in order to her get help."

Adair: (Sniffling and more in control) "I knew you would know what to do, thank-you."

Practice:

Practice remaining calm in intense situations. Pretend you are watching a movie and step back from the heat of the emotion. Think outside the box as to how to handle various crises that are presented to you. Be reassuring, affirmative, and directive when providing advice to others as to how to react or respond to the crisis at hand.

When should I Use This Interactional Role?

The interactional role of The Firefighter is best used when others are in crisis. During these times and circumstances quick, directive actions are appropriate and necessary. The interactional role of The Firefighter allows you to help the others take action so that they can move out of a crisis so that they can return to a level of "normalcy.

The Journalist

Steps to Becoming the Journalist:

1. You need to like listening to the stories of others.
2. Begin by asking others to tell the stories of how their differences began.
3. Remain calm and neutral when tensions grows in and between others
4. Be curious and listen as others share their stories.
5. Practice asking inquiring questions to calm tensions and clarify ambiguous information.
6. Observe the nonverbal behaviors of others as they share their stories.
7. Remain neutral as differences of opinion are presented.
8. Try to get as many viewpoints as possible about the differences.
9. Practice asking tough questions about the differences when necessary.
10. Do not be afraid to ask tough questions.
11. Encourage others around you to speak directly with each other.
12. Work with those around you in a collaborative fashion to find solutions to the differences presented.

Situation Example:

Mandy's mother recently passed away and her father is beginning to date a new woman. Mandy is angry and does not like this new woman and becoming very disrespectful to her father. She has just called her aunt (Mother's sister) to see if she can move in with her as she, "hates her father." The Aunt invites her for tea and moves into the interactional role of **The Journalist**, to try to understand why Mandy is so insistent that father not date another woman.

> Mandy: "I just hate him! He is so mean! and I do not even want to be around him. Please let me live with you."
>
> Aunt: (Looking at Mandy with soft eyes) "Share with me how your father is mean?"
>
> Mandy: "He just is not there for me anymore. He has no time for me and all he wants to do is to be around *her*."
>
> Aunt: "Her? Can you tell me about her?"
>
> Mandy: "Someone at work. They go out for coffee all the time. I have not met her so I have no idea about her, but I do this I do not like her at all."
>
> Aunt: "Sounds like you are missing your father and afraid that he may be too interested in another woman. Tell me about what you are missing and what you use to enjoy doing with your dad."
>
> Mandy: (Crying) "We use to do a lot together. On Saturdays, we would go fishing and have a picnic...."

Practice:

Listen and observe the nonverbal behaviors (actions) of those who are in intense disagreement. Be inquisitive, curious, and unafraid to ask difficult questions about how their concerns or differences developed. You need to practice asking open questions that will help to reveal the history of Key-Relation"s differences and how the differences began. Lean forward as people tell their stories and give good eye contact. Encourage people to speak by slightly nodding of head, saying, "Hmm hmm" or "Can you tell me more?"

When should I Use This Interactional Role?

The interactional role of The Journalist is good to use in almost all situations, presented by Key-Relations. This interactional role is especially useful with those who experience panic or helplessness in various life circumstances. By asking questions you provide opportunities for others to share their stories and perceptions about situations. You would introduce hope and a sense of calmness into a highly charged situation that permits those around you to relate to each other on a more functional interactional level. Through using this role, you would help others to examine the good and bad aspects of various situations without judging. You would also serve as a model for others on how to be curious, inquisitive, and open to all information that is presented. The interactional role of The Journalist would help you to remain poised when tensions arise, and regardless of how serious a situation may be, you are able to bring out hope. Because you present to all as inquisitive, curious, and unafraid to ask difficult questions, you are able to win the confidence of a wide variety of people.

The Judge

Steps to Becoming The Judge:

1. You need to have a code of ethics based on right and wrong.
2. You need to have good listening skills.
3. You need to be patient and not rush to judgment.
4. You need to be able to listen calmly and without bias to the differences of each person in conflict.
5. You need to be able to ask questions that will help you gather sufficient information about the differences presented.
6. You need to be detailed oriented and like to problem-solve.
7. You need to be able to think analytically.
8. You need to be willing to make judgment about other people's behaviors.
9. You need to be able to cope with the fact that some people may be come angry with you.
10. You need to be very articulate and clear when sharing your decision and judgment to others.
11. You need to be able to stand firm on your judgment, so others do not question you.

Situation Example:

Elvis and his father are in a heated argument. Fifteen-year-old Elvis wants to extend his curfew to 2:00 am from 11:00 pm. His father is dead set against changing his curfew and both are being very unreasonable. Elvis' mother listening in the kitchen enters the room and serves as **The Judge** in order to stop the conflict.

> Elvis: (Angry) "You are so unreasonable. I can't even talk to you."
> Father: "There is nothing to talk about, there is no way you are extending your curfew. Are you crazy?"
> Elvis: (Face reddening) "Crazy? None of my friends has a curfew."
> Father: "I am not responsible for your friends, but I am responsible for you. No son of mine is going to be out until 2 am and that is the end of the discussion."
> Mother: (Entering from the kitchen). "Elvis your father has a point, there is no good reason you need to be out until 2:00 am. However, I know there are times when you go to school activities such as dances that end at 11:30 pm and you need time to get home. On those nights, we shall extend your curfew one hour?"

Practice:

Listen to the presenting disagreements of other's without interrupting. Ask questions pertinent to the situation. Give both sides a chance to speak. When you believe that you have enough information, render a mutual decision as to how you believe each person present should act in the situation.

When Should I Use This Interactional Role?

The interactional role of The Judge is best used in situations where one or more persons are demonstrating inappropriate and even severe or abusive behaviors. In these situations, The Judge may need to gather information quickly, and render an opinion about the best response to the inappropriate situation or behaviors in order to insure the safety of all family members. The problem is that there can be different opinions about what is labeled inappropriate or abusive. The primary role of The Judge is to create a safe environment for all to be heard prior to rendering an opinion. The Judge must be aware of the fact that once he renders a decision, he has sided with the one he agrees with and others who are present may feel alienated. After the safety of those involved in the tense situation has been secured, The Judge may explore the dynamics as well as what happened to prior and after the inappropriate or abusive behavior.

The Mediator

Steps to Becoming The Mediator:

1. You need to be able to problem-solve.
2. You need to like to do conflict resolution
3. You need to develop good negotiation skills.
4. You need to practice adopting a neutral position when tensions arise.
5. You need to rehearse remaining calm when tensions surface between and with others.
6. You need to practice active listening skills.
7. You need to allow people to speak without interruptions.
8. You need practice taking information at face-value.
9. You need to stay in the moment when differences develop.
10. Practice read and interpreting the nonverbal behaviors of others.
11. Develop good negotiation techniques
12. Practice reframing the differences of others into positive out comes.

Situation Example:

Jolene's mother, Lisa, has moved into the family's home. Jolene and her mother have never gotten along and she views her mother as being quite dominant. They argue over the smallest of details. In order to please both women and to return calm to the atmosphere in the home, Patrick, Jolene's husband has moved into the role of **The Mediator** in order to resolve differences and stop the bickering between them.

> Lisa: "I think the dishes should be moved into this cabinet as it is closest to the table."
> Jolene: "I prefer they be in *this* cabinet as it is closest to the stove, and when I cook it is easier for me to grab a dish."
> Lisa: "That may be Jolene, but I have more experience in the kitchen."
> Jolene: "But you never cook anymore so what difference does it make to you."
> Patrick: (Sitting at the table reading a newspaper). "Listen the cabinet by the sink is in between the stove and the table. Let us move the dishes there

and see how that works out for both of you."

Practice:

You need to begin by taking a less responsive role when differences surface among those around you. You will need to practice listening to the differences of those around you. Develop negotiation techniques that can become a model and be implemented when people's differences look unresolvable. Shy away from making unilateral decisions as to what should or should not be done. You will need to learn how to be curious and ask questions about the issues that exacerbate the presenting concerns. You will need to rehearse reflecting the desires and wishes of those present and then present a solution which will make everyone present happy.

When Should I Use This Interactional Role?

The interactional role of The Mediator is most useful in highly charged emotional situations. This role is best to use when Key-Relations quarrel other over rules, expectations, or life preferences. The Mediator role is particularly useful at the onset of an issue when those around you are disagreeing especially with adolescent children, who need to learn negotiation skills. In this latter circumstance, the primary value of the interactional role of The Mediator lies in the ability to reduce tensions in and between others and model negotiation skills. By so doing, opportunities are created for others to more calmly discuss presenting issues (e.g., parental expectations, rules around the adolescent's freedom).

Potato Hot-Head

We firmly believe that this is a very detrimental and dangerous interactional role for anyone to assume. Therefore, we do not endorse any of the skills displayed by this interactional role and will not address this interactional role any further.

The Peacemaker

Steps to Becoming The Peacemaker:

1. Practice being neutral and unresponsive in tense situations.
2. You need to dislike conflict.
3. You need to be easy-going in life.

4. You need to be approachable and display an unassuming manner.
5. Practice carefully monitoring and listening to the voice volume of others.
6. Practice observing the nonverbal body language of others and what it means.
7. To obtain others attention, speak in a soft, quiet voice.
8. Practice maintaining an atmosphere of calm and minimizing the differences of others.
9. Intervene when voices are raised by others, reminding them to calm down and stop the expression of all negative behaviors.
10. Practice reframing tense situations into neutral situations, so people remain calm.
11. Offer to do the work of other's if it will make them feel less stressed.
12. Be careful not express any level of dismay or anger.

Situation Example:

Phil and Andre are arguing over who will clean the bathroom area at the factory while on coffee. Both are custodians, and Andre is new to the job. Phil cleaned it last night. Andre says it is not his responsibility. Terry is listening to their exchange and realizes that tempers may get out-of-control. Terry moves into the interactional role of **The Peacemaker** in order to calm the tension.

Phil: (Nose flaring, voice raised) "Listen ass, the bathroom is not just one person's responsibility we take turns around here."

Andre: (Glaring at Phil) "Listen you aren't my boss and no one said any thing about cleaning toilets when I took the job."

Terry: (Calm voice) "Hey guys, cool it. Obviously there is miscommunication here. Phil, I agree it is not the most pleasant job in the world, Andre, it was always a shared job between Phil and the other custodian before he retired. Listen, I think you both need to review the job description duties and see what it entails and then decide how the bathroom will be cleaned. I have extra time, let me work with you Phil tonight cleaning and then tomorrow you both can check out the job description and make a plan from there."

Practice:

Be alert to others nonverbal behaviors (actions). Listen attentively to their differences.

Pretend you are watching a movie and step back from the emotion, remain **calm** and speak with firmness. Clarify each other's position, reframe the situation and offer a new perspective or approach to handling the differences so all present will be satisfied. Be open taking on the tasks or needs of others so that a sense of serenity and calmness is maintained by all present.

When should I Use This Interactional Role?

The interactional role of The Peacemaker is most useful in crisis situations when a calm atmosphere is needed in order for decisions to be made quickly. This role is best to use when Key-Relations are in a highly confused or emotional state and are unable to be proactive in a situation. The Peacemaker role is particularly useful at the onset of an issue, as The Peacemaker has a natural gift for seeing many different points of view, seeing all the shades of gray in any given situation. The Peacemaker has a special way of diffusing conflict by remaining calm and steady. The primary value of the interactional role of the Peacemaker lies in the ability to focus on similarities rather than differences. The Peacemaker is rarely if ever, drawn into conflict and avoids being pressured to react. By so doing, opportunities are created for others to remain calm so that presenting issues can be discussed and analyzed.

The Preacher

Steps to Becoming the Preacher:

1. You need to have a sense of how people "should" behave in various situations.
2. You need to practice lecturing and directing others.
3. You need to practice remaining calm in times of stress.
4. You need to rehearse observing the behaviors of others.
5. Practice sharing your opinion with others.
6. You need to have a well-established belief, moral, and value system.

Situation Example:

Lindsey was visiting another country for the first time and was overwhelmed by the number of poor people living on the streets or in shanty towns. She began to speak of her disillusionment with the country and began to blame all the citizens for the state of poor. Steve moved into the interactional role of The Preacher to help her understand what the poor think of their living conditions.

>Lindsey: (Crying). "This state of the poor is horrid, and the government needs to be held accountable. How can they let so many people go hungry and live in such horrible conditions."
>
>Steve: "The government is doing all they can but the country as a whole is very poor. They work with the commodities that they have and daily food is flown into assist the poor."
>
>Lindsey: (Still crying) "But they need so much, how can things ever be turned around?"
>
>Steve: "I appreciate your caring, but you know Lindsey crying in front of these people does not help them. Many do not understand how badly they have it as they do not know your world, so they cannot make comparisons like you do. When you cry you confuse them and they feel ashamed, but they do not know why they are feeling ashamed. You must accept their way of life, what they have, and know that they are actually very strong people. They make the best of what they have."

Practice:

Begin by listening to others' beliefs and value systems. Allow others to express their family, political, or religious views without being interrupted. Then practice sharing with others your ideas, beliefs, values, and cultural norms. Be firm that others need to follow your religious, political, beliefs, customs, and values. Serve as a model for others by behaving in a manner that you reflect your values, beliefs and customs.

When Should I Use This Interactional Role?

The interactional role of The Preacher is best to use when others appear to lack moral direction in responding to an important matter or when role models are needed, but are unavailable. Strong ethical, political, and religious values can provide support and guidance particularly in stressful emotional situations. In such circumstances, the Preacher may be able to help those with differences and identify a course of action consistent with well-established values and ethical behaviors.

Note:

The interactional role of The Preacher is particularly useful in working with those from other countries, whose values and belief systems are different from those of society-at-large. The Preacher can help immigrants learn about the dominant cultural beliefs, values, and social norms in an effort to smooth their transition to a new country with different rules and expectations. The Preacher role can help immigrants to achieve stability and balance in a new culture resulting in improved levels of functioning at home, school, work, and within the larger society.

The Recorder

Steps in Becoming The Recorder:

1. You need to like multi-tasking
2. You need to listen and observe the communications and nonverbal interactions of others during conflict.
3. You need to remain calm and aloof intense situations.
4. Practice being neutral and not taking sides when others express their differences.
5. Practice mentally recording your observations.
6. After you leave the situation, write down or list what you have ob served in detail.
7. Practice expressing your emotions and feelings to other's differences on paper
8. Analyze your writings for self-reflection, and decide the best course of action for a particular situation.

Situation Example:

Sharon's siblings were in a very heated situation. In the past, she has observed her siblings argue to the point where they have physically harmed each other during a fight. Both of her siblings are older, and she is afraid to speak or stop the fighting for fear of being hit by her brother, who has a very quick temper. One time she shared with her mother what happened between her siblings, and the next day her brother screamed at her and threatened to hurt her if she ever told again. In order to protect herself, Sharon had moved into the interactional role of **The Recorder** so she could safely write about her fears and thoughts in her diary.

Dear Diary:

I am really scared. My brother and sister are fighting, and I know that one day they will really hurt each other. My brother has a very violent temper and is constantly in trouble at school. My sister tries to help and solve his problems, but he turns on her with such rage. Tonight he had her on the floor and was hitting her. I did not know what to do, and I know I cannot tell my mother or he will hurt me. Please Dear Diary, I am afraid what can I do? I want to tell someone at school or my Grandmother. Do you think they can help me?

Love,
Sharon

Practice:

You need to practice being silent when in the presence of intense highly charged emotion between others. Pretend you are watching a movie, and step back from the emotion. Observe what people do (actions) and mentally record what they say. When away from the situation, reflect on what you observed and/or heard and begin to write in a journal about what you saw, heard, and felt. In other words describe your feelings, thoughts, desires and wishes. Use your writing as a reflection board. Re-read what you wrote and begin to reflect upon or analyze about what happened, how you responded and how might you best approach the situation if it should happen again.

When should I Use This Interactional Role?

The interactional role of The Recorder is perhaps most useful when those around you are in very intense heated situations and you are afraid of being hurt. In such circumstances, you may intentionally want to record what is happening or being said mentally, and later use a diary to reflect upon the situation before responding. Through the process, you can safely express your emotions and reactions on paper. This strategy may serve to help you moderate the intense situation while establishing boundaries so that you are not pulled into the conflict.

The Referee

Steps to Becoming The Referee:

1. Practice observing others when they disagree
2. Listen to and follow the flow of conversations
3. Observe as the tension builds who interrupts who
4. Remain neutral in intense situations.

5. Monitor and mentally note who speaks, when, for how long and who is interrupted.
6. Practice using a firm voice and ask those in disagreement to silence while you speak (e.g., "Hold it a minute, let me say something").
7. Be willing to take control of situations by interjecting rules of communication.
8. Share that they each need to take turns talking one at a time without interrupting each other.
9. If a person is interrupted by another hold your hand up to silence the other person and say, "Wait."
10. After one person fully expresses their differences, ask the next person to speak, and so on.
11. Continue in this manner until the differences are fully discussed.
12. Switch into another interactional (e.g., The Mediator) to help create solutions for the differences.

Situation Example:

Trudi, Frank, and Dick are arguing about whose turn it is to use the computer. None of them is listening to each other, and they are interrupting and breaking off each other's conversations. Harry has been monitoring their interactions and then decides to move into the interactional role of **The Referee** so that the chaos, arguing, and interruptions fueling the differences among those present will stop.

> Trudi: (Sniffling) "But, Frank...I told you that...."
> Frank: (Interrupting Trudi) "I don't care what you said you are lying, and you..."
> Dick: (Interrupting Frank) "I told both of you...."
> Harry: (Placing a hand up in the air). "Hold it everyone! Frank you will get a chance to speak and so will you Dick, but for now you have the floor Trudi, and the rest of us will listen quietly without interrupting each other. Trudi, it is okay, now calm down, and you were saying...."

Practice:

Begin by listening to the flow of conversation and observing the nonverbal behaviors (actions) between those present. Who speaks when, to whom, who interrupts who, who dominates the conversation. Once you have a feel for the flow of the conversation and interactions (verbal and nonverbal), emphatically stop all conversation and take control of the heated situation by indicating who can speak when and for how long. Create a space for all to be heard. Use a hand motion of placing your hand up in the air to silence a person if they attempt interrupt another. If they refuse to stop interrupting, ask them to leave or physically change where they are sitting so they are less intrusive. Structure the content as to how and when information is imparted by others. Set up an atmosphere where one person speaks at a time.

When Should I Use This Interactional Role?

The interactional role of The Referee is often engaged into action when those in conflict interrupt each other and have a tendency to speak for each other. During these moments, there is a sense of confusion and chaotic interactions occur among those involved in the highly charged emotions, especially children, consistently interrupt each other. When you instruct others not to interrupt, you may hear those around you silence but replace the voice with deep disruptive sighs or exaggerated body movements to create nonverbal interruptions. Through the process, the Referee decides who speaks to whom and when. This helps to create opportunities for those present to listen to each other. Families with adolescents or children may benefit most from having a person present such as The Referee who creates conditions that help reduce tensions and provide opportunities for family members to display mutual respect for each other. By virtue of his ability to restructure rules and communication interactions, the Referee is positioned to halt diversions of Key-Relations that tend to intensify conflicts, particularly those related to child rearing practices, so that issues can be discussed and analyzed. This helps to establish meaningful connections among those present.

The Runaway

Steps in Becoming The Runaway:

1. Listen and follow the flow of conversations of those in conflict.
2. Be alert to when conversations with and between others become too heated.
3. Observe the nonverbal behaviors of others.
4. Decide if there is anything you can do to help solve the differences of others.
5. When overwhelmed or panic sets in, remove yourself from the situation.

6. When overwhelmed or if you feel your anger building to a point of no control or panic sets in, remove yourself from the situation until you can calm yourself down and deal rationally with the situation.

7. Reflect upon the situation and determine a course of action for the future.

Situation Example:

Juanita and Amber (her sister) had spent the day shopping and going to lunch. Jose verbally exploded when he learned that Amber spent about $500.00 on clothes. Jose and Amber are screaming at each other at the dinner table. Juanita has been sitting quietly, observing, and not saying a word. In order to protect herself, Juanita moves into the interactional role of **The Runaway** in order to remove herself from the situation and have time to think more clearly.

> Amber: (Eyes bulging) "And, who the hell are you to tell me what buy or not buy?"
>
> Jose: (Red faced) "I work my ass off so you can sit home all day and watch your soap operas, that is who the hell I am. Every time you and Juanita get together, you act like we are millionaires."
>
> Amber: (Interrupting Jose) "Do not bring Juanita into this. You knew when we married that I would stay home and not work. So stop your complaining and I will buy what I want. Get a second job if you have to."
>
> Juanita: (Having trouble breathing picks up her purse). "I need to go" and quickly ran out of the house."

Practice:

Begin by listening to the flow of conversation and observing the nonverbal behaviors (actions) between those present. When you have a feel the flow of the conversation and/or interactions (verbal and nonverbal), are too intense, you are becoming overwhelmed and/or you are about to lose your temper excuse yourself from the situation (e.g., go to another room, take a walk, a drive, or go to a friend's house). Once you have removed yourself from the situation, reflect upon your reactions, thought and feelings in a calm manner and determine a course of action that can help you to express your feelings and thoughts without anger or fear to others.

When should I Use This Interactional Role?

Despite its obvious limitations, the interactional role of The Runaway can be very useful in highly charged emotional or abusive situations. There are times when minimal reaction is better than trying to confront a situation openly. During these moments, it may be best to remain silent, and remove yourself from the emotionally charged or abusive situation in order to be able to think and then select a plan of action. However, if you try to escape through the use of drugs, alcohol, or gambling these activities are very self-destructive and will only prolong or worsen the state of affairs for you.

The Savior

Steps to Becoming The Savior:

1. You need to like people.
2. You need to have a strong desire to help and assist others.
3. You need to enjoy being highly involved with others and their problems.
4. You need like being in charge of and taking responsibility of others.
5. You need to be willing to put the needs of others before yourself.
6. You need to remain calm and hopeful during times of intense differences.
7. You need to be able to identify a "Victim" to save and protect.
8. You need to create a "safe" environment for the "Victim."
9. You need to accept the "Victims" issues at face-value.
10. If the discussion of others is hurtful to the victim you need to practice stopping all conversation.
11. You need to practice having all communication directed toward you for monitoring of all spoken content.

Situation Example:

Elizabeth has learned that her neighbor, Margaret's husband has just lost his job and they are having trouble making ends meet. The children are hungry and have one meal a day. Elizabeth begins cooking dinner for the family on a nightly basis. She is on a limited budget and is highly involved in a number of volunteer activities that take her away from the home especially on weekends. She fails to tell her neighbor that cooking every night is a strain on her. Elizabeth, in order to protect her neighbor from depression and desperation, has moved into the interactional role of **The Savior**.

> Margaret: (Sniffling) "I do not know… how we will ever repay you'.
> Elizabeth: "I am glad to do it."
> Margaret: "We would be so hungry if it were not for you. And you're
>   preparing and cooking of the food saves me so much
>   time. I really am not myself and this gives me time to
>   spend in bed."
> Elizabeth: "You have enough to worry about, I like to cook and will
>   gladly prepare a hot meal for your family every night for as long
>   as you need me to."
> Margaret: "But you are so busy and are hardly ever home."
> Elizabeth: (Ambivalently) "Not an issue. I always have time to be there
>   for you."

Practice:

You need to take time to learn the basis for someone's difficulties. When others express pain, you need to demonstrate curiosity and try to understand what does that person really need to "feel" better. You must practice listening carefully, objectively, and with a "third ear" for distortions of their problems and concerns. You will then need to make decisions or take responsibility for the care of others. Be open to accommodating your schedule to meet the needs of others.

When Should I Use This Interactional Role?

The interactional role of The Savior may be best used with family members, spouse, significant other, friends, co-worker or acquaintances who may be emotionally or physically abused and
with those who require extra support or guidance, such as elderly clients. In such circumstances, you may need to intervene quickly to insure their safety or well-being. The Savior role may also be useful when working with refugees and immigrants, whose knowledge of the host culture and public resources or services may be limited. In this case, you must careful not to "do" for them by personally contacting agencies etc. but guide them into self-directed behavior.

The Superman

Steps to Becoming The Superman:
1. You need to have a high level of confidence.
2. You need to practice being highly responsible for others.
3. You need to rehearse making decisions for others.
4. You need to like giving advice to others.
5. You need to remain controlled during times of intense emotion.
6. You need to be very knowledgeable about a number of topics.
7. You need to draw from your own experiences and knowledge to guide others.
8. You need to become comfortable in not allowing others to speak.

Situation Example:

Gabriella has recently taken a new position at work and has issues with the new chair of her department. She has very few friends and typically uses her husband, Xavier, as a sounding board. Xavier has very little patience listening to her issues and often moves into the interactional role of **The Superman** in order to limit the amount of information he hears.

> Gabriella: (Frustrated) "So, now he wants me to teach four new classes, and do the class preparation as well. Do you know how much work that is?"
>
> Xavier: "Do you know how to say the word, NO?"
>
> Xavier: (Stating firmly) "You can and you will! Phone him on Monday and tell him you are only teaching two classes, and to stop dumping on you. You have more power than you think. Now where is the newspaper for me to read. I do this all the time without a problem so should you be able to as well."

Practice:

Begin by listening to others about their differences or concerns. Practice deciding a course of action that those present need to follow in order to resolve their differences. Learn to present your decision in a firm manner and with authority. Learn how to stop others from questioning you at any level. Convey expectations that you know what is best for everyone.

When Should I Use This Interactional Role?

The Superman is best to use in highly complex, emotionally charged situations where no one seems to be able to make a decision and immediate action is required. Employing this interactional role can help deploy crisis situations, and return a highly charged emotional atmosphere into one with structure, where people can feel safe and have time to reflect upon events with less emotion.

The Teacher

Steps to Becoming The Teacher:

1. Be willing to learn about a variety of topics via the internet and various resources.
2. You need to become well versed on a number of subjects.
3. You need to like to share knowledge with others.
4. You need to have good oral and written communication skills.
5. Practice remaining aloof and controlled in various emotional situations.
6. Practicing teaching new ideas to others.
7. Practice teaching using multiple sources and techniques.
8. Know how to use the internet so that information can be accessed quickly.

Situation Example:

Kaiden, age 16, is visiting his cousins for a week. He is amazed how much Chase, age 15, and Tristan, age 13, argue about the household jobs that they each have to do on a daily basis. There are no "assigned" tasks just things that need to be done before their mother arrives home from work. Sometimes they even get into pushing contests with each other. On day two, Kaiden had seen enough, and decided to move into the interactional role of **The Teacher** to help clarify the daily house tasks.

> Kaiden: (Firmly but without emotion) "Okay enough guys. Let's think this through. Come here and sit." (Kaiden grabs a blank piece of paper from the computer printer).
> Chase: "What the hell are you doing?"
> Tristan: (Whining) "Must I?"
> Kaiden: "Listen, every day you guys argue over the same thing. Whose

turn is it to do what for "Mom?" Okay let's begin by listing
what your mother wants done by the time she gets home from
work. (As his cousins state a list, Kaiden writes the chores on a
piece of paper.) Ok now Tristen, what three chores do you like
to do?"

Tristan: "Take out the trash, feed the dog and make my bed." (Kaiden
puts Tristan's name by each job he likes).

Kaiden: "Okay Chase, what three jobs do you like to do?"

Chase: "Well if I must, feed the fish, make my bed, check the house for
dirty dishes and bring the dishes to the kitchen sink."
(Kaiden puts Chase's name by each job he likes).

Kaiden: "So that leaves vacuuming the TV room and putting the dirty
dishes in the dishwasher. Okay I am going to make a weekly chart.
Now your Mother is home on Wednesday so you do not need to
do these chores. So, I am Xing out Wednesday. Now on
Monday and Tuesday, Tristan you do the dishes and
Chase you vacuum. On Thursday and Friday, Chase you do the
dishes and Tristan you vacuum. When the jobs are done, place
an X on the chart so neither of you needs to ask or argue
over who has done what. (Kaiden looks affirmingly at his
cousins) Okay today is Tuesday, look at the weekly chart and
tell me what you are to do. As you picked jobs that you like
to do, those are done every day by you. This chart is only for the
dishes and vacuuming but I am listing the other chores with
your name by them so you remember what you picked."

Practice:

Begin by listening to the concerns and differences of those around you. When you have
an understanding of the issues, use your knowledge in order to help others grow in a
physical, intellectual, and even spiritual level. You may need to practice a lecturing style
or be open to suggesting books others *should* read in order to help "fix" their situation.
Teach through multiple approaches (e.g., talking, writing thoughts down on paper, using an instructional board, graphs, etc.). Practice multi-tasking. Try to remain emotionally aloof form the situation and use your intellect to guide you.

When should I Use This Interactional Role?

The interactional role of The Teacher is best to use when others have limited life experience, are uncertain of what to do, or when they present with highly charged complex concerns or differences. For example, a friend's child is having trouble focusing in school and the friend is worried as the child is failing in school and may be held back. The friend is overwhelmed, and she shares that she punishes the child by taking away "everything" and the child still does poorly in school, it is like he "doesn't care." The friend may need to be educated about attention deficit concerns and how the disorder can negatively impact children's ability to do well in school. In this situation, the Teacher can help the friend locate professionals to assess the child and determine if an attention deficit concern is present and how best to intervene, so the child can be successful in school.

Reflection:

Now that you have had an opportunity to review each of the interactional roles discussed in this book and insight as to how practice each interactional role it is time to release the power from within you. Begin by:

1. Completing the Self-Reflection Form below. This form will help you to process, analyze, and reflect on your growth.
2. Put selected interactional roles into action.
3. Try out the selected interactional roles in a number of different settings and with different people.
4. Observe how people respond differently as you change.
5. Do not give up if the interactional role is not successful. You will need to practice more than once for the interactional role to come across smoothly and with confidence.
6. After you have practiced those interactional roles that are pretty comfortable, add new interactional roles to your repertoire until eventually all interactional roles have been tired out.

As you change your interactional role(s) with others, you will begin to notice that you have adopted those actions/behaviors and interactional roles that seem to work well for you; using them unconsciously and with flexibility. Further, with time and patience you will be able to adapt, change and identify reactions of others that continue to make you uncomfortable in highly intense emotionally charged situations, which will lead you to trying out new interactional roles.

Self-Reflection Form:

Think about each interactional role described above and what skills are needed to begin to practice each role then complete the section below:

Which Interactional Role would I like to begin practicing?

_____

_____

What must I practice or remember when using this interactional role? (List)

_____

_____

_____

_____

After trying out the new interactional role take time to reflect:

1. How effective was I in using the new interactional role?

_____

_____

_____

2. Did I feel less anxious, overwhelmed, or uncertain in the situation?

_____

_____

3. What seemed to work well for me in this new interactional role?

_____

_____

_____

4. What do I need to do in order to practice the interactional role better?

_____

_____

_____

5. What did I notice about how other's responded to the new interactional role.

_____

_____

6. **If** the interactional role was not effective, think about the situation. What was happening in the situation and what type of responses, emotions, or feelings were you experiencing?

_____

_____

_____

7. Review the other interactional roles described in this book and select new roles to practice, that may help to you be more effective in interpersonal relationships.

_____

_____

_____

_____

_____

PART FOUR

Highly Complex Emotionally Charged Relationships

Chapter 26

Can Shifting of Your Interactional Role Really Work in Complex Situations?

Thus far we have given a case story for every interactional role introduced and tried to let you, the reader, experience how to look at difficulties in your relationships from the perspective of a particular rigid interactional role when tensions develop between key relations. We also tried to guide you into learning how to shift your position into a more flexible interactional role in order to bring about positive change with others resulting in feelings of more power within your relationships and creation of happiness from within.

In the following three case stories we will show you how, by changing your own interactional role, you can influence change in others, even in very complex and rigidly ingrained situations that appear completely hopeless. We will describe the problems in each case from the perspective of the person who seems to suffer the most in his rigid interactional role within the key relations. You must remember that when you try to change yourself complexity can enter into a situation. Key relations may become resistant and when this occurs you may need the assistance of a therapist for support. In highly complex situations, change is not impossible but may be more difficult. In some situations like story one and two, the individuals in pain could not heal a cut-off or estranged relationship with someone they loved but eventually were able to look at their own responsibilities in the situation which brought change and healing to themselves which led to being freer and more happier in life. In story three the individual had to distance themselves from a key relation in order to maintain stability.

We will also reveal that we, as therapists, are not immune from becoming rigid when faced with highly complex and intense emotional situations in our own lives as we can be seduced into very rigid role(s) when key relations speak with us about their problems. We will explain how we attempt to get out of these rigid interactional role(s) in order to introduce flexibility and light into very heavy, complex, confusing, and intense situations with others.

The Caretakers

When key relations have severe on-going mental health or physical conditions, you may automatically take upon yourself the interactional role of " The Caretaker" (e.g., The Angel, The Saviour, The Firefighter, The Judge, The Doctor, or The Superman). You may discover that at times you are so overwhelmed in "The Caretaker" interactional role that you will avoid the situation or confronting of others and become "The Birdwatcher", "The Recorder" or "The Runaway". As a child, you may have been invited or assigned these interactional roles by your immediate family members as they needed you to take care of them. Overtime, others that you have come into contact with began to EXPECT you to behave in one of the interactional role(s) related to a caretaker. The more you "saved" or "took care" of another, the more key relations became dependent on you. Before you knew it, "The Caretaker" interactional role became cyclic in nature. You may have discovered that when you tried to get out of "The Caretaker" role, you were met with severe resistance, verbal abuse, or the possible manipulation of another threatening suicide.

Untenable Complex Situations

As you move through life you may encounter situations that are more complicated than you are used to dealing with. When this happens relational problems take on an extra dimension and some situations create feelings of complete helplessness. When face-to-face with situations which are rigid and highly complex you may find yourself very ambivalent. You feel you would like to shift to another interactional role but the pressure from those around you is so great that alternative interactional roles become threatening for your key relations so you remain fixed in one of the caretaking or avoiding interactional roles. At this point problems become so difficult as you believe the attitude of your key relations transcends who you are, what you desire, or whom you want to be. This is particularly true when a key relation is mentally ill, for example with severe depression, bipolar illness, psychosis, physical illness, or displays what you observe to be criminal-like behavior. Sometimes you may be dealing with key-relations who are being led by forces more or less coming from the outside, such as with addiction (e.g., alcohol, drugs, gambling), or the victim of the domination of a sect or a fanatic religious order.

When a situation is untenable, you will need to re-think (or re-frame) the interactional roles and behaviors which are being displayed by others. There may be situations that seem so impossible that you may lose contact with another. When this happens and you feel totally powerless, reflect upon your relationship with the person whom you are missing. How was the relationship in trouble prior to someone controlling or influencing the person to dismiss you, and most importantly think how life would change if the person who was "lost" to you re-entered your life again. Is it really for the best for you or through distance do you have the possibility to live your life more openly and freely being less connected?

Case Stories

We will describe below three case stories where very difficult, complex problems occur and demonstrate how you can challenge yourself to have the courage to change your interactional role or keep a particular interactional role in order to creates greater peace inside. The first two stories are about good friends who came to us for advice, knowing full well our professional qualifications. The third story is about a couple who sought psychiatric help from one of us for their family problem.

It is up to you, the reader, to think and reflect upon the interactional role of the person who seems to be at the center of the problem and to contemplate about other interactional roles that might be more useful in helping the person shift away from their very rigidly ingrained response patterns. Guided questions will be presented for your reflections as you proceed through the case stories. Of course you may see yourself in one of the presented cases. If this happens and you recognize yourself, or parts of your behavior, you may develop doubts or have feelings of heaviness, be unable to breathe, and hopelessness may develop about the situation you are reading. If this happens do not panic, sit back, inhale, think about why the case is too close to you and then reflect about your own interactional role(s) in this type of situation. Find the courage to listen to the suggestions and ideas that might help guide you out of your highly complex situation by reframing your relationship within the lost relationship.

Story 1

The Unwanted Sister

Laurentine, a good friend, came to visit me at my home in Ohio. While talking about our families she shared a story about a family situation where she did not feel comfortable. She felt that she had been stuck in a position regarding her sister and the rest of her family that has made her very unhappy for many years. She had read with interest our latest book, *Shake-UP; Moving beyond Therapeutic Impasses by De-Constructing Rigidified Professional Roles* which presented altering professional roles in various therapeutic relationships with clients in order to move out of situations that seemed to lack movement. With the content of the book in mind she desired to speak to me.

"I do not want you to solve my problems, just listen to my story," she stated. With these simple words, she pushed me into the interactional role of "The Bird Watcher". "I come from a very nice family. My sister, Mary, is five years my senior and even though there is a large age difference between us we always had a good relationship. As my "big" sister she defended me when necessary, (sometimes even when it was not needed). We both had a good relationship with our parents, even though we perceived them somewhat differently.

Mary, for example, looked upon our mother less positively than I did. However, I never observed any real conflicts between my sister and my parents. Once when my sister broke off a long standing relationship with her boyfriend, my mother was not happy as she was quite close to this man. My sister was a good looking woman and soon found somebody else, or maybe she had already met him before she broke off her relationship. I do not know, because I was studying away from home at that time. Mary married in harmony with the family and after a while her husband became a very respected part of our family. I thought of him as interesting, exciting, and even looked up to him. He was a man of the world, did not live an ordinary life, and enjoyed doing practical jokes on his friends.

As the years passed, I also married and we both had children. We rarely saw each other, because of distance. However we would get together to celebrate Christmas, other holidays, or our parents' birthdays. I always thought of Mary's family as being close knit. Sometimes though I had problems with my sister's behavior towards her husband."

With this minimal information what would you describe Laurentine's problem to be?

_____

_____

_____

"When we visited I would observe her being very sharp tongued and insulting towards her husband. I always felt I should defend him, so I tried to alleviate the tension by taking on the role of "The Clown" or "The Runaway" as I would introduce humor or would attempt to change the subject. Now I realize that I did not have the courage to use the interactional role(s) of "The Mediator", "The Judge", "The Teacher", or "The Journalist" which would have been proactive. I never asked my sister why she behaved the way she did toward her husband and why her husband did not mind. It seemed, at the time, not necessary to intervene because the family was not under any excessive pressure. And, Mary never asked me for advice." Laurentine paused and took a sip of her white wine. She sighed and continued her story.

"In the mean time life went on, and my father died. The family relationships did not worsen. My mother became more and more involved with Mary's family. Mary's children stayed several days a week with her after school. The oldest child, Sylvie, and grandmother became very close. Because of distance the relationship between my children and their grandmother was not as close, but still very good. Unfortunately, I divorced but this did not seem to harm my relationship with my mother or the rest of the family. After a couple of years I found a new partner and this also did not create any problems for my family.

The bond between my mother, Mary, her children, and her husband became even closer. My mother aged and eventually moved into an old person's home. Mary had a lot of connections and found a place for our mother close in proximity to her home. This made it easier for Mary to visit. I still lived too far away for frequent visits."

"This seems to be a long story," I interrupted my friend and told her that I still had no idea what her problem was. She smiled and said she was happy about this as she also thought there was no problem. "But wait awhile the riddle will come," she stated.

"One day while I am at my mother's home together with my sister. We were about to say goodbye and were walking towards our cars. Normally we have a drink at Mary's place. But she said,"I have to tell you something that is not so nice." I am concerned and ask her what is wrong. I became quite worried and began to think maybe she has problems with one of the children? Is her husband Percy ill? Are there problems at work? Or, is she herself ill?

None of this. Instead, she tells me, " Percy has asked me to tell you, that from now on, you, your children, and our mother are not allowed to enter our home anymore."

I laughed because he is the one who liked to play practical jokes. Sometimes he even sent letters to his friends on official note paper from bureaucrats, telling about draconian changes that were being implemented and how these changes would cause a lot of trouble for them when implemented. When his friends panicked and asked him for advise he would tell them it was all a joke. But as far as I know he had never been negative towards his close relatives. On the contrary, he was always ready to help and had an elaborate network to do so.

Mary shared it was not a joke. I was surprised and shocked. Of course I asked Mary what was going on. What are the reasons for such drastic and strange decisions? Mary sighed and told me that she did not have a clue. She then stated, "Please if you really care about me, as a sister, do not ask anymore about it and do not get me into trouble by asking me to speak to Percy. I cannot influence him to change his mind, you know that."

What is Laurentine's problem now? How has it shifted?

_____

_____

_____

Through this request, she placed a lot of pressure on me. I realized that the interactional roles of "The Journalist", "The Detective", "The Peace Maker" or even "The Mediator" as you call them in your book, are now impossible to implement. Not even the roles of "The Firefighter" or "The Preacher" would help. As "The Firefighter" I could have rushed into their home and confronted him. As "The Preacher" I could have shown him the unjustness of his behavior.

Laurentine was silent for a moment, sighed and then continued. "As the situation unfolded I felt I was stuck in the roles of "The Runaway", or even "The Bird watcher " as you describe so nicely in your book. I felt totally powerless. I knew that if I tried to use a more active interactional role(s) with Percy I would endanger my relationship with Mary as she would have distanced further from me. She let me know that she having problems with Percy's decision but asked me _not_ to intervene."

Which quadrant of roles does Laurentine's family dictate in highly charged intense situations?

_____

_____

_____

Laurentine takes another sip of her wine and pauses; she seems to be very sad; as if the situation occurred just some weeks ago rather than many years ago. I immediately asked, "You still have no questions for me?" She just nodded "No" and continued her story.

But I interrupted her, "Mary, I would like to ask you why did you accept this behavior and why did you ascribed an interactional role of avoiding to me? You counter my questions before I can even present them to you." Mary responded, "Do not ask me to confront Percy with all kinds of questions. You know what he is like." I think to myself, obviously I do not know what he is like, but I remain silent. Completely flabbergasted I leave Mary.

Laurentine is silent again. As a friend, I have a strong urge now, to let go of my interactional role as "The Bird Watcher" as I want to become "The Journalist" or even the "The Detective". But I feel Laurentine is not ready for this so we both are silent for a while.

By requesting her friend to be "The Bird Watcher" does Laurentine entrap her friend into a similar helpless stance in solving of her problem as she is in? Reflect.

_____

_____

_____

After a while Laurentine continued. "Percy has not changed his ideas and fifteen years have now passed. My mother was unable to visit my sister. No, I am lying. When Percy was on business travel our mother was allowed to visit. Neither I nor my children have ever been permitted to visit Mary when Percy was at home. Mary occasionally came to visit me, but these visits were very rare. We did not see each other socially, except when there was "family business" to attend to. The strange thing is, as far as I know, neither Mary nor her children have ever questioned Percy about his decision. When Mary's oldest daughter, Sylvie, married my mother and I were not officially invited to the wedding. One day, Sylvie phoned me and asked me to come to the wedding and bring her grandmother saying that her father would not dare protest or make a fuss about our presence on her wedding day. My mother and I agreed to go as she wanted to attend her beloved granddaughter's wedding. We slipped in during the reception. My mother was in a wheelchair and I pushed the chair. We felt like we were beggars or criminals crashing the wedding. Sylvie immediately embraced us and seemed very happy that I had arranged this for her. To this day I harbor a lot of ambivalence. Can you imagine my niece's wedding and we were not invited?" Laurentine started crying when she described this situation which was still very painful for her. I poured her another glass of wine and she continued her story.

How did this situation become cyclic in nature:

_____

_____

_____

When our mother died, Mary and I, arranged the funeral together. All the children were present. But Percy did not come to the funeral of his mother–in-law. I never understood his sudden decision and never have I chosen another interactional role that would have confronted him. Through the years I have remained steadfast as "The Runaway" or " The Bird Watcher". Sometimes I have shared my story, as you call it in a kind of "The Recorder" role, with my friends. They felt sorry for me and found Percy to be "derailed", "crazy" or they even expected a deep, dark secret to be revealed. Their responses did not help me very much. Throughout the years, I have been very careful not to put Mary under any pressure by asking her to confront her husband nor have I pushed to get closer to her children, afraid of creating a loyalty conflict for them. I have the idea that they do not understand why I avoided them and may even blame me for not giving them more attention. But, I do not know that for sure. And never have I confronted Percy with any of this. I am sure this is "The Runaway" interactional role," she laughingly and sadly stated.

From what you have read, through selecting interactional roles in the avoiding quadrant did Laurentine actually try to protect her sister from further emotional harm?

_____

_____

_____

"I am telling you the story now because I have doubts about my choice of inter-actional roles. I have only one sister and would like for us and our children to be closer and have more contact. Now, what do you think about Percy's behavior?"

Would selecting another interactional role actually have been more effective in this situation? If so, which one?

Laurentine invited me, halfheartedly, with a question to step into the role of "The Teacher". She expected me to give a reason for Percy's behavior and how to cope with it, without revealing any more information. By offering advice, I would have become " The Superman" an interactional role that I try to avoid most of the time. Rather, I carefully assumed the interactional role of "The Journalist". "You have had this problem for some time, so you must have some ideas yourself about what happened? What do you think influenced Percy to make these decisions?" I ask prudently.

"I do not know," she said. "Sometimes I think he really is disturbed. Some have said that he suffers from *paranoia*. I looked it up on the internet. A couple of the symptoms I recognized, but people who suffer from this usually do not function as well as Percy was doing in society. Further, the article indicated that spouses, other family members, or close friends would start to have doubts about the judgment and critical qualities of a paranoid person. To my knowledge, Mary, her children, or others that know him do not seem to think he is "crazy" nor have they expressed any doubts about his judgments".

Do you believe Mary and her children can truly judge or admit Percy's shortcomings without fear of punishment?

She sighed. "I almost think, after all this time, that I have made this whole thing up and that I am the one who is "crazy"", she laughed.

I reflected and said, "So you have a tendency, like a lot of your friends, to play "The Doctor" and make a psychiatric diagnosis. Listening to your story I can imagine your reaction, but you are not a psychiatrist, so the interactional role of "The Doctor" would be a bit risky for you nor will it bring you any closer to Mary or Percy."

At this point, I feel the need to change the subject but I do not want to scare Laurentine. After all it is a big step for her to discuss her problem with me. Especially knowing that I am a psychologist and a family therapist. Our book has pulled her over the threshold to re-address her problem, but she was still ambivalent about making changes. So I said, "Can I ask you some questions, Laurentine?"

"Yes, just ask," she said hesitantly. "My question is, why are you looking for the solution by finding a reason for Percy's unexplained behavior? To me it seems an impossible task, especially since you do not have enough information. Only a conversation with him would shed some light on his bizarre decision, but it does not appear that he or you are very eager to do this. The fact that your sister had to convey the message to you says enough. So I agree with you that the interactional role of "The Construction Worker" in which you confront him with your wish for a solution, has very little chance of succeeding. If you did question him, I suspect he probably would choose the role of "The Runaway" and avoid your questions or even worse he would choose the interactional role of " Potato Hot-Head" and become very angry."

Do you agree that if Percy was confronted that the situation may become very angry?

_____

_____

Laurentine agreed. At least for now she had been heard and taken seriously. She even relaxed a bit. "Yes...Yes but what to do? Continue the way it is?" She asked.

"Not so fast," I stated. "Why did you chose the role of "The Runaway" with your sister? Have you ever wondered why she has not taken any steps, in all these years, to overcome this problem between the two of you? Do you have an explanation, coming from your family history, the very low priority your relationship has for her? You told me that you were always close, but I cannot see that in her behavior towards you."

Do you wonder if the problem may have laid hidden between the siblings and that the husband in his own way, perhaps even unconsciously, was protecting his wife?

_____

_____

_____

Laurentine looked shocked and after some thinking she stated, "You are right.

All this time I only saw my relationship with Percy as being the problem. In this way I have kept my sister and even her children outside of the problem." She is silent again. "But with rethinking, I must admit, there were times that I have wondered about her behavior towards me. When our mother died I received a couple of nasty letters from her, concerning the inheritance. I had looked after parts of the estate and she was angry about some of the things. I did not understand it very well. She even voiced suspicion that I would not take care of things correctly.

It appears that Mary had most of the responsibility for the care of her elderly mother. Is it possible that Mary was actually resentful toward her sister for not helping more with their mother's care? And, is it possible that she complained to her husband about this situation? Reflect.

_____

_____

_____

As I look back, I now see that I chose to avoid the confrontation and, to my relief, things turned back to normal. Apparently, I loved and felt safe in the interactional role of "The Runaway".

My impression was that Laurentine liked to think that her relationship with Mary was closer than it was in reality. The facts spoke for themselves. The relationship must have been for more ambivalent than Laurentine believed or even consciously perceived. I suspect that Mary and Laurentine never faced their differences and always blamed other people when their relationship came under pressure.

Is it possible that Mary was unhappy, resentful, and would complain to her husband about her mother and sister? And, in order to protect himself from listening to the complaining and his wife from harboring responsibility Percy simply refused for her family to be a part of their lives? Reflect.

_____

_____

_____

Can Shifting of Your Interactional Role Really Work in Complex Situations 263

I do not tell her this of course and continue my interactional role as " The Journalist". "Have you ever imagined what life would have been like if you had a closer relationship with your sister and would have seen her more frequently?"

Laurentine took her time thinking. "Well, since you ask, it is difficult to say... I do not think we would have seen each other more often as we do not live close to each other. Also our views on life are quite different and sometimes I reflect about how different our friends really are. I cannot explain it clearly. On the other hand, I am now wondering if we had been closer, perhaps our relationship would have worsened."

"Yes, possibly," I replied and offered her some snacks as we paused for some moments. Then I asked her, "Did you ever think that your sister needed the distance in one way or the other, that somehow it made her, and you, feel better?" Laurentine looked at me surprised. "What do you mean? No, I cannot envision that!" Obviously this question was too heavy, so I left it at that.

"A final question, "Do you have any idea what would change in your life if you and Percy were friends again? Would you have more contact with Mary and her children? And, how would it influence you and your children's lives in the long-term?"

Laurentine looked surprised, again. "What difficult questions. No... I do not think I would have a lot of contact with Mary or Mary with me. The children have their own lives now. I do not really have an important place in their lives. I do not think you can turn back time and change. The same for my children. If, by a miracle, Percy would decide that he wanted to have contact with me and my children, it would not bring Mary, Percy and I or their children much closer. They have a different social network."

Laurentine is silent for some time and then smiled. "You could perhaps say that because of Percy, Mary and I were able to create our own lives. I have a lot of respect for Mary's friends and her social life, but I would not want to be a part of it. I admire the things she and her friends are doing, but it is not "my cup of tea" as they say. And I guess Mary thinks, deep in her heart, the same about my friends."

Do you think that Laurentine understands that the difficulties between her and her sister are much deeper than "social networks" and is she still in "The Runaway" role?

_____

_____

_____

Laurentine laughs again, almost relieved. "It seems you can not bear to think of belonging to the life of Percy and Mary," I said with a smile. Laurentine hugged me spontaneously. " Oh my God, I would not want to think about that. Do not get me wrong, my sister has a lot of very nice and well known friends. There is nothing wrong with them. But they do not fit into my life." Laurentine laughed out loud. "You know what I suddenly thought of? You know the television series, *Keeping up Appearances?* I feel like the sister who is married to Onslow and she is the rich sister! If needed, I come but I happily return to my own social surroundings when I leave them. Every one has his own "niche" so they say. Mary is happy in the "niche" she and Percy created for themselves and I am very happy in my own niche."

Was the conflict which was highly complex reframed into a satisfactory relationship? _____

_____

_____

"Seriously, I am grateful that, one way or the other, you have shown me that I can have peace with the relationship that I have with Mary, Percy, and their children. I just now understand, we do not have a conflict. Percy has helped us to understand that we were both brought up differently and had very different desires and social contexts. If we really need each other, we are there for each other, but we do not have to be a part of each others lives on a daily basis. If we would be part of each others life I think we soon would have conflicts because we have a totally different view on life. Thanks to Percy we can continue feeling our close bond without the pressure of too much proximity. We can live our own lives without hindering each other. Mary will always be important to me. She is there when needed and the other way round. We both know that. Mary chose more the way of my mother. She preferred being important. Showing off, a bit, although she denies that too. I am more like my father who did not care for status. Of course I realize there are more nuances than I am mentioning. But, that does not matter."

I asked, " What are your plans now?" "Not a lot different than what I have done so far. But I now feel as if it is more my choice and I feel less anger towards Percy. I am at peace with the way Mary and I have shaped our relationship. I just hope she feels the same way! I think that my new sentiments will show in our, even though infrequent, contacts with her and her children. Strangely enough, I can even be friendly to Percy. The only problem of course is that my mother had a lot of trouble coping with it. But, you cannot win them all. And, secretly, I think that she really did not mind that she had infrequent contact with Percy, because she did not like him that much. She always preferred Mary's first boyfriend. Anyway, mother is dead, so there is no problem anymore." Laurentine stood up from her chair and gave me a huge hug and shared that she had to go home to think about all this.

Impressions:

In the case above it is interesting that the problem scenario shifted to the siblings and possible undetected differences or even hard feelings which may have been harbored for years by Mary towards Laurentine and perhaps vice versa. The most revealing aspect is that Mary asked Laurentine not to contact Percy and her request was taken at face-value. By adopting the various interactional roles located in quadrant III, Need to Avoid, Laurentine protected Mary. Mary was not questioned about her request and Percy was never confronted to find out if in fact he had made the decision that Laurentine and the mother were unwelcome in their home. It was automatically assumed by all that Percy was the issue, he was labeled as, "mentally-ill" (paranoid) and that his illness resulted in the dismantling of a family perceived as close. Now one must wonder what Mary's influence was on the decision and was Percy actually acting on her conscious or unconscious wishes. It is possible that Mary's unhappiness about caring for her elderly mother may have placed too much responsibility on her and in order to protect her, their marriage, and their family from her unhappiness (and or complaining), he may have severed her family's relationships with her family. Knowing Laurentine for as many years as I have, she has a tendency to be very optimistic toward others. I suspect that Laurentine may have unconsciously been unaware of or ignored differences which were voiced through the years by her sister assuming all was, "well or normal". Therefore, her sister's resentment and anger may have gone unresolved for many years.

Through the use of the interactional roles in quadrant II, The Need to Be Curious, "The Journalist" and "The Detective", Laurentine was able to reflect upon the situation from a new perspective. As a friend I also played the interactional role of "The Angel" as hope and a new perspective was interjected into a hopeless situation. As Laurentine discovered that even though Mary and she were not as close as she thought, and this caused her much pain, she realized that in reality their lives were quite different and she was satisfied with whom they were and whom they had become. She also recognized that if she needed Mary, she would be there and vice versa. This allowed Laurentine to become free and move beyond the cyclic nature of the family's dysfunction, pain, desire to "do" something and the strong need to avoid conflict.

Story 2

The Creation of a Devil

"I cannot tell you the exact date, time, or hour that Frances interfered with and destroyed my father's relationships with his children, grandchildren, his best childhood friend of sixty years, friends, relatives, or other social contacts but I can tell you over a period of years it happened," started my friend, Clarence, as she shared her story with me.

She was clearly very upset even though the situation happened several years ago. She asked me to discuss her interactional role(s) in this sad situation because she felt trapped and was unhappy about it; she was having problems letting go of her anger. I remember very well how we sat in her beautiful garden in Amsterdam on one of those rare warm evenings in September. We agreed that I would be "The Bird Watcher" and just listen as a good friend with therapeutic expertise. I promised her not to become "The Doctor" or "The Teacher" and that I would absolutely try to avoid the interactional roles of "The Preacher" or "The Savior". I poured her another cup of tea and she eagerly continued.

"My father used to be an amazing man and one of the things I admired most was his ability to connect with all ages and make them feel comfortable, welcomed, and good about themselves. My childhood friends adored him and my mother, and they remained connected with them well after I had married and moved to another city. My father made people laugh and they loved to be around him. He was comfortable in the interactional role of "The Clown" and he knew how to make all social classes feel good, accepted, and important. There was no one and I mean no one that was closer to me than my father. If as a child or adult anyone asked me if my relationship with my father could be destroyed to the point where he would cut-off, I would have laughed in their face and looked at them like they just landed from out-of-space. But over time, slowly, with manipulation, and planning it happened. Our relationship became totally estranged and I was unable to speak to, contact, or connect with my father at any level. As "The Bird Watcher", as you call it, I watched and knew what was happening but when I tried to intervene, the rage of an individual with sociopathic borderline Potato Hot-Head behaviors would silence me.

Which interactional role does Clarence take here?

"Over time I feared her reaction and possible loss of my father as when I tried to be "The Detective" my questioning made life unbearable for him and he was forced into an either/or position." Clarence was clearly very emotional now.

What was Clarence's problem and why did she become frozen into the interactional role of "The Bird Watcher?"

_____

_____

_____

It became immediately clear to me that Clarence had chosen to give her father's new wife the interactional role of "Potato Hot-Head" at least, or even stronger, that of "The Devil" and she strongly protected her father by becoming silent.   However, I do not know if she realized this and so I became "The Detective" and asked her to make her position clear to me. "Did you ever question the interactional role of your father in these issues or even blame him for the interactional role he took?" Clarence looked at me for some time as if I suggested something very malicious. "No, no of course not, she had him totally under her spell! That bitch!" Her choice was to give her father the interactional role of "The Victim". She did not experience him as a person who had his own responsibility for and strength to stop his second wife's incessant interfering behavior in family matters.

By denying acceptance of her friends proposal to re-frame the interactional roles being played out by her father and his second wife, was she in fact reinforcing a very ridged framework from which to understand her circumstance? Expand.

_____

_____

_____

Interestingly as a friend I quickly noted that when I offered a new perspective or attempted to re-frame a new way to reflect on things presented, I was immediately forced back into the interactional roles of "The Bird Watcher" or "The Runaway". It soon became apparent that she was rigidly frozen into her view of how things were as she described them.

Did you sense that the avoidant roles prescribed to her friend above are the same roles that Clarence was prescribed unconsciously by her father or family when she tried to intervene?

_____

_____

_____

Clarence continued her story. "I did not keep a journal as I am not "The Recorder". I did not write down specific dates or times as I ALWAYS believed as "The Angel" that before my father died he would connect with me as I knew he loved me. He said it many times as you will see in what I tell you."

I did not react to this statement but I did wonder how her father could be a totally loving person to his daughter and at the same time hurt her so deeply. I did not dare ask this question as Clarence was too fragile.

"As "The Bird Watcher," I observed as my father was being belittled, threatened, and coerced by his second wife to the point where he had no choice but to cut-off from all he knew, especially his children. I have no idea what Frances, that is her name, I hate to even pronounce _that_ name, threatened him with but whatever it was, it was _powerful_. He was afraid to be alone and she was constantly threatening to leave him. "I asked her why she suspected a secret exists" and she shared that she could not talk about it, at least not now.

Can you imagine a secret so powerful that it would be used to coerce someone away from all key relations of more than sixty years?

_____

_____

Clarence totally confused me. What was she implying? Did she know of or could she imagine that there was a very powerful secret that only her father and his second wife shared? Surely she knows or suspects something herself, she obviously observed something but is hesitant to share as it was too deep and painful for her to talk about. Does Clarence have the idea this secret is strong enough to force her father to cut-off from his children whom he supposedly loved very very much? I felt seduced to take the role of "The Detective", but refrained as it was too obvious a choice and not appropriate at this time. So, I just nodded and Clarence was eager to tell more. She stepped into the international role of "The Archaeologist" and shared her family history with me.

"Back in the early 1970's Frances appeared on the scene after I had left for college. My mother (in the interactional role of "The Savior") would speak of Frances and how she would go to her sons' school on "grandparents" day and she spoke of how Frances and her children began to always be around, especially at our boat in Muiden. They began to stay on a regular basis with my parents at our summer home in France. Initially, my mother wanted to help Frances, who was the same age as me and who had a very poor upbringing. Some of her siblings were in jail. She wanted to be there as a "mother" figure for Frances whose own mother died at a young age. When I returned from college in the summers, Frances and her children came only once to our home and when I returned to college they re-appeared again frequently in the lives of my parents. My mother grew weary of Frances and confided in me that she did not like or trust her anymore. She did not want her at her boat, her summer home, or in her primary home. But Frances did not go away. She would always be at the boat dock, waiting without her children and would end up on the boat with my father to go lobstering. This went on for about fifteen years."

Do you believe that in actuality her father might have been having an affair with Frances and maybe the relationship with his wife was already in trouble behind the scenes?

_____

_____

_____

Hearing this I very much wished to ask more "Detective–like" questions. Very obvious ones like: Why did your mother need to help Frances and her children so much? How do you explain to me that a woman who you always experienced as a very strong and wise mother had no courage or power to set limits on a poor and hardly educated woman? On whose "shoulders" do you think Frances was "seated" to be so dismissive of your mother's wishes? Not just for some weeks or months but over fifteen years? Why did your mother not share her sorrows and worries with her husband who supposedly loved her so much? If she did, why did he ignore her? Why did you personally not speak with your father when you learned that your mother felt uneasy with Frances being around? You must remember what made you hesitate. You remember all that happened so intensely and well, except you do not explain why you took the role of "The Runaway" from the first moment of learning about Frances' behaviors. You must have realized that you let your mother down when she shared her uneasiness with the presence of Frances and you did nothing to help her.

Or even more heavy questions came to mind such as: Did you realize back in college that your father betrayed your mother with Frances? Try to be honest, how long did you suspect that your father was having an affair with Frances? Did you ever share this with him or your mother or with your siblings? If not what stopped you? (I knew Clarence had a younger brother and a younger sister). Did your siblings ever speak of the same concerns with you? Did you feel helpless and stuck because of your loyalty to your father? As the oldest sibling did you in your own way try to protect everyone? Did you ever think, now, that you secretly allied with your father so he would not abandon you as he (perhaps) did your mother? All of these questions were so obvious.

If her friend had posed these questions to Frances what do you think her reaction might have been?

_____

_____

I felt immediately that Clarence would become very angry if I presented these questions. Clearly, she has chosen to give Frances _Devil-like_ proportions and power. So I stayed in my role as "The Bird Watcher". But I have to admit that I became more and more uneasy with it. Clarence did not notice my growing uneasiness and continued her story.

"In May of 2000 I had visited my parents' home and my mother shared that Frances had become a serious concern. She believed she was having a relationship with my father. My mother was very upset and was thinking about divorcing my father. She was crying, she was angry, and very hurt. THIS was not my mother's normal behavior. In July of 2000 my mother shared with me she had decided to divorce my father and had told him so a few days earlier." At this point Clarence was visually sad. She sighed deeply, started crying, and could not continue her story for some minutes.

What do you think might be causing Clarence so much pain and why is she still stuck in an avoidant behavior from Quadrant III?

_____

_____

_____

To be honest, I felt sorry for Clarence. The interactional role of "The Detective" shouted from within me as I silently reflected to myself: Did Clarence ever ask her siblings to help her to find the courage to challenge her father's behavior? Did she believe the idea of her mother, that her father was having an affair? I was curious and wanted to be "The Journalist" by asking what prevented her from speaking about these things with her father and mother? What was the division in the relationship between her parents that had resulted in this affair? Why would a well-educated, strong and involved daughter become "The Runaway"? How could her father have such a "spell over her" that she did not dare to confront him with her ideas about the way he treated her mother. Rather than to ask these questions, I decided to take the role of "The Teacher" and then The Journalist/Archaeologist for a moment to find out if Clarence could tolerate a new perspective.

Do you believe that these are the best interactional roles for her friend to adopt at this point in the conversation?

_____

_____

I shared with her, "You know it is nearly impossible to find out why your father would take such an interactional role in a relationship that you thought to be strange and destructive, without having an honest discussion with him. Even if he should want to do that, it is difficult to solve your problems as long as you are stuck in a position that makes it impossible for you to change your view of your father and the role of his second wife. Instead, you can try to understand why the interactional roles you selected in this situation were important for you to the point that you could only protect your father. Can you also tell me how it is that for all these years you were and still are seduced into the role of "The Runaway" or "The Bird Watcher"? Did you ever dare to imagine what would have happened if you changed your interactional roles? Were you ready to accept the consequences in your relationship with your father, mother, Frances, and your siblings if you decided to change your interactional role into more of a challenging and/or confronting one? Like "The Detective" or "The Firefighter" which may have helped your mother to cope better with the divorce and feel less alone or "The Preacher" confronting your father about his disloyal and abandonment behaviors?"

Do you believe that these questions might help Clarence reflect on her behaviors and fears in regards to taking on new more healthier interactional roles with her key relations?

_____

_____

_____

Clarence listened carefully when I changed my interactional role from "The Bird Watcher" or "The Runaway" into "The Teacher" and then "The Journalist/Archaeologist". She seemed shocked and confused. She even started to cry again. I supported her for a moment. Then she said, "Later I will think about all of that. But please you must listen to me for a while as I need to get my story out." She forced me rigidly back into the interactional role of 'The Birdwatcher'. To be honest, I did not know for sure if I would be able to really _listen_ to her story as I had the idea she would not share with me about her interactional roles in this sad situation. Rather, I am more or less convinced that she will try even harder to give Frances a more powerful and devilish interactional role. Even if Frances is indeed a very evil person (which I also think she is), prescribing or obsessing about this interactional role will never help Clarence find peace with her own interactional role or the interactional roles of her parents, which are the only important things for her at this time. I knew it was very important for Clarence to share the whole story with me so I allowed her to seduce me again and I agreed, so she continued her story.

"Listen, the morning of the day my mother died she had gone to the dentist to have her teeth cleaned. She had a heart murmur and therefore she had to take medication before and after her teeth was cleaned. I spoke to my mother the day of her death and she said she had just walked with her friends and was going to the dentist. Somehow she had spoken to Frances who worked for a doctor. Frances had phoned her "out of the blue". During the conversation she said she could bring the necessary medication to her, which apparently she did. I remember my mother saying she appreciated this as she was running late but thought it odd that Frances called or would do this as their relationship was less than "cordial". I am mentioning this as my mother, a very healthy lady, died in her sleep that night after taking the medication and my father refused an autopsy. It all seemed suspicious to me but I did not question it at the time, I only observed as I respected my father. But as "The Detective" I did wonder--was there a connection between the medicine, the death, and the announcement of the divorce?"

Was this the powerful secret that Clarence spoke about above between Frances and her father that she seemed to be afraid of surfacing?

_____

_____

_____

Clarence stopped her story and was looking at me as if she wanted to make sure I understood that she suspected Frances had some hand in her mother's death. I cannot deny that I indeed had my own thoughts about Frances' role but immediately understood that this was not a helpful road to travel with Clarence as Frances' behavior was not her problem but the issue was her own interactional role in her family. And I understood more and more that she would never be able to free herself as long as she stuck to her ideas that her father was a very loving husband (although perhaps involved in killing his wife), father, and a kind of Angel who, unfortunately and unknowingly, was seduced by Frances to follow her lead. But I wonder to myself how can I get the courage to change my interactional role without chasing Clarence away as a friend and shutting the door to her freedom even more? I do not know and with some resistance, I decided to listen to her story again.

Clarence was still very much involved in it. Her face had reddened and she was crying a bit. "The day my mother died I arrived with my family at my father's home and Frances was there in the kitchen. I thought it odd that Frances was sitting there as it was a very emotional and private time for our family but my father said that when Frances learned of my mother's death she, "Ran out of the doctor's office and straight to him." Even as the family arrived, Frances did not leave. When she did go home that night, she had gathered his personal clothing "underwear" and said she was taking it home to wash. Early the next morning she was at the house with his cleaned underwear and she stayed for several hours. This went on day after day after day. After my mother's funeral, I had to return to my home which was in another city about six hours away. The next weekend I returned to my father's home and I did this for several weeks off and on. Every time I came, Frances was there, she began cooking for my father, sitting with him constantly, and even when we spoke about his finances and what was in the family safe-Frances was there. My father sat with me and asked me to write down all of his accounts (he was a quite wealthy man). He reviewed my mother's will with me and said it would stay exactly as my mother had left things; he would never change it. Frances was always present during these discussions.

I thought it strange as when I called my father, Frances would also be on the phone. I never got to speak alone with just my father. This seemed weird and I was concerned but my father would say, "No, Frances needs to be on the phone" or if he answered he would call Frances who was always there and say, "Pick up the phone."

The following summer my husband and I went to my father's summer home with Frances and my father. Frances was cordial but cold. I knew I was unwelcome by her but I stayed anyway. Shortly after we left, Frances had the summer home remodeled so that the second and third bedrooms were taken away. I asked my father why and he said, "Frances does not want company". And, I knew that a place where I had been grown up and spent my summers was no longer open to me as was our family home which was two hours away.

After my mother died, friction seemed to appear between my younger brother and father over the next few years. It was obvious, through Frances' behavior; she did not like my sibling. Frances had by now quit her job and my father told me he was paying Frances € 3,000.00 a month to "be" with him. When I asked why he responded, "She is going to take care of me if I become ill and I am paying her in "monthly, installments" ahead of time." I let him know we would always be there and he would never be alone and that he did not need Frances but he would say, "No, Frances has said she will take care of me, it is all arranged."

Whenever I came to my father's home it was apparent that Frances was annoyed and she did not like me but she knew I was very close to my father and she had to tread water with me. No matter where we went, Frances came, if my father sat on the couch, she sat right next to him; *she never left his side.* I am sharing this as all of a sudden my father began to speak of his distrust of my younger brother. How he was going to steal from the estate, control him, take the family summer home from the family etc. As he spoke Frances would go on and on and on about my sibling and how horrible he was and how he would "get everything". She was nonstop and would say, "Allen you need to do something" or "Clarence your brother will betray you." This did not stop and before I knew it, there was friction not only between Frances and my brother but also between my brother and father like I had never seen before.

One day we were on my father's boat and my brother and his family was tied up next to us in their boat. Frances was agitated and angry that he was there. I cannot recall exactly what happened but I know she became so angry that she stated, "He has no idea who the hell he is dealing with. I shall win in the end. I shall get everything. Just wait!" I was in total disbelief about what I heard and what she said. I remember my father knew I heard this and he said, "Don't worry I shall protect you. I am smarter than that." He said that in front of her to me many times.

Further, I remember Frances sitting on the couch at our family home telling my father, in front of me, how his children did not love him, wanted nothing to do with him, and only wanted his "money". I denied this, I challenged it but Frances went on and on and on-she badgered, she belittled, she ranted. But most importantly she would laugh and say to my father, "Your children want nothing to do with you when you are sick, they will not take care of you." And I remember again saying Dad, "I will be here-you will never be left alone." So I wonder, if she said this in front of me, what did she say when I was not there."

Do you believe that Frances was the source of the evil or that her father was giving Frances permission to behave this way in order to help him distance him from his children?

_____

_____

"As time went on the division between my brother, Ralph, and my father grew. Then Frances started on my younger sister, Melanie. Actually Frances saw Melanie as less of a threat then Ralph or I, but she would belittle, and badger my father about my sister. She would openly attack my sister (verbally) and treated her with such disregard and disrespect it was sad. But Melanie, as "The Savior, "did not want to alienate my father so she took Frances' verbal abuse. Soon, my sister was partially estranged from my father, but she never stopped trying to connect with him and on rare occasions was able to speak to him or visit but only with Frances' "permission". Until one day Frances became very angry at her and cut her off from our father 100%.

Do you begin to get the picture that her father may have been no Angel and in collusion with Frances? Thinking this how might this influence your interactional role towards Clarence?

_____

_____

Again, Clarence paused and looked at me. And she asked, "Are you *now* convinced that Frances **IS** the Devil?" I have to admit I indeed had the idea that Frances was not a very trustworthy or nice person. But I knew I had to be as neutral as possible if I wanted to help my friend. It is obvious that she denied her father's responsibility for this story as well the lack of responsibility that she and her siblings' demonstrated. How was it possible that she more or less accuses her father of having a relationship with the Devil and conspiring with her to possibly murder her beloved mother without ever challenging her idea that he is a very loving and admirable person? Not that I want to re-shape him into another Devil, but at least Clarence could be aware of his full responsibility for his behavior towards her mother, herself, and her siblings. Which family secret could make her so powerless? I have no idea of course. But I know that continuing to assume the interactional role that she wants me to play will not help her. But also I know that any other interactional role could undermine our relationship.

I guess, my dear readers, that you sometimes can become trapped into very stressful interactional roles that you do not wish to be in and there may seem like there is no way out. I know now for sure that if I allow her to continue her story she will tell me stories that are all the time more and more proof of the devilish qualities and power of Frances. But even if it is true that this woman is a criminal and she has stolen money from Clarence's family, or did even worse things, it is clear that these deeds are not the real and very painful problems for Clarence. She has to find the courage to redefine her father's and mother's relationship towards each other, towards her, and her siblings. Of course the most important thing is that she must develop the courage to challenge her most valuable and important belief that her father feels as close to her as she to him. I realized that eventually I must step into the interactional role of "The Doctor", "The Savior" or "The Therapist" if I am completely to travel this road with Clarence. But at this point I decided to continue the interactional role of "The Bird Watcher" and let her end her story. But I also decided that after she finishes it, I must have the courage to take the interactional role of "The Doctor" for just a little bit.

Do you think it was helpful for her friend to allow Clarence to finish her story?

_____

_____

_____

Indeed Clarence continues telling all kind of terrible actions of Frances towards her, her siblings, and her father's friends. She made clear that neither she nor any other family member or friend had the courage to confront directly or indirectly, her father with his interactional role in the whole story. The powers that Clarence attributes to Frances become absolutely Super-Human. She becomes "The Devil in all his dark glory". And, in her story, her father, herself, her siblings and all father's friends become weak and powerless victims of the Black Goddess, Frances.

After she finishes her, indeed, very sad story I tell her that it has impressed me enormously. And it did. But, I say, "What impressed me the most was your readiness to accept the interactional role of being "The Total Powerless Victim". That is not the way I know you. You are a strong, powerful person and know exactly how to get what you need and how to defend yourself. So I want to give you advice, against our agreement, in the interactional role more or less of "The Doctor". Go and find a person, professional, who can help you to find out how your family history and your relationships in your family were able to take away your powers. I can tell you that I am sure that Frances is not responsible for that. She perhaps is the tyrant who was placed on the throne in your family's land but she was a puppet placed there by the forces within your family system. But who am I? Go and find out yourself. It will give you a lot of peace in your future life. And perhaps it can guide you to choose another interactional role, a more helpful one, towards your father and other family members. It will also be important for your children to experience that you are not a powerless victim and they also are not at mercy of the tricks of the Devil but can choose to change their interactional roles when confronted with very difficult situations."

Clarence looks at me totally astonished. I think for a moment she will hit me on the head. But then she sighed very deeply. "I knew you were a terrible person," she said with a smile. "I will think about your advice and words. Now please go home. I need time for myself." I give her a tender hug and leave her house as requested.

I did not hear from her for over year. When she connected again with me she shared that she had not sought therapy as of yet but had done a lot of self-reflection and she realized and agreed that through the years she was very loyal to her father and never protected her mother, who at times she became very angry with when she complained about her father's lack of attention and warmth toward her. Yes, there was much in her family, many secrets within the family history including her grandparents' history that needed to be revealed. She is now ready to ask the painful memories and stories of her siblings and also to research and do a family genogram with the help of a therapist. She knows now there is much that she closed her eyes to and even questions whether she lived in a "Pollyanna" dream world. Her family was in trouble for years and she never acknowledged or had the courage to confront the observations that she saw or the verbal stories that she heard. She was shocked to learn two things: (1) Her father had died and she was only informed several weeks later by a family friend after he was buried and, (2) He had never married Frances but allowed her to act like and respond as his "wife" to many. Frances did inherit her father's entire estate, wealth, including all of her mother's heirlooms. The good thing that she shared was that in an attempt to understand what has transpired for more than thirty some years, I have now assumed the roles of "The Recorder", "The Detective", "The Journalist" and "The Archaeologist" and have discovered that the roots of our family tree are so well grounded that evil destruction has resurfaced as re-struction. We are closer, more committed, and well connected with each other at every living generational level, you see, we are truly a **FAMILY.** She said with a strong and steady voice to me. I was happy, as I could see that she was succeeding in regaining power within herself, and her family system was in the process of becoming closer and healing together.

Impressions

In the case above it is interesting that the problem scenario shifted to the father's lack of loyalty to the mother and possible undetected family secrets which may have been harbored for years. What is most revealing is that Clarence was trapped into avoidant interactional roles by her unconscious and unquestioning loyalties to her father, a man she had placed on a pedestal her entire life. By adopting the various interactional roles located in quadrant III, Need to Avoid, Clarence protected her father and failed to understand and protect her mother, who was not as strong as she appeared but quite helpless in her relations with her husband and very needy of attention. There was no question in my mind that Frances exacerbated the problem between the father, mother, and later the father and children and abused it to fulfill her own personal needs. But the father had to have given her permission at some level to behave as she did as he never stopped her. Suggesting he was a very needy and cruel man, also. Even if there was a "secret" which strongly connected him to Frances, this only fused their relationship and the need to dismiss the children was a paramount goal between them.

I was surprised to learn of how helplessly rigid Clarence had become in this situation as did her siblings who are also very strong. I know Clarence as a very strong, intelligent, and sensible woman and I saw how her need to blame Frances whom she imputed Superhuman, Devilish Powers as the solution of her internal loyalty struggles, seduced her into a very rigid, unproductive, and painful role.

When I tried to challenge the interactional roles that she had assigned to her father and Frances it was difficult as Clarence needed to be heard as she had not shared her story which she carried silently inside of her with many people. As in relations like this, the requested interactional roles of the friend resembled, and even mirrored, the interactional roles she had chosen in this conflict and within her family. She denied that Frances might be a normal, poor, and uneducated person but instead ascribed her to be a person with sociopathic borderline behaviors. One thing became very obvious to me that her choice to give Frances superhuman, devilish powers would never help her to heal. Even though the story she shared indeed portrays Frances as an evil and cruel woman. The truth is that Frances along with the father was "the true devil"!

By holding on to this belief Clarence protected not just her father but also herself, her siblings, relatives, and close friends of her parents. As you see you can be seduced very easily into an interactional role that your friends or relatives like you to take. And, you hesitate or refuse to change the assigned interactional role as you feel that your relationship with your beloved family member or friends will be in danger if you do.

I must admit I risked challenging Clarence when I used the roles of "The Detective", The Journalist", "The Archaeologist" "The Teacher" and "the Doctor". Clarence was in pain and she needed to understand her responsibility in this situation as well as the interactional roles she assumed. I risked costing a friendship which I hold dear, but I believed at some level she was ready to hear my thoughts or she would not have shared her story. In these interactional roles I believed I helped her to see the whole story from more of a family- oriented perspective. This allowed her to decide how to change her definition (re-frame) of what had been going on and still is going on. Through this process, she would be able to change her interactional role in a way she could ask the questions of her family members to gain more understanding of the family's pain and secrets. Through this she herself would be able to really feel her pain and disappointment about her father's and perhaps also her mother's interactional roles towards each other but mostly towards her. This could perhaps change her behavior and free her from her role of "The Powerless Victim of the Devil".

Although, Clarence still believes firmly that Frances is the devil but she now understands that Frances was allowed to enter their family space as there were hidden family secrets, long before Frances was on the scene, which opened the door to her.

After hearing her story and what she had transpired the following year, I believe Clarence is on the road to healing and she will look forward to a life filled with connection and fulfillment with the generations of the future and not look back to the generations of the past. She has clearly faced the true devil and now she has found redemption.

Story 3

The Language of Music

The reason for my contact with the family in this story was rather dramatic. The doctor of the psychiatry department of a general hospital asked if he could transfer a female patient to the closed ward. He was unable take care of her anymore because the department was not safe enough for her. The woman, we will call her Titia, was in her early 30's and had tried to commit suicide. She had sliced her left wrist while on the toilet in the hospital ward. A passing nurse had seen the blood seeping underneath the door. Titia was taken into surgery where the cut was taken care of. In the process of cutting her wrist she had also severed a major nerve vessel, which resulted in her left hand and wrist becoming paralyzed.

Titia stayed in the surgical ward for observation, but while nobody was watching she took a knife and almost cut out her tongue. Her tongue was badly sutured. After that the surgeons did not dare to keep Titia on their ward for safety reasons. Even the psychiatrist did not think it was safe for her on his ward. So they asked if she could be admitted to our closed ward.

What was the issue for the psychiatric and nursing staff at the hospital?

_____

_____

_____

Even though our closed ward could not offer much more security, we agreed to take Titia. We asked the physicians to ask Titia to bring as many family members with her to our first meeting which would be scheduled upon her arrival to our hospital. Our psychiatric ward worked according to family-therapeutic principles.

The next morning Titia was brought to our hospital by ambulance. We received her at the outpatient building where we had planned a session with her and her family before the official admission. She was tied to a stretcher and accompanied only by her husband, Eric. Eric was in his early fifties, physically handicapped, and walked with a stick. I proposed to have a conversation and interview with Titia and Eric, accompanied by the psychiatric nurse who was responsible for the closed ward. Other psychiatric team members would observe the interview behind a one way mirror. Titia and her husband willingly agree to this proposal.

Upon arrival I had requested that the ambulance staff untie Titia however they refused because according to the referring psychiatrist she was too suicidal and unpredictable. The ambulance staff demanded that Titia be taken to the closed ward immediately and thus forced me into the professional therapeutic role of *The Doctor*. In other words I needed to convince them that as a *Doctor* I knew what was best for the patient.

Was it the patient's behavior or the professional medical staff that was determining the interactional roles of those in the situation?

_____

_____

_____

From the ambulance staff's perspective the idea that I wanted to talk to this "mad" woman and her husband was according to them *insane*. To be honest, the pressure to agree to take the professional therapeutic role of "The Doctor" was quite reasonable and would have offered me much security as she was acting very unstable. I hesitated, and almost complied with the request, but with the help of my psychiatric team I withstood the pressure and choose another professional therapeutic role to use with the couple.

At this point the ambulance staff wanted *me* to untie Titia and to take full responsibility of her. Seeing that they were non-compliant, I agreed and I untied Titia. She shifted unsteadily off the stretcher. She took a seat next to her husband. In the background I could hear the ambulance staff grumbling while they entered their vehicle and then left.

Through the ambulance's staff noncompliant behavior which Quadrant IV professional role was the psychiatrist forced into?

_____

I welcomed the couple and agreed that they had severe, even life threatening problems. I took the professional therapeutic role of "The Journalist"/"The Archaeologist" and told them I wanted to learn of their family history and while they spoke I would draw on a piece of paper a "family genogram" or "family tree" in order to get to know them better. This would help me to visualize and see various relationships in and among the family members.

Titia and her husband are relieved to tell their family story and openly talk about what they believe is happening in their family. They both, especially Titia, agree that the problems in their family greatly impact their lives.

Titia shared that she was desperate because she believed that her mother wanted to kill her daughter, Jana. Her mother would not accept that Titia now gave more attention and love to Jana than to her.

What was Titia's problem? _____

_____

_____

Eric agreed, but did not think that his mother-in-law would go as far as to "kill" Jana. He shared that his wife had slowly developed these ideas overtime and now the doctors say that she is " psychotic". The couple shared that her mother indeed had problems accepting the birth of her grandchild. She only came to visit the infant after a couple of weeks had passed. Her mother was described as quite needy throughout Titia's life. She demanded constant attention from her husband, son, and daughter. She often felt unappreciated, abandoned by her family and if left at home alone for any reason she would react intensely, often through a suicide attempt. Titia shared that her immediate family had to constantly be home in order to give her mother the attention she demanded.

What interactional role did the mother force Titia into and was this similar to the role the psychiatrist played when Titia was removed from the stretcher?

_____

_____

Titia was very involved in trying to help her mother because she had much pity on her father. Titia shared that she often felt more like the "mother" of her mother than a daughter. She always had to be with her mother. It was clear Titia was rigidly in the interactional role of "The Saviour" as she tried to support her father and protect him from pain. She also was trying to "save" her mother from committing suicide. Titia's own wishes and desires were subordinate to that of her mother. She reported that she developed much anger and resentment toward her mother. But never spoke of her anger with her parents.

Titia also described situations where she took on the interactional role of "The Mediator" or "The Peacemaker" between her father and mother in order to keep peace; negotiating differences between them. In this way she became more of a partner to her father than her mother was. She always had to be at home. She shared that her brother was not as involved as she was. He was her mother's favorite, but her mother never pressured him as much as the others to attend to her needs.

Do you believe that Titia's interactional role became rigid as a result of an underlying family message or belief?

After her father died, Titia was basically the sole support of her mother and she moved into a very rigid "Saviour" role. When her daughter Jana was born Titia had the feeling she was stuck. She wanted to give her daughter attention but she had the feeling that if she did, her mother would demand even more attention. Her hope that her mother would take on the role of grandmother evaporated quickly. To the contrary, Titia had the feeling that her mother was jealous of her daughter. Titia became more and more stressed and was afraid that her mother would kill Jana. She did not know how to handle this problem, and it was hard to speak to her husband as he did not believe or support her ideas.

Titia then shared that she developed the idea to kill herself. That would end the mother-daughter-granddaughter triangle. She believed this would force her mother to switch her attention to the granddaughter and she would need to keep Jana alive as support for her. That way Titia would save the life of her daughter, Jana. At this point she was locked into a very extreme rigid "Saviour" role. A role that was comparable to the role Jesus played which was to die to save mankind. Instead, Titia would die to save her daughter.

Titia shared her thoughts with her husband who then called a doctor. Titia was admitted to the psychiatric ward with the diagnosis of psychotic depression with severe suicidal intentions. While in the hospital, Titia became more and more anxious and feared for her daughter's life. She decided that the only way that she could protect her daughter would be to commit suicide immediately; she was overwhelmed with fear.

As the couple spoke, we discussed her role in her immediate family, the role of her brother, her husband, and her mother-in-law. It became clear that when Titia was younger she was pressured by her family not to marry Eric. He was twenty years older than her and handicapped. She had known him since childhood. He was her piano teacher and Titia was his most gifted pupil. Later on she started to confide in him and he started to act like her "Saviour". Eventually they married. His mother was a tremendous support for them in this process. Eric shared that his mother had always supported him. He was born handicapped. His grandparents advised his mother to let him die when he became ill as there was no future for him, being handicapped. After this, his mother cut-off from her parents. He said, "I was my mother's biggest and only project; her sole purpose in life. She continuously affirmed my strength and my healthy qualities." Going through life was heavy, but his mother gave him the courage to persevere. He was very musical and was taught by the best teachers. He became a gifted and successful piano teacher. Now he gives master classes to the best piano players in the world.

Throughout their marriage, with his support and his mothers', Titia distanced herself slowly from her mother. She agreed with that the distancing was good for her. But then after her father died, her mother tried to commit suicide several times. She blamed Titia and said that she was selfish and did not care about her mother. It was her fault that she was trying to commit suicide and she tried to make Titia feel guilty by saying, "Your father would resent you".

Did the "cut-off" seem to help or hinder the situation for Titia? How did the mother successfully bring back Titia to the interactional role of "The Savior"?

_____

_____

_____

Successfully guilt set in and Titia immediately shifted back into the "Saviour" role. Again, her attention shifted to her mother and her needs. As "The Saviour" she knew that her reactions and behaviors within this role would harm her own interest and desires; but she felt trapped. Eric tried to persuade her to take on another interactional role towards her mother. For example, he described behaviors that were consistent with "The Journalist" or "The Teacher". But she refused. He did not dare pressure her too much as he could see she was vulnerable so he began to take on the interactional roles of "The Mediator" and "The Peacemaker" between his wife and her mother to help keep peace. He also adopted the role of "The Saviour" towards his wife to try and protect her as best he could.

Did the husband's interactional roles help or hinder Titia? Would another interactional role have been better for him to assume?

_____

_____

During this time, Titia became pregnant, unexpectedly. Because of her husband's handicap they did not have frequent sexual intercourse. Their relationship was more spiritual and they experienced intimacy through music. The couple was emotionally very close. They also enjoyed the husband's mother who visited and supported them often. Upon learning of the pregnancy, Titia's mother stated that she was afraid that the baby would also be born handicapped. Titia and her mother's relationship became strained and deteriorated quickly." At this point I tell the couple I want to have some consultation with my team members behind the screen. They agreed.

As the psychiatric team reviewed this case it was obvious that there were severe family problems. Titia was stuck between her loyalties to her daughter; need to fill the demands of her manipulative and needy mother, as well as loyalty issues toward her deceased father. After consulting, the psychiatric team decided to create a "family sculpture" where the psychiatric team members would portray in action the role of the missing family members. The team wanted the couple to visually experience how "stuck" they were in their relationships and in their interactional roles with others.

After the family sculpture I decide to continue in the professional therapeutic role of "The Journalist", and I asked the couple to take on the role of "The Recorder". I ask them to write down the family relationships and the role of the family members in their own specific language: _the language of music._ The couple was asked to write a melody that described each of the characters in the family that personified the interactional roles of the closest family members. When that was completed, I asked them to write a composition describing the family events of the last few years and describe through melody which steps had been taken. Obviously not an easy task, but they were musically gifted and they loved the idea. They immediately understood what was asked of them.

To complete this task, the couple would stay together on the psychiatric ward. They were able to use a piano during part of the day and the whole of the evening. Titia asked if she had to continue with her medication. For a moment I felt seduced to step in the role of "The Doctor", but I was able to keep my role as "The Journalist". I told her that she herself could decide if medication is necessary. She could stop the medication, if she so desired. She shared that she wants to stop. But because of her back pain wanted to continue with Anodyne. They asked if their daughter and mother-in-law could visit them. I explained to them that the visit had to have a positive influence on them and if so, they were welcome to visit, often. I also shared that the couple would be allowed to visit them at their home. But they preferred the use of the offered rest period with the task at hand at the hospital.

Over the next three weeks the couple worked hard on their composition. They were very social towards the other patients. I checked on them every day to see if any stress had developed because of the task and to monitor Titia's stability. There were no specific problems. When I visited, I remained in the therapeutic professional role of "The Journalist".

The next family session was held approximately three weeks later. The session was held in the room with the piano. The couple entered the room happy and laughing. Titia walked up straight and had no further back pains. The husband made jokes and easily took on the role of the "Music Teacher", towards me and my psychiatric team. He explained how a piece of music could be written in major and minor and that sentiment could be expressed through it. Titia agreed with him and made jokes about him not being able to let go of his "Master Teacher" role. They explained that they had made a melody for her mother, mother-in-law, brother, themselves, and Jana. And then a composition, putting all of the melodies together.

Titia sat at the piano. I was assigned the role of "The Pupil" and maintained the professional therapeutic role of "The Journalist". Titia started playing the piano with one hand (the other hand was still paralyzed). First, she played the melody and explained each melody as she played. Eric commented and agreed with her analysis. He said that Titia had written the melodies and together they created the composition. After the melodies, of which she played twice, they together played (each with one hand) the music composition piece. It was a very emotional and moving experience.

Through the melodies, Titia identified important themes as her role as; (1) " Mother" in her family, (2) her relationship with her mother, (3) her intense, anxious behavior, (4) the relation between herself and husband, (5) the birth of Jana and, (6) the latest dramatic events including the suicide attempt were translated into sound.

After the very passionate and informative experience, I asked the couple if they had any ideas how to proceed with their life. The couple decided they would go home the next day. Titia said she did not want to see her mother for at least a year. She would write to her mother and let her know of her wishes (a first!). She also asked if I would talk to her mother, if she so desired. I agreed.

The couple's desire to go home was quite a surprise for me. I almost jumped back into my role as "The Doctor" and wanted to ask them if it is wise and safe to do go home without further treatment. After all she entered the ward being diagnosed as having a psychotic depression with severe suicidal intentions. But I resisted and did not take the role of the "The Doctor" with Titia and the results were positive. Instead, I agreed with their wishes and allowed them to take control and responsibility for their lives.

The couple returned, after two weeks, and shared that everything was well. Titia had taken back her role as mother, no suicidal thoughts were present and she had not seen or spoken to her own mother but had written her a letter. All seemed to be going well for the couple so further contact was not necessary unless something happened and they needed support.

Years later the couple consulted with me again. This time the problem was concerning the husband. As we spoke, we looked back at the former problems and the incredible recovery of Titia. As "The Journalist" I asked them what they thought had worked so well. They shared what helped the most was the fact that they were given responsibility for their own lives and that I had not played the professional therapeutic role of "The Doctor". By being flexible and believing in Titia, I was able to create space which allowed them to think about their interactional rigid roles in the family and how their interactional roles were developed to "protect" Titia's mother. One of the most eye opening experiences for Titia was to learn how she had become so rigidly and unconsciously appointed by her family members into "The Saviour" role in her family. Through the process she was able to learn other more flexible interactional roles which helped to give her power to become free from the guilt of her mother's issues. As she stepped out of the role of "The Saviour" she was able to find happiness and felt more complete. She had even learned to express her desires openly to others without fear.

Impressions:

Throughout her life, Titia's primary purpose was to make "others happy". She was even subordinate to her brother. After her father died, Titia was basically the sole support of her mother and she moved into a very rigid "Saviour" role. When her daughter, Jana, was born Titia had the feeling she was stuck. She wanted to give her daughter attention but she had the belief that if she did, her mother would demand even more attention. Titia understood that her mother was jealous of her daughter. As a result, Titia was afraid that her mother would kill Jana. She did not know how to handle this problem, and it was hard to speak to his husband as he did not believe or support her ideas. So Titia, like her mother, also became needy and looked for a "saviour" to protect her and her daughter. The husband stepped into the role of "saving" her and she sacrificed herself to "save" her daughter. Even the hospital staff and ambulance personnel became "saviours" in this incidence. They would not untie Titia or keep her at the hospital as it was not "safe" for her. Titia was stuck between her loyalties to her daughter; need to fill the demands of her manipulative and needy mother, as well as loyalty issues toward her deceased father. Music became the ultimate "saviour" for the couple as they could visually and creatively experience how "stuck" they were in their relationships and in their interactional roles with others in her family. Through the process she was able to learn other more flexible interactional roles which helped to give her power to become free from the guilt of her mother's issues. As she stepped out of the role of "The Saviour" she was able to find happiness and felt more complete. She had even learned to express her desires openly to others without fear.

Personal Reflection Questions

As you, the reader, can see some situations are painful and may not be able to be resolved or completely understood. Especially if your key relation has a mental health or physical illness. Cut-offs from key relations are the most hurtful and destructive of all relationship patterns. And you will experience much pain, sadness, confusion and helplessness. You may even obsess about a situation that is intenable. But there is a way to bring understanding and change for yourself in complex highly emotional rigid situations if you are willing to reflect and think about your interactional roles and be willing to re-frame the situation, not blame, and look at yourself. The following questions can serve as a guide but you may need to adapt these questions to your particular situation, or ask yourself new questions. If you have intense difficulties, we highly recommend the assistance of a mental health professional who is trained to help you re-think and re-capture a sense of who you are. When seeking self-reflection the following questions can serve as a guide:

1. What is there in the relationship that creates a level of unimportance toward you from whom you are trying to connect with?

2. Are you participating in interactional roles (especially avoidant or caretaking behaviors) that place you into a rigidly helpless or limited situation?

3. Are you able to look at your complex situation from more of a positive re-frame?

4. When the individual cuts-off or you cut-off the relationship, what is there that causes so much pain that you are placed in an either-or situation?

5. When someone presents in your key-relations has a highly complex mental illness or physical condition, how rigid is the interactional patterns within and/or prescribed by family members?

6. Do you reach out to other key relations to gain additional understanding of your family's history and their perceptions of how to deal with the concerns from a different approach or do you submit yourself to a limited avoidance or caretaking interactional role?

7. Have you consciously or unconsciously colluded with a member of the family to either protect their secret or protect them in other ways which places you in a rigid avoidant or savior-like interactional role?

8. Are you open to re-frame so that the cyclic nature of the relationship can be disrupted into a more effective communication?

9. Are you willing to seek out your family stories becoming "The Detective", "The Journalist, "The Archaeologist" and ask questions from a historical perspective to help you gain understanding of the family "secrets" or other painful experiences that are directly or indirectly influencing the current relationship of which you are struggling?

10. Most importantly, when a relationship is severed or cut-off, can you see how the process may in fact be helping you to move on with a life that is free and allows you to create a more open relationship with others?

11. And lastly, are you willing, when in pain and internal conflict, to seek out therapeutic assistance in order to gain insight of your situation with a deeper and more intimate level of understanding?

PART FIVE

How Did My Preferred Interactional Role Develop?

Chapter Twenty-Seven

Learning a Preferred Interactional Style

How you develop your preferred interactional role in specific social interactions is based on the interactional roles that you have assumed within a variety of contexts throughout your personal life (see figure nine: Development of Preferred Interactional Roles). As you progress along the continuum of life from birth to present, interaction with family members, friends, as well as interactions within the school context and participation in social clubs, help to shape you into the person you are today.

Figure Nine
Development of Preferred Interactional Roles

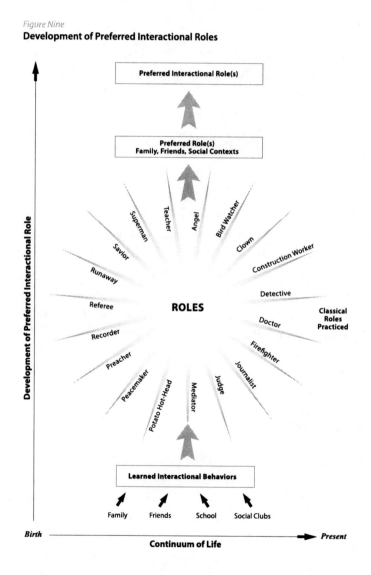

Throughout the developmental years, you practiced several interactional roles, through every relation that you encountered. From these enactments, especially when disagreements developed, one or more of the interactional roles became your preferred way of engaging with family, friends, within the school context and/or in social organizations. This interactional role(s), or the way that you responded with verbal and nonverbal behavior to others, developed unconsciously, as feedback was received by you from a variety of people in different settings. This preferred interactional role(s) or typical interactional patterns (style) were later transferred from your childhood life to your adult life and finally to your professional life. Thus, without realizing it, you employ a certain set of preferred interactional roles when you engage with everyone you meet.

Interactional Style:

Your interactional style or pattern can fall under four areas as described in earlier chapters (e.g., Quadrant I, Need to Intellectualize, Quadrant II, Need to Control and Manage Information, Quadrant III, Need to Avoid, and Quadrant IV, Need to Save others). As described in chapter 5, employing a particular style can be healthy, as you will automatically shift from one interactional role to another within the preferred quadrant as you engage with Key-Relations. You may even flexibly change to interactional roles within other quadrants without thinking. This is a very healthy interactional stance to have with others. However, of special note, if you stay on a daily basis primarily in Quadrant III, Need to Avoid and Quadrant IV, Need to Save Others, you may be prone to developing high levels of stress, anxiety, anger, and depression. As the interactional roles described in these quadrants do not allow you to express your thoughts, feelings, and reactions to, especially your Key-Relations openly. You may even become overly responsible to the point of putting other's needs before your own which can develop resentment. Therefore, *be careful* as these quadrants place you at risk as they mask your identity, feelings, and true-self. The problem arises within the four quadrants when you become rigidly adhered to one or two interactional patterns when stress, tension and differences develop within and among your Key-Relations. It is at these moments when you feel powerless, helpless and at a loss of how to improve emotional differences.

Living and Presenting Culture:

DiNicola, 1997 referred to the vast array of possible interactional behaviors that you can implement throughout life as your "Living Culture" (see figure ten: Living Culture). Each person's "living culture" is highly distinctive and is created via the interactions and relationships that you were exposed to during your lifetime. The different relations with every family member or individual that has entered and left your life become part of your unique "living culture". Therefore, you always carry your own "living culture" with you which is dynamic and constantly changing as people enter and leave your life. This "living culture" influences how you react and respond to verbal and nonverbal behavior that is received from others.

Figure Ten
Living Culture

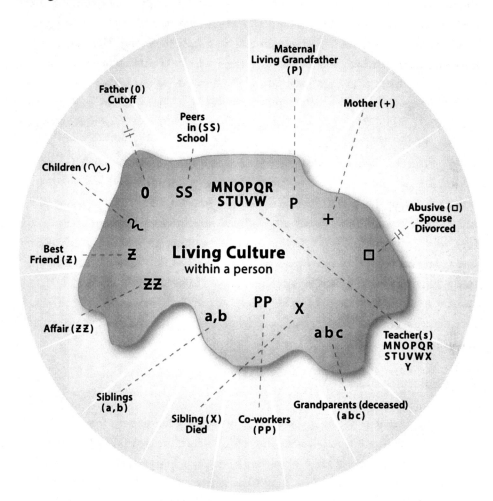

When in a face-to-face context, phone conversation or even social media connection with another person(s), your "living culture" presents itself, and you will unconsciously draw upon various parts called your "presenting culture" (subset of your "living culture") as you engage with others. When engaged with another you will automatically activate certain elements of *their* unique "living culture" while another person may draw upon an entire set of different elements within their own unique "living culture". For example, using Figure ten as a backdrop, Jillian is in a deep conversation with her new friend Lilly. Lilly reminds Jillian of her mother, and as she speaks to Lilly her body posture is rigid, and she basically uses one-word responses. As they speak, Jillian is drawing upon behaviors and manners that she used when her mother asked her questions. Lilly, on the other hand, perceives Jillian to be like her sister whom she loved speaking to so Lilly speaks nonstop often asking Jillian a lot of personal questions. Julian later meets Timothy, a male friend, for tea and her friend reminds her of a previous boyfriend which she very much enjoyed. As she speaks to Timothy she giggles and laughs freely, as these were behaviors that she used when speaking to her former boyfriend. Timothy, also perceives Jillian to be like his good friend, Shelly, whom he loved laughing with. So he responds to Jillian in a very light-hearted and jovial mood. So, as each person interacts, they will bring forth or "present" different aspects of their "living culture" as you will of your "living culture". Therefore, you behave differently in different situations depending on who is present and which part of your "living culture" is activated.

Figure ten is an example of how the different subsystems of your "living culture" (e.g., relations with mother, father, siblings etc.) interact together to solidify certain interactional behaviors that are used throughout your life. These subsystems also include those in your life who are emotionally cut-off or no longer present with you. Thus, your "living culture" is a collection of all interactions experienced during your lifetime and serves as the backdrop from which you will respond to others. Therefore, you need to reflect upon your own "living culture" as you carry parts of it into each interaction that you have with others and determine how your communication and behaviors are a reflection of your "living culture" which includes negative and positive aspects of all previous relationships.

Emotional Differences:

When others become upset, angry, sad, or are in need of your support: to protect yourself from discomfort, you draw upon specific interactional role(s) (subset of your "presenting culture") or a specific interactional style to help you work through times of differences and stress. Yet there are times when you get stuck in this interactional role (s) and feel too much in charge, anxious, overwhelmed, angry, or even depressed. At this point, you have no idea how to get out of the situation. It is at this point, that you need to state to yourself, *"I can EXPAND and I have the power from within me to change"*.

Yes! Yes! You do have the ability to change your interactional role(s) at any time throughout an interactional engagement with Key-Relations to draw upon your vast, complex dynamic "living culture" within yourself in order to create new levels of communication and nonverbal responses when in tense situations. The "presenting culture" you select from your vast "living culture" will determine the interactional roles that will be assumed in your inter-relational engagements. You must realize that you *cannot* change others; you can only change *yourself, your interactional role, and how you respond in highly charged situations.* Changing your interactional role will impact others and through the process they will also change via responding to your new interactional role.

Reflection:

Take time to reflect on the following questions in order to bring a part of your own unique "living culture" to life:

1. Which people would I describe within my "living culture" as those with whom I have a positive relationship?

2. Which people would I describe within my "living culture" as those with whom I have a negative relationship?

3. How did I behave or respond when in the presence of each person within my "living culture"?

4. List each person that you view as responding negatively to, and list what aspects you must be careful of when in the presence of another person who activates a similar negative response.

5. Identify the interactional roles that you shift into when in the presence of others who activate negative responses.

6. Identify other interactional roles that you can draw upon to shift to when you respond to those who bring out negative affect.

Morgan came into therapy sharing that she wanted to leave her husband. She was tired of their disagreements and felt overwhelmed because he constantly interrupted her. They had been married for five months, and she felt as though she was becoming more and more depressed. She was crying all the time, felt anxious, and angry. She even "hated" looking at her husband. When asked about their dating and engagement she shared things were pretty good, their fights were minor, and when they fought she just did not say much and let him have his way, she never saw it as an issue between them. But since they married, they have many disagreements. When asked how she responded to these disagreements she shared, "I become quiet, I do not say much, in fact, I often get in the car and leave for hours. It is like I need to "runaway." When she returns home, she goes to her room, and nothing more is said. So each time they fight there is no resolution. The therapist began to explore carefully what life was like for Morgan as a child, especially when her parents disagreed. Morgan eventually shared that her parents were very unhappy and fought a lot. When they fought, she watched and said nothing (what we call assuming The Bird Watcher interactional role) as she learned early, if she tried to intervene she would get "slapped" especially by her mother. So when the fighting really became bad she would "leave" (what we call assuming The Runaway interactional role). A few times she even ran away for a day or two but then came back. She finally left home for good at age sixteen.

In later sessions, Morgan began to discuss how she responded to stress with her peers as well when she was involved in various school or social settings. She then spoke about how she now responds in her work environment when conflict arises. She is a hairdresser stylist and often in training sessions many will argue about one style over the next. In all situations, she becomes quiet, watches and says nothing. She does not get up and leave, but many times she has the desire.

In each situation described above she enacted the interactional roles of The Bird Watcher and The Runaway. The therapist then referred back to her current response to her husband when he disagrees with her, and began to speak about the risks that she must take to change her interactional roles so that she could be heard. From there, the husband was invited into the therapy session, his history was explored and his interactional roles identified. The couple began to role-play new interactional roles, which EXPANDED new levels of communication for both of them, helping them to feel more successful and connected in their marriage.

Looking back at the initial session, the therapist realized Morgan had to "EXPAND" her preferred unconscious interactional roles of The Birdwatcher and The Runaway, which were leading to ineffective levels of anxiety and depression within her marriage. She had been seduced by her family not to react or express her feelings as a child, which was leading to feelings of ineptness and helplessness in most situations when tensions arose. She was drawing on those aspects of her "living culture" and her "presenting culture" of times of stress with others, and connected to the negative aspects of her reactions toward her parents' fights. Over time, Morgan and her husband were challenged to change their preferred interactional roles and through the process of adopting new interactional roles, Morgan did not have the impulse to "need out". Expanding their interactional role(s) was imperative if their marriage was to survive.

The Risk Associated With Changing Your Interactional Role

Changing your interactional role requires you to take a risk, and the thought of taking risks may result in anxiety or fear. "If I change, what may happen?" We would suggest taking small steps. Select the interactional roles that you are most comfortable with and begin there. Remember if you do not like a particular interactional role you have the possibility from *the power from within you* to alter or change to a new one. All of the interactional roles presented in this book have positive and negative aspects. Every interactional role can be effective, with the exception of the role of Potato Hot-Head, and every interactional role, if used rigidly and in all interactional settings, can lead to feelings of ineptness, frustration, stuckness, and even depression. As you try out each interactional role you may want to follow the steps outlined in Part III, Chapter twenty-five, EXPANSION, and do several role-play scenarios in your head so that you can become familiar with the various classical interactional roles prior to engaging with other people. This will allow you to experience what each interactional role feels like before using.

EXPANDING:

One thing is for certain, within various social situations; you will engage in more than one of the interactional roles described within the following chapters. This means that you have the ability to EXPAND fluidly from one interactional role to another that will create a healthy interactional style. It is when tensions arise that you must begin to analyze and determine which interactional role(s) you unconsciously assume when experiencing stress. Emotional concerns (e.g., anxiety, fear, panic attacks, depression, etc.) develop when tensions between others or within you build and the interactional role becomes solidified to the point where it is the *only* way you can interact and communicate with these others when there are disagreements. During such situations, you need to realize that you are stuck and are engaging in a very rigid and inflexible interactional role.

By shifting from your preferred presentation of your "living culture" to another interactional role within your "living culture", you will be open to take a risk and engage new interactional roles that can help you become more confident, self-assured and heard when disagreements arise within and among others. Thus, it is vital for you to learn how to implement in a flexible way as many possible different interactional roles from your own "living culture" as well as how to EXPAND the richness of your "living culture". Learning to engage in different interactional roles in different contexts, will allow you to shift comfortably in and out of a variety of interactional roles with others.

Abusive Relationships

If your spouse or significant other is verbally or physically abusing you (Potato Hot-Head), then you must be very careful about changing your interactional role. When you are in an abusive relationship, we highly encourage you to seek out psychotherapy with a therapist, and **do not** attempt to change your interactional styles without support. The abuser may feel threatened by the releasing of your power from within and may try to intimidate you back into a submissive role. Therefore, we as a psychiatrist and psychologist, encourage you to partake in psychotherapy sessions and under the careful monitoring of an expert decide how best to make changes so, you remain safe. You must remember that abuse at any level is never justified, so you should never feel that it is your fault. You will need, with the assistance of a therapist, to convey to your abuser (1) how hurtful words can be and, (2) that physical abuse will not be tolerated at any level, and is unacceptable to you. You will need to set boundaries on what you will and will not accept from your abuser.

You must remember you are not alone, and you will need to surround yourself with a support system of family and friends. Discuss with them what is happening and how you are feeling. Do not feel ashamed or believe that it is your fault and that no one will understand. If the verbal abuse escalates to physical abuse, immediately enact the role of The Runaway and **LEAVE** the situation. It is imperative that you do not engage in the conflict. If your abuser becomes angry, become The Peacemaker temporarily, and stay calm, do not agitate, and then walk away as soon as you can. If setting boundaries, getting therapy and refusing to engage do not stop the abuse, then it is time to consider leaving the relationship and breaking all ties. Your personal safety is far more important than the relationship. Remember, you *can* do it, and you do have the **power from within you** to protect yourself and/or your children.

Also in situations when you feel pushed into a role where you feel powerless and forced to use anger and risk abusing another, the role of Potato Hot-Head, you need to take the role of The Runaway to get out of the intense situation and calm down. When this happens regularly you should seek out a therapist, and ask for help to avoid the interactional role where you could hurt someone else.

Costs and Benefits of Changing Your interactional Role

Change is a big risk, and before you actively decide to alter the way you interact with others you must stop and think. What are the costs and the benefits of changing? Those around you may be confused with your newly found "power" and work hard (consciously or unconsciously) to convince you to return to your preferred interactional ways (homeostatic pattern described earlier in this book). There is the risk that others may not like the "new" and stronger "you; you will need to be strong and resist returning to former interactional styles that resulted in your being ineffective in situations where tensions arose in emotionally charged situations. It is important to remember that you cannot change anyone else nor can anyone else change *you*.

A flexible use of the interactional roles described in this book gives you several benefits. You will feel more confident, more in control, and able to respond in highly charged situations with compassion, empathy, and control. You will create an atmosphere where differences in and between others can be discussed, analyzed, and interventions or alternative ways of engaging can be developed that will lead to lasting change. Through the process, you will improve and develop more satisfying relationships with family members, spouse, significant other, friends, co-workers or acquaintances.

Are You Happy?

One of the primary questions that you need to ask yourself is, "Am I happy"? Change is not easy; it takes patience, practice, and willingness to put forth the effort. If you are unhappy in your Key-Relations, then you need to change who *you* are by EXPANDING to a new interactional role. Other people will not change to make you happy. Change comes from within as does happiness. Through the use of this book, you will learn how to deal with tension, highly charged emotions and crisis situations in a more effective way. The changes you make in your interactional style with others can be life altering. If you have seriously reflected on your life, whom you are, and how you interact with others and are saying to yourself, "**I am not happy**" then it is time to **EXPAND *and*** *change your interactional role(s) in your personal and professional relationships in order to be more effective.*

A Personal Note from Us to You:

As you try out new interactional roles, do not give up after one or two tries. The interactional roles introduced in this book take practice and remember you are not alone. Together, as a psychiatrist and psychologist, we have over sixty years of professional experience, helping people to change. We know that these interactional roles work. We are there behind you, helping you, and guiding you to EXPAND and release the power from within yourself.

Dr. Lars Brok & Dr. Audrey Ellenwood

References

DiNicola, V. (1997). *A stranger in the family.* New York: W. W. Norten Company.

Koenig, K. (2001). Getting style conscious in therapy. *Focus Newsletter.* Retrieved from
     http://www.naswma.org/displaycommon.cfm?an=1&subarticlenbr=356
     on 9-4-13.

Send in The Clown theme song with lyrics retrieved from:
     http://artists.letssingit.com/stephen-sondheim-lyrics-send-in-the-clowns-
     ms8d5sh
     on 10/3/13.

Superman theme song with lyrics retrieved from:
     http://videosift.com/video/Superman-Theme-Song-With-Lyrics
     on 10/3/13.

About The Authors

Audrey E. Ellenwood, Ph.D. Angel, Teacher, Doctor

Dr. Ellenwood has been a licensed psychologist since 1988 and has a clinical private practice. Prior to 1987 she was an elementary teacher and worked as a school

 psychologist. She has received family therapy training and supervision from two world re-known family therapists, Maurizio Andolfi, M.D. and Jay Haley, Ph.D. Her specialties include family, couple, and individual therapy, psychological and neuropsychological assessments, women's support groups, and dealing with children's behavioral or emotional issues. She was the Director of the School Psychology Program at Youngstown State University for three years, before retiring, and prior to that she was Director of the Bowling Green State University School Psychology Program for

twenty-three years. She is *director of Project Learning Around the World,* (www. platw.org) a 5013c charity which provides educational material and equipment for children in developing third world countries. She has served as president for various local, state, national, and international psychological associations. She was recently the recipient of the Clyde V. Bartlett Award which recognizes an Ohio school psychologist for outstanding services or achievement in the profession. Dr. Ellenwood is editor of the *Ohio Psychologist* and co-chair of the Communication and Technology Committee of the Ohio Psychological Association. Dr. Ellenwood is co-author of the book, *Shake-UP: Moving Beyond Therapeutic Impasses by De-Constructing Rigidified Professional Role.* As a hobby she writes children's books. Dr. Ellenwood resides in Sylvania, Ohio, USA.

Lars Brok, M.D., Doctor, Teacher, Savior

Dr. Brok is a Family Therapist, Psychodrama Therapist and Psychiatrist and, with R.Pluut, Co-Founder , trainer and supervisor in systems therapy and Director of  the ISSOOH, a 26 year old family Therapy training institute in the Netherlands. Dr. Brok is a former member of the Board of the Dutch association of Family Therapy and its Training Committee. He was editor of the Dutch Journal of System Therapy. He specialized in working with clients with psychotic experiences and their families. He also specialized in working with families and clients from different cultures and in migration related issues. From 1991 until 2007 he was head of a Multi-Functional Psychiatric Center part of Delta Psychiatric Center, in Rotterdam. He retired in 2007 but is still working about 4 months a year in centers specialized in the treatment of clients with psychotic experiences. Dr. Brok serves on the International Committee of the Academia Della Terapia Familiare in Rome, head: professor Andolfi. He has written several articles and chapters in books about family therapy and psychiatry. Dr. Brok is co-author of the book, *Shake-UP: Moving Beyond Therapeutic Impasses by De-Constructing Rigidified Professional Role*. Dr. Brok is participating in *Project Learning Around the World* (www.platw.org). This project supports the education of children in underprivileged positions. He is living partly in Antwerpen, Belgium and in Le Pontreau, France. Among many other things, he is writing a cook book.

CPSIA information can be obtained at www.ICGtesting.com
Printed in the USA
BVOW01s0408131014

370379BV00007B/6/P